Barça: The

By Nic Aldam

Published by Barçacentral Press

barcacentralpress@gmail.com

C/Manso 70 2° 1ª, Barcelona 08015, Spain

ISBN 978-1494445119
Cover design Carmen Iglesias Feijóo

ABOUT THE AUTHOR

Nic Aldam moved to Barcelona in 1989 and he has been following FC Barcelona ever since. In 2007 he began blogging about the club at FCBNews.com and in 2010 he started the Barçacentral website (http://barcacentral.com/) where he continues to write match previews and reports to all of Barça's matches as well as opinion pieces. Barça: The Guardiola Years is his first book.

CONTENTS

CHAPTER 1 – Hibernian 0 Barça 6

Futbol Club Barcelona ended the 2007/2008 season in a terrible mess. On May 7 2008 a 4-1 defeat to Real Madrid at the Santiago Bernabéu stadium exposed the gap between the two great rivals of Spanish football and showed how far Frank Rijkaard's team had fallen since winning La Liga and the Champions League in 2006. The Barcelona fans wanted to know who was responsible for the change in fortunes and the club's president Joan Laporta was under a lot of pressure. Rijkaard's relaxed approach was being seriously questioned as it seemed as if some of the team's players had lost their ambition. Ronaldinho Gaucho, who had been responsible in many ways for the rise of Rijkaard's team from 2003 to 2006, also had to take his part of the blame for Barça's fall. As the Brazilian's form dropped so did the team's, and rumours of his partying lifestyle and missed training sessions did nothing to help team spirit.

Moves from club members to remove Laporta as president were under way and Laporta and his board of directors needed to do something. Rijkaard's days had been numbered for quite some time now and the day after the humiliating defeat at Madrid news was leaked that ex-Barcelona captain Josep 'Pep' Guardiola would be taking over as first team coach for the 2008/2009 season. Guardiola had arrived at the club in 1984 at the age of 13 and had been a key part in Johan Cruyff's dream team in the early 1990s. He later played under Bobby Robson and Louis Van Gaal before moving to Italian team Brescia in 2001 after a total of 379 games for Barça. He also played briefly under Fabio Capello at Roma, had two years in Egypt before ending his playing career in Mexico in 2006. In June 2007 he returned to Barça to coach the B team and in his one season in charge he had taken the young team to the promotion play-offs. However, his appointment to the job as first team coach was not greeted enthusiastically by some fans. He had only one season as a coach under his belt and that was in the Spanish Third Division, many wanted an experienced coach such as Jose Mourinho to take over, and Laporta's decision was seriously questioned. However, Laporta had faith in Guardiola, after all very few knew the club as well as Pep did.

On 9 May club member Oriol Giralt officially presented a motion of no-confidence against Laporta which meant that a vote of club members would be taken where the president could be removed from office if Giralt's group could obtain two-thirds of the vote. On 11 May Barça played their last game at Camp Nou under Frank Rijkaard and managed to throw away a 2-0 lead to lose 2-3 in the last minute to Mallorca. Less than 40,000 turned up to see the game, and sections of the public showed their displeasure with Joan Laporta during the match. At the end when Dani Güiza scored Mallorca's third there was a bigger display of protest. It was a sad end for Rijkaard, and the moves against Laporta gathered momentum.

There were obviously problems within the club. A few days after the Mallorca defeat Deco, who had been one of the stars of the team, declared his intention to leave. There were rumours that other big names such as Samuel Eto'o and Ronaldinho would also be leaving in the summer. Plans to bring in new players were also well under way and on May 26 Barça announced that the Malian international midfielder Seydou Keita had been signed from Sevilla for €14 million. The following day Gerard Piqué was signed for €5 million, the 21-year-old defender returning to the club after four years at Manchester United. But these were not the big name signings that might have appeased the disgruntled supporters.

Guardiola, who was still with the B team preparing for the promotion play-offs, was officially signed as first team coach for two years on May 29. It was also announced that Tito Vilanova, who was his assistant at Barça B, would continue as his number two with the first team. In the next

—

8

couple of weeks Barça confirmed the signings of Uruguayan defender Martin Caceres for €16.5 million from Villarreal and Brazilian full-back Daniel Alves for €32 million from Sevilla. While the signing of Alves may have caused a bit more of a stir amongst supporters there were still questions being asked about spending so much money on defenders. Meanwhile, the offloading of players began as Gianluca Zambrotta moved back to Italy to play for AC Milan, José Edmilson moved to Villarreal and Giovani dos Santos was signed by Tottenham.

On Sunday 15 June Barça B won their promotion to the *Segunda División B* and the following day Guardiola was officially presented as first team coach to the press. However, with the vote of no-confidence against Laporta set for 6 July, the mood within the club was still very uncertain. The only joy for Barça fans was the form of players Xavi Hernandez, Andres Iniesta and Carles Puyol for the Spanish national team who were impressing in Euro 2008. Spain lifted the trophy at the end of June beating Germany 1-0 in the final and Xavi was voted Player of the Tournament by UEFA. Iniesta and Puyol were also included in a list of the 23 best players of the competition.

On July 1 Deco signed for Chelsea for a fee of €10 million, while Santiago Ezquerro and Lilian Thuram both left the club after reaching the end of their contracts. On Sunday 6 July Joan Laporta held on to the presidency of the club by the skin of his teeth. Twenty-four thousand members turned up to vote and Oriol Giralt fell just short of the two-thirds majority needed to oust Laporta, polling 60.6% of the vote. Only 37.75% of the voters cast their vote in favour of Laporta. Two days later the local press was full of reports that Laporta was about to resign, but at a board meeting on July 10 Laporta insisted he was staying put. Laporta's stance brought about the resignation of eight members of the board including three vice-presidents Albert Vicenç, Ferran Soriano and Marc Ingla.

With the club seemingly in crisis, fifteen players turned up at Camp Nou on July 14 for their physical examination for the new season. Some players had been given extra time off for holidays after international duty, but Víctor Valdés, Albert Jorquera, José Manuel Pinto, Thierry Henry, Rafa Márquez, Oleguer Presas, Sylvinho Mendes, Bojan Krkic, Gabi Milito, Eric Abidal, Eidur Gudjohnsen, Touré Yaya, Gerard Piqué, Martín Cáceres and Marc Crosas all reported for work. Leo Messi would arrive the following day for the team's first training session. Ronaldinho was also absent but by now it seemed certain that he was about to leave the club.

At just past 11 pm on July 15 Joan Laporta and AC Milan's vice-president Adriano Galliano announced that they had reached an agreement for the sale of Ronaldinho for €21 million. Ronaldinho had given Barça so much since joining the club in 2003 but at the end few were sorry to see him go. It brought to an end the Barça career of one of the greatest players ever to grace Camp Nou. From his home debut against Sevilla in September 2003 when he scored with a fantastic shot from 30 yards after a run from within his own half, Ronnie thrilled fans with his shimmies and flicks. He was responsible for bringing Barça out of the doldrums of the Gaspart era, pride was restored for the fans and this reached its crescendo in May 2006 when Barça beat Arsenal in Paris to win their second European Cup. On the way, there were two La Liga titles and two Supercopas, a dazzling two goal display in the Bernabéu that had the home fans applauding their greatest rivals, countless free-kicks that left goalkeepers standing, backheels, powerful runs that left defenders for dead and pinpoint 40 yard passes. It was sad to watch his decline over his last two years at Barça when it seemed that his partying lifestyle was catching up with him. It was clear to the Camp Nou regulars that he had lost his once superb physical condition.

There was more movement in the transfer market as Barça signed Alexandr Hleb from Arsenal for €15 million and Oleguer Presas was offloaded to Ajax. The only remaining question was whether Samuel Eto'o would stay at the club, and who would replace him if he left. Eto'o was a confrontational character with an explosive temperament. He had publically criticized both Rijkaard and Ronaldinho in February 2007, had come close to walking off the pitch at Zaragoza a year earlier after receiving racist abuse from the crowd, and in May 2008 he had been accused of headbutting a journalist while on international duty for Cameroon. Pep Guardiola, in his first press conference as coach in June, had included Eto'o, along with Deco and Ronaldinho, as one of the players he didn't need at the club. Didier Drogba, Emmanuel Adebayor and Dimitar Berbatov were all rumoured to be possible replacements.

However, Eto'o travelled with the squad to Scotland on Monday 21 July where Barça would play the first pre-season friendlies against Hibernian and Dundee United. There was still plenty of uncertainty amongst fans but signs that Pep Guardiola was working the players hard in early training sessions which included a run from the hotel to the training ground, offered signs for optimism. The sessions appeared to be more intense than they had been previously under Frank Rijkaard. Guardiola ran a tighter ship. There would be fines for players arriving late for training, and a much stricter control of the players' diets.

As usual for early pre-season games Barça included some youngsters from the B team in the squad to give them some experience. Abraham Gonzalez, David Corcoles, Victor Vazquez, Pedro Rodriguez, Jeffren Suarez and Sergio Busquets were all known well by Guardiola from his time coaching them the previous season. The only first team players missing were Xavi, Puyol and Iniesta who were still on holiday after winning Euro 2008 with Spain, and Gabi Milito who would end up missing the entire season through injury.

There was a lot of expectation for the first game at Hibs. How would the team play and how would the new signings fit in? Pep Guardiola chose a starting eleven of Valdés, Alves, Marquez, Pique, Corcoles, Vazquez,

Busquets, Gudjohnsen, Messi, Henry and Pedro, but there would be plenty of changes during the game with Pinto, Abraham, Caceres, Crosas, Hleb, Toure, Keita, Jeffren, Bojan and Eto'o all getting a chance.

The team began in the familiar 4-3-3 formation that had been used by Rijkaard but there was a freshness about the way Barça played, with a higher tempo and very good off the ball movement. After just four and a half minutes Dani Alves crossed from the right and a poor clearance went straight to Eidur Gudjohnsen who controlled on his left foot before cracking the ball home with his right from just outside the penalty area. In the fifteenth minute Messi shimmied in from the right in typical fashion before firing low past Hibernian keeper Andy McNeil. Two minutes later a fantastic build up involving Messi and Alves on the right led to Messi finding Henry who knocked the ball back for Gudjohnsen to score his second with the help of a deflection. The Alves-Messi understanding was immediate and would prove to be a key link throughout Guardiola's time in charge.

Victor Vazquez shot wide from Gudjohnsen's cross soon after. However, it was not long before Barça scored a fourth. In the 27th minute Messi dribbled inside and found Pedro on the left and the youngster beautifully curled a right-foot shot inside the far post. Messi continued in splendid form, forcing an excellent save from McNeil and then being denied what would have been a terrific goal by the linesman flagging a disputed offside.

There were the expected numerous changes at half time and Barça were not quite as dominant after the break. However, in the 48th minute Jeffren jinked his way through to set up Bojan to net the fifth. Hibs forced Pinto into the first Barça save after 56 minutes and eight minutes later Steven Fletcher missed a great chance firing over from close range. Toure wrapped things up with Barça's sixth on 69 minutes after exchanging passes with Jeffren.

The game was an excellent beginning for Guardiola and set the pattern for things to come. Barça would continue to impress throughout the preseason winning comfortably at Dundee Utd (1-5) and Fiorentina (1-3) before flying out to the USA for two victories against the Mexican team Chivas (2-5) and New York Red Bulls (2-6). Samuel Eto'o scored five goals in these games and shortly before Barça played Wisla Krakow in the Champions League preliminary round Pep Guardiola announced that Eto'o would be staying at Barça "because he wants it and I want it".

Hibernian: McNeil (Grof, min.83); Van Zanten, Jones, Hogg (Canning, min.73), Hanlon; Murray (Chrisholm, min.46), Stevenson (Thicot, min.46), Shiels (Rankin, min.73), Nish; Fletcher (Morais, min.65), O'Brien (Cropley, min.83).

Barça: (first half) Valdés; Alves, Marquez, Pique, Corcoles; Vazquez (Crosas m30), Busquets, Gudjohnsen; Messi, Henry, Pedro.

Barça:(second half) Pinto; Abraham, Caceres, Pique, Corcoles; Crosas (Hleb m66), Toure, Gudjohnsen (Keita m66); Jeffren, Bojan, Pedro (Eto'o m66).

Goals: m5 Gudjohnsen 0-1, m15 Messi 0-2, m17 Gudjohnsen 0-3, m27 Pedro 0-4, m48 Bojan 0-5, m69 Toure 0-6.

CHAPTER 2 – Barça 6 Atlético Madrid 1

Barça would face Wisla Krakow in the Champions League preliminary round without Messi who was at the Beijing Olympics competing for gold with Argentina. There had been controversy as Barça and the Argentine Football Association argued over their need for the player. Barça wanted their best player for the Champions League as there would be serious financial consequences if they failed to get through. By the time FIFA had declared on the matter saying that Barça were correct in their claim to have the rights to the player, Messi was already in China and had played in Argentina's first game. Guardiola had won a gold medal with Spain in the 1992 Olympics and he knew how much it meant to the player, "the most important thing is that Messi is happy". So Messi stayed on to win gold and he would not forget Guardiola's decision.

Guardiola showed his faith in the *cantera* (Barça's youth academy) by playing Pedro in Messi's place for the first leg against Wisla and Eto'o scored another two with Henry getting another in a 4-0 win. Eto'o scored again as Barça clinched a thrilling 2-1 injury time win over Boca Juniors in the annual Joan Gamper tournament. Not too much importance was given to Barça losing the return leg at Wisla 1-0. With qualification secured for the Champions League, the focus turned to the start of the Liga and the question of whether Barça could improve on the previous season's third place.

For the opening game of the 2008/2009 league season at newly promoted Numancia Guardiola put out what would seem to be his best eleven with Valdés in goal, a back four of Alves, Marquez, Puyol and Abidal, a midfield trio of Xavi, Toure and Iniesta, with Messi , Eto'o and Henry up front. Things didn't go to plan, Numancia scored an early goal and then defended the lead heroically for the rest of the game to win 1-0. It could not have been a worse start for the new coach and there was now a two-week break for internationals before the next match.

For the following game at home to Racing Santander Guardiola played four of the new signings, Alves, Piqué, Keita and Hleb, while taking a big gamble by bringing in both Pedro and Sergio Busquets. Rijkaard had given Pedro a three minute debut as a substitute the previous January, and he had also played in the first game against Wisla. This, however, was his first start in La Liga while for Busquets, the son of Barça's keeper of the mid 1990s Carles Busquets, it was an unexpected debut coming in to replace Toure. Both players would perform well but Barça could only draw 1-1 and Hleb had to come off with an injured ankle which would signal the start of a miserable season for the Belarusian.

With just one point from two games there were plenty of questions in the press about Guardiola's ability. Johan Cruyff publicly supported Guardiola, saying the Racing game had been the best Barça performance in many seasons. This might have been a slight exaggeration but Cruyff pointed out the strengths of the team as being the positional play, the rhythm at which the ball was moved and the pressing game, stating that the only problem was with finishing.

The goals started coming, however, as Barça earned a straightforward 3-1 victory over Sporting Lisbon in the first game of the Champions League group stage. Then the team achieved the first big score of the season with a 1-6 win at Sporting Gijon. Frank Rijkaard had first played Messi as the central striker for part of the away game at Athletic Club the previous season while Guardiola had first given him the role in the preseason game at Fiorentina, but this was the first time Messi played the false nine role for 90 minutes and he responded with two late goals while Samuel Eto'o was sacrificed to the right wing. Sergio Busquets was back in the team for his second game and he again performed well, while Xavi and Iniesta were both very dominant. It seemed both players had grown in confidence since winning Euro 2008 with the national team and they were now filling in the roles of Ronaldinho and Deco as the orchestrators of Barça's play.

Messi again began in the middle for the next game at home to Betis with Eto'o starting on the right. However, they switched positions early on and the move paid off with Messi assisting Eto'o with two goals. Toure was back in place of Busquets while Martin Caceres got his first league start alongside Rafa Marquez in defence. The defence looked shaky and with the score at 2-0 Barça relaxed and allowed Betis to equalize with two goals in eight minutes. Guardiola brought on Busquets and Eidur Gudjohnsen in place of the disappointing Toure and Keita and the team reacted with Gudjohnsen grabbing the winner 10 minutes from time.

Barça needed an even later winner to beat local rivals Espanyol in the last league derby between the sides at the Olympic Stadium on Montjuic, a game that needed a nine-minute break in the second half due to crowd disturbances caused by Barça fans firing flares into the Espanyol section. Ferran 'Coro' Corominas had put Espanyol ahead on 20 minutes with a disputed goal and Barça struggled to find a way back despite playing the second half against ten men due to the sending off of Espanyol's Nene. An equalizer finally came in the 76th minute thanks to Thierry Henry. Then in the very last minute Samuel Eto'o, who had come on as a second half substitute, won a penalty. Leo Messi held his nerve to send keeper Carlos Kameni the wrong way and the ref blew for full time before Espanyol even had a chance to kick off.

With games now coming twice a week Pep Guardiola continued to make changes and try out new things. For the Champions League game at Shakhtar Donetsk he played a defence of three for the first time with Piqué, Marquez and Puyol, while Dani Alves was given a more advanced role on the right side. Eto'o and Henry played as a dual strike force while Messi was rested and started on the bench. The plan didn't work, and with Barça a goal down Guardiola brought on Messi with half an hour remaining. Even with Messi it seemed it wasn't going to be Barça's night. Then in the 87th minute the Shakhtar goalkeeper Andrei Pyatov dropped a cross from Bojan Krkic and Messi had a simple tap in for the equalizer. As the clock moved towards 94 minutes Xavi sent a trademark pass into Messi on the left, and as Pyatov came out to narrow the angle Messi sent a sublime chip over the keeper's body for his second last-minute winner in a week.

Five wins on the trot had most fans happy. Messi had scored six in the first seven games and looked well on his way to beating his best season's total of 17 goals in the 2006/2007 season. Eto'o was also impressing, working hard for the team while banging in four goals. Xavi and Iniesta were both in excellent form while Busquets had also been very composed when he played. Of the new signings Piqué was fitting in well, and while Alves was a bit inconsistent there was plenty of promise.

However, the need for late winners against Betis, Espanyol and Shakhtar suggested some things were still not working. Barça had moved up the table to fifth place but were still two points behind the old enemy Real Madrid and three points behind early front runners Valencia and Villarreal. The team had still not kept a clean sheet and the defence looked vulnerable at set pieces. Toure had been magnificent in his first season under Frank Rijkaard, heroically playing on through the pain of a herniated disc. Now he was struggling to find his form, and with the emergence of Busquets he did not have the continuity in the team to regain it. Thierry Henry had shown some improvement on his poor first season with the club but he had only scored once and was still a long way from the level demonstrated at Arsenal for so many years. Eric Abidal had started reasonably well after signing for the club in the summer of 2007, but his form dropped in the second half of the 2007/2008 season and many fans began to see him as a weak link. He hadn't started too well under Guardiola but that was about to change with a magnificent match against Atlético Madrid.

Meetings between Barça and Atlético had a history of being high-scoring incident-packed games. Atlético had begun the season strongly but a defeat at home to Sevilla the previous week had seen them slip below Barça to 7th in the table. Coach Javier Aguirre had to make do without Maniche, Forlan, Simao, Seitardis and Pablo for the visit to Camp Nou but with players such as Sergio 'Kun' Agüero and Maxi Rodriguez in their ranks they were still likely to be dangerous. The game had been billed as a duel between Agüero and Messi, and it is true that Agüero had destoyed Barça in a 4-2 Atlético victory the previous season at the Vicente Calderón.

Guardiola made four changes to the team that had started against Shakhtar with Abidal, Gudjohnsen, Busquets and Messi recalled in place of Toure, Keita, Henry and the injured Dani Alves, which meant Puyol moved to right back and the team returned to the classic 4-3-3 system. Barça began the game at a terrific pace. After just two minutes Iniesta won a corner on the left which was taken by Xavi and headed in at the near post by Marquez. A minute later Messi was brought down inside the area by Tomas Ujfalusi and Eto'o sent Atlético keeper Gregory Coupet the wrong way with the penalty. Then with just eight minutes on the clock Messi made it 3-0, taking a quick free kick while Coupet was still trying to organize the defensive wall.

A mistake from Busquets allowed Maxi Rodriguez to burst through and curl a beauty past Valdés to make it 3-1. However, any chance of an Atlético comeback was dispelled in the 18th minute when Eto'o controlled Xavi's pass with his chest before turning the defenders this way and that and shooting low past the hapless Coupet.

Just before the half hour Iniesta and Messi swapped wings briefly, giving Iniesta the chance, after receiving from Xavi, of running at the defence before firing a left foot shot against the base of the post. Some days everything goes your way, and in this case the ball rebounded sweetly to Gudjohnsen who fired into the empty net to make it 5-1. Iniesta had another try a couple of minutes later but this time his right footed curler from the left came back out off the far post.

It was stunning stuff. There was still time before half time for Gudjohnsen to come close after excellent work from Xavi, and then Messi went on a tremendous run from inside his own half which ended with him just clipping the ball wide: a great shame as it would have been one of the goals of the season. Thirty seconds later Messi got another chance for a run on goal, but he seemed to have not recovered fully from his previous effort and the defence responded in time.

The second half could not match the electrifying football of the first 45 minutes though Guardiola brought on Thierry Henry and Bojan Krkic and the game improved for a while, culminating in the goal of the night from Henry. The Frenchman began the move himself pushing the ball forward to Xavi who flicked it on to Bojan who'd cut inside from the left. Bojan touched the ball square to Henry who had continued his run to meet the ball with a tremendous first time rocket shot from outside the area which gave Coupet no chance.

All in all it was a marvellous display from Barça. There were leading roles from the usual stars, Messi, Eto'o, Xavi and Iniesta, while other players who had received a lot of criticism such as Gudjohnsen, Abidal and Henry all performed very well. The following day Real Madrid could only draw 2-2 at home to Espanyol and so Barça stayed above them in fourth place on goal difference, with Valencia, Sevilla and Villarreal still ahead. However, Barça had demonstrated against Atlético the levels at which the team could play when things started clicking, it was the team's sixth straight win but the first real exhibition. There were plenty more to come.

Barça: Valdés; Puyol, Marquez, Piqué, Abidal; Xavi (Keita m74), Busquets, Gudjohnsen; Messi (Bojan m69), Eto'o (Henry m59), Iniesta.

Atlético: Coupet; Perea, Heitinga, Ujfalusi, Antonio López; Luis García (Pernía m46), Assunçao, Raul García, Maxi Rodríguez (De las Cuevas m21); Agüero (Banega m58), Sinama Pongolle.

Goals: m3 Marquez 1-0, m5 Eto'o (pen) 2-0, m8 Messi 3-0, m13 Maxi Rodriguez 3-1, m18 Eto'o 4-1, m28 Gudjohnsen 5-1, m74 Henry 6-1.

CHAPTER 3 – Barça 2 Real Madrid 0

A year before the 6-1 win over Atlético Madrid Barça had also played host to Atlético in the last match before an international break. Barça comfortably won 3-0 with goals from Deco, Messi and Xavi and moved into second place in the Liga with five wins and two draws from seven games. Rijkaard's team had been playing well but slipped up after the international break in a 3-1 defeat at Villarreal and the season went downhill from there.

Now with thirteen points from 6 games Barça were in a similar, though slightly worse position going into an international break, though being above Real Madrid, albeit only on goal difference, made things seem better. With Guardiola in charge there was a better team spirit and there had been fewer injuries which suggested a better preparation.

However, after the break the so-called FIFA virus left Barça without Xavi, Gudjohnsen and Pedro for the always difficult trip to Bilbao to play Athletic Club at San Mames while Leo Messi had played twice in Argentina that week and was left on the bench. Victor Sanchez played alongside Toure and Keita in midfield though Busquets came on when Keita injured a knee after half an hour and Barça ground out a 0-1 victory thanks to Eto'o's second half goal. With Piqué and Abidal impressing at the back it was Barça's first clean sheet since beating Wisla Krakow in August. Valdés had needed to make two splendid saves in the first half but the performance had generally been very solid. It was the type of game that Champions won and Barça were looking the part.

Four more victories followed and the goals began to flow. There were two for Bojan and a first goal for Busquets in the 0-5 Champions League win at Basle. The team then produced a fantastic display to beat Almeria 5-0 with all the goals, including a hat-trick from Eto'o, coming in a spectacular first 37 minutes. Bojan scored again in a narrow 0-1 win at Benidorm in the Copa del Rey and the following weekend Barça went top of the league with 1-4 on a waterlogged pitch at Malaga. With Abidal out injured Guardiola preferred to play Puyol rather than Sylvinho at left back and the captain responded with a typically courageous performance.

The winning run came to an end at the start of November with a disappointing 1-1 draw in the return match with Basle. The worst news, however, was a thigh injury for Iniesta which would see him sidelined until the New Year. The team remained clear leaders of Champions League Group C so perhaps it was normal that there was some relaxation. The day before the match the solidarity within the squad was demonstrated when the entire first team travelled to Navarra for the funeral of goalkeeping coach Juan Carlos Unzue's father.

Guardiola's biggest win yet came in the next game as Barça hammered Valladolid 6-0. Camp Nou was treated to another exhibition especially in the first half with four goals all thanks to the lethal finishing of Eto'o. There followed a disappointing 1-0 win over Benidorm in the return game in the Copa del Rey and then Barça extended their run of league wins to nine with a 0-2 win at Recreativo and went five points clear at the top of La Liga. Messi scored the first, breaking off the wall in a well-rehearsed free kick with Xavi while Keita scored his first goal for the club to wrap things up. Messi's dribbling skills that day prompted *Canal+* commentator Michael Robinson to declare that Messi dribbles past top class defenders with the ease with which the good player in the school playground goes past the rubbish ones.

With 28 points from 11 games it was Barça's best ever start to a league season. However, the following Friday Messi strained a thigh muscle in training and without him the nine-game winning streak in the league came to an end with a 1-1 draw at home to Getafe. Bojan got his first league start in place of Messi but was substituted after a poor game. His face when he came off revealed how upset the 18-year-old was. In his first season with Frank Rijkaard he had had more opportunities due to injuries to Eto'o and Messi, and he had responded with an impressive ten goals. This season Eto'o and Messi were fit while Henry was improving, Iniesta was also used quite regularly as one of the front three, and then there was competition for places from Pedro and Hleb. Bojan seemed overanxious to impress and his disappointment when taken off was evident.

Despite the draw with Getafe Barça still held a three-point advantage at the top of the league. However, there were doubters who claimed that Barça hadn't played any tough opponents yet. In the run up to Christmas Guardiola's team would be properly put to the test with four league games against Sevilla, Valencia, Real Madrid and Villarreal, the four closest challengers in the race for the title.

First there was Champions League business as Barça secured top place in Group C with a 2-5 win at Sporting Lisbon. Messi was back with a goal and two assists, and Guardiola showed his intelligence by bringing on Bojan with the score at 0-2 and the youngster got a boost to his confidence, scoring with a penalty.

The eagerly awaited game with Sevilla arrived with many outsiders hoping to see Barça fall. Eto'o broke the deadlock in a closely fought first half and then Barça controlled the game more in the second half with Toure back to his dominating best in midfield. For the last 30 minutes Guardiola switched Eto'o to the right side with Messi playing through the middle, and the Argentinian responded with two cracking late strikes as Barça ran out 0-3 winners. It was a good weekend for Barça with Madrid losing at Getafe. The only bad news was that Eto'o picked up his fifth yellow card which ruled him out for the following week's game with Valencia.

Hleb came into the team against Valencia and combined the right and centre forward positions with Messi while Henry generally continued on the left. However, it was the Frenchman who rose to the occasion in Eto'o's absence, scoring his second hat-trick for Barça in an impressive 4-0 win. As Madrid succumbed 3-4 at home to Sevilla, which led to the sacking of coach Bernd Schuster, and Villarreal could only draw 3-3 at home to Getafe, Barça's lead at the top extended to six points.

It was good preparation for the *Clásico* with Madrid. Alves, Marquez and Toure were all finding their form and Abidal was back from injury looking strong. Xavi and Puyol were as consistent as ever, while lesser fancied players such as Gudjohnsen and Hleb both performed well against Valencia. Most impressive was the number of goals being scored. Between Liga and Champions Leaugue the team had totaled sixty-four goals in twenty-one games with a remarkable forty goals from the three main forwards. Eto'o was leading scorer at this point with 17 goals, Messi was on 14 while Henry had bagged 9.

On the Tuesday before the Madrid game Guardiola had the luxury of resting all his key players for the final Champions League group game at home to Shakhtar. Only 22,763 turned up to see Barça go down 2-3 and a 20-game unbeaten run came to an end. The following day Madrid also had an inconsequential Champions League game against Zenit St Petersburg but with important players such as Ruud Van Nistlerooy, Pepe, Gabriel Heinze, Lass Diarra and Wesley Sneijder all out injured new Madrid coach Juande Ramos played seven of the players who would start at Camp Nou as Madrid won 3-0.

Madrid were also without the suspended Arjen Robben and Marcelo for the *Clásico*, though they received a boost when Sneijder was declared fit. Sergio Ramos was moved to left back to replace Marcelo with Cristoph Metzelder coming in to partner Fabio Cannavaro in central defence, Royston Drenthe replaced Arjen Robben while Sneijder returned in place of Rafael Van der Vaart. Barça were at full strength apart from Iniesta who was not quite ready. Gudjohnsen was preferred over Keita and Busquets to start in midfield alongside Xavi and Toure.

Barça began the game very strongly. In the sixth minute Messi went past Sergio Ramos with ease and Iker Casillas had to make a diving save. Then a couple of minutes later Cannavaro had to make a saving tackle to deny Messi after a slick one-two with Eto'o. Madrid were sitting very deep and concentrating on keeping Barça out and Messi was fouled four times in the first fifteen minutes. Puyol and Toure were often allowed space to bring the ball forward but the ball was not arriving anywhere near Eto'o.

In the 24th minute Madrid had their first chance when Sneijder hooked Drenthe's pass towards goal but Valdés responded well to tip the ball over. Then two minutes later Raul played in Drenthe who got the better of Alves for the only time of the game to get a clear run at goal. Valdés had to come out and make an excellent one-on-one save. Then from the resulting corner Higuian had another chance but shot over the bar. Barça and the crowd seemed a bit shocked and Madrid began to look more confident. Henry and Toure managed shots on goal but Casillas dealt with both efforts comfortably and now Barça were struggling to break through. The risk of playing Sneijder turned out to be a bad one for Madrid as the Dutchman limped off in the 36th minute. Barça began to look the better team as the first half came to an end but the referee Luis Medina Cantalejo frustrated the crowd by inexplicably blowing for half time on 45 mins and 5 seconds despite Sneijder being subbed off and some subtle time wasting from Madrid.

The second half began with a powerful shot from Eto'o which Casillas parried but the chances were few and far between. Eto'o was playing more on the right where Metzelder followed him, and Messi tried, but usually failed, to get past the Madrid defence through the middle. Madrid, however, were playing deeper and deeper and it seemed that sooner or later they might pay for it. In the 69th minute Busquets, who'd come on for Gudjohnsen, played the ball square to Xavi and was blocked by Salgado as he looked for the return. Medina Cantalejo signalled a penalty which many referees would have ignored. Eto'o took the kick but his shot was not good and Casillas dived to his left to palm the ball away.

Eto'o nearly made up for it three minutes later but Casillas made another good save this time low to his right. At the other end Valdés had had long periods without touching the ball but he needed to be alert in the 78th minute to save superbly in another one-on-one with Madrid substitute Miguel Palanca.

With time running out it looked as though the game would end goalless. Then, in the 83rd minute, Barça won a corner on the right. Xavi swung the ball to the far post where Puyol made a magnificent leap to head the ball down towards Eto'o who scored with his knee from about two yards out to send Camp Nou into ecstasy. Madrid were too tired now to come close to an equalizer and in injury time Hleb began a counter attack sending Henry away on the right. The Frenchman played the ball left to Messi and as Casillas closed him down Messi flicked the ball over the Madrid keeper with just enough power to beat Cannavaro's desperate lunge on the line.

Barça hadn't played the beautiful football seen in previous games of the 2008/09 season, mainly due to Madrid defending well with man-to-man marking of Metzelder on Eto'o, Ramos on Messi and Fernando Gago on Xavi. However, Madrid couldn't keep up the aggressive marking for the entire game and they tired near the end allowing Barça's quality to show. However, things might have been very different if Victor Valdés had not stopped the two one-on-one chances.

It was Barça's first win over their rivals since Ronaldinho's exhibition had the Bernabéu applauding in a 0-3 victory in November 2005, and the first at Camp Nou since 2004. The following week Barça won a heroic 1-2 victory at Villarreal, holding on for the final 20 minutes after Piqué was sent off which left Barça with a massive ten-point advantage over second placed Sevilla going into the Christmas break.

Barça: Valdés ; Alves , Marquez , Puyol , Abidal ; Xavi (Keita m90), Toure , Gudjohnsen (Busquets m63,); Messi , Etoo (Hleb m88), Henry.

Real Madrid: Casillas; Salgado, Metzelder, Cannavaro, Sergio Ramos; Gago, Guti (Javi Garcia m73), Sneijder (Palanca m36), Drenthe; Raúl, Higuaín (Van der Vaart m77).

Goals: m83 Eto'o 1-0, m91 Messi 2-0.

CHAPTER 4 – Barça 5 Deportivo de La Coruña 0

Barça began the New Year with a league game at home to Mallorca. Pep Guardiola had allowed the South American players a couple of extra days Christmas holiday so Alves started on the bench while Messi watched the game from the stands alongside Argentina national coach Diego Maradona who had attended the game with the hope of seeing Messi play. Victor Sanchez came in to partner Marquez in central defence and Puyol replaced Alves at right back, while Hleb was given another chance in place of Messi. The game was somewhat bad-tempered and it only improved after Alves and Iniesta were brought on to substitute the disappointing Sanchez and Hleb with the score at 1-1. Iniesta celebrated his return from injury with a goal 15 minutes from the end and Toure wrapped things up with one of the goals of the season, weaving past three defenders to finish off a fine team move.

Maradona followed the team to Madrid to see the following Copa del Rey game against Atlético. This time Messi did play and the Argentine coach was treated to a display that he himself would have been proud of. Messi was quite simply sensational, his understanding with Alves was really beginning to flourish, and he ended the night receiving an ovation from the Vicente Calderón after grabbing a hat-trick in a 1-3 first leg win.

Barça took their run of away victories to thirteen with an epic 2-3 win over bottom-placed Osasuna on a freezing foggy night in Pamplona. The game turned out to be more complicated than might be expected when top of the table play bottom despite Eto'o firing Barça into the lead on the stroke of half time. Second half goals from Flavio and Pandiani gave Osasuna a surprise lead and Xavi didn't equalize until the 80th minute. Four minutes later Alves forced an error from Osasuna and Messi picked up the loose ball about 40 yards out. He cut in from the right, skipping past defenders on the way, before unleashing a bullet of a shot that screamed into the far corner for the winner. Valencia's 3-3 draw at home to Villarreal meant Barça's lead at the top increased to 12 points with Madrid moving into second place.

There were plenty of changes for the return Copa del Rey game with Atlético, with only the in-form Alves and Busquets remaining from the eleven starters in Pamplona. Goals from Bojan and Gudjohnsen gave Barça a 2-1 win to complete the job and earn a place in the quarter-finals against Espanyol.

Barça finished the first half of the league season with a home game against seventh-placed Deportivo de La Coruña. Guardiola preferred Piqué over Marquez in defence, Toure and Keita started in midfield with Xavi, while Messi, Eto'o and Henry continued up front though Henry played most of the first half as centre forward with Eto'o on the left side of attack.

Barça began at a tremendous pace and Deportivo keeper Daniel Aranzubia had to save twice from Henry in the first two minutes. After just 26 seconds, Xavi sent a superb pass inside the full back for Messi who squared to Henry on the penalty spot but the Frenchman's first time shot was saved by Aranzubia diving to his right. A minute later Henry exchanged passes with Abidal on the left before cutting inside and letting fly but Arunzubia was there to parry.

Barça continued to control the game with a very high percentage of possession. In the 14th minute Eto'o made a good run in from the left, turning the full back this way and that before shooting just wide of the far post. Then in the 24th minute Xavi won the ball inside the Barça half and played a quick pass forward to Messi who set off on a diagonal run. There were four Deportivo players near to Messi but none could get close enough to attempt a tackle. Henry was in a good position to receive but Messi just sped on until he reached the edge of the penalty area and cut a shot back across the keeper and in off the far post.

There was very little seen of Depor's promising Mexican Andres Guardado as Alves was very dominant on the right. Then in the 25th minute Guardado had to limp off injured, and before a substitution could be made Barça had taken advantage with a second goal. Messi played the ball back from near the corner to Alves who sent in a delicious cross with the outside of his right foot which Henry met with an immaculate firm header which gave Aranzubia no chance.

Messi should have scored again after Alves delivered another fine cross from the right but the Argentinian made poor contact with his header and the ball went wide. Keita then received a superb through ball from Abidal but he failed to get a shot on target. Next, Eto'o had a chance but after going round the goalkeeper the angle was too tight to shoot and the defence had the chance to close him down.

Barça's insistence paid off in the 41st minute. Messi headed the ball down the line for Alves who crossed to Keita whose header was parried by Aranzubia but Eto'o was on hand to stab home the rebound from close range. It might have been four just before half time but Keita unfortunately couldn't get out of the way of Alves's powerful goalbound shot. Barça were so superior in the first half that Depor did not manage one shot at goal or even one corner.

Barça's level had to drop a little in the second half and Valdés was finally called into action, tipping over a shot from outside the area, while at the other end Messi's curling effort forced a fine diving save from Aranzubia. Barça seemed content to control possession and the game dropped in intensity. However, this all changed when Iniesta was brought on in place of Toure in the 70th minute.

Iniesta had only been on the pitch a couple of minutes when he found Henry out on the left before darting into the area to meet the Frenchman's cross with a sidefoot volley that brought an excellent save from Aranzubia. In the 82nd minute Barça played a short corner between Xavi and Keita, Xavi then played the ball inside to Iniesta who sent a splendid reverse pass back for Xavi's run into the area and Xavi pulled the ball back for Henry to score his second of the game. Two minutes later Iniesta again created another goalscoring chance, this time for Puyol who had made a splendid run forward from his own half. Puyol would probably have scored but Aranzubia rushed out of his goal and took Puyol's legs away. The ref had no choice but to award a penalty and show the keeper a red card. With all their subs used Juan Rodriguez was forced to don the goalkeeper's jersey and Samuel Eto'o gave him no chance whatsoever from the penalty spot to complete the rout.

It was an excellent team performance with plenty of style and elegance, speed and skill. Alves had a phenomenal game on the right side while Keita probably had his best game so far as a blaugrana. The defence was hardly troubled but dealt well with everything that came its way while the forwards were still banging in the goals. Barça's lead at the top remained at twelve points and everything was looking rosy. From the 19 games played in the first half of the season the team had scored 59 goals while conceding only 13, accumulating a record-breaking 50 points. Since taking just one point from the first two games, the team had won every single league game except for the 1-1 draw at home to Getafe. However, no medals or cups are won for the first half of the season. Could Barça last the pace?

Barça: Valdés; Alves, Piqué, Puyol, Abidal; Xavi, Toure (Iniesta m70), Keita; Messi, Eto'o, Henry.

Deportivo: Aranzubia; Manuel Pablo, Lopo, Zé Castro, Filipe Luis; Sergio, Juan Rodríguez; Cristian (de Guzmán m63), Verdú, Guardado (Lafita m28); Bodipo (Riki m76).

Goals: m21 Messi 1-0, m27 Henry 2-0, m41 Eto'o 3-0, m82 Henry, m86 Eto'o (pen) 5-0.

CHAPTER 5 – Barça 5 Olympique Lyon 2

On Monday 19 January the first team officially moved to the new training facilities at the magnificent Ciutat Esportiva Joan Gamper in Sant Just Despí. Two days later on the morning of the Copa del Rey quarter final first leg with Espanyol a problem between Guardiola and Eto'o in training was reported, with the player being sent back to the dressing rooms before the session was over.

Espanyol had just sacked their coach Mané and brought in ex-player Mauriccio Pochettino in his place. The last ever derby at the Olympic Stadium on Montjuic ended in a goalless draw, bringing to an end Barça's run of 13 away wins. It was the first evidence that Pochettino's Espanyol would prove to be a difficult opponent for Guardiola's Barça.

The second half of the league season began with Barça gaining revenge over Numancia for the opening day defeat. The front three of Messi (twice), Eto'o and Henry scored the goals in a 4-1 win. With the lead at the top of the Liga still at twelve points and the team playing so well the idea of a possible treble began to emerge. Guardiola played a stronger team for the Copa del Rey return match with Espanyol and it seemed to pay off as Barça took a 3-0 lead through two goals from Bojan and another from Piqué. However, two quick goals from Espanyol left Barça holding on for a nervy last 20 minutes, as one more away goal would have seen the treble dream disappear.

The Espanyol game was played on a Thursday night and Barça almost paid for the effort the following Sunday at Racing Santander. Messi was left on the bench until a 55th minute penalty gave Racing the lead. Guardiola called for the Argentinian who came on to turn the game around with two goals, Barça's 4,999th and 5,000th in La Liga. It was this performance from Messi that prompted the Barcelona based sports daily *El Mundo Deportivo* to run a poll asking if Messi was the best Barça player of all time. Ninety-four percent voted in favour of the 21-year-old.

Two home games followed. Goals from Marquez and Henry gave Barça a decent 2-0 lead in the Copa del Rey semi-final first leg against Mallorca, then a 3-1 win over Sporting in La Liga maintained the lead at 12 points as Madrid kept winning too. Alves and Iniesta were in particularly good form while Eto'o continued to find the net, scoring twice in the win over Sporting. However, the day after the Sporting game the first rumours of a possible bid for Eto'o from Inter Milan appeared in the press.

On the following Saturday, St Valentine's Day, Barça dropped points for the first time since November in a 2-2 draw at Betis. For the first time all season Barça were overrun in a spectacular first 25 minutes in which the home team took a two-goal lead. Eto'o pulled one back, firing in the rebound to his own penalty on the stroke of half time, but it wasn't until the introduction of Henry and Messi, who had again started on the subs' bench, that Barça began to play, and it wasn't until the 84th minute that Eto'o grabbed the equalizer. Madrid won again the following day and the lead at the top of La Liga was down to ten points.

On the Tuesday, Iniesta, who was arguably the most in-form player at that time, pulled a thigh muscle in training and he would be sorely missed in his two week absence. It was Espanyol again in the next league match, Pochettino still hadn't won a game with his new team and Espanyol had slipped to bottom of the table going into the derby at Camp Nou. It was a bad-tempered game with Abidal coming off with a thigh injury which would see him sidelined for two months, while Keita was sent off for a rash challenge on Moises Hurtado before half time. Ex-blaugrana favourite Ivan De La Peña scored twice early in the second half, the second a perfect chip punishing Valdés for a poor clearance. Barça's ten men managed to pull one back through Toure but Espanyol held on for their first league win at Camp Nou for 26 years. Madrid had beaten Betis 6-1 earlier that evening so the gap was down to seven points. Doubts began to creep in. Two years earlier Espanyol had ruined Barça's title dreams with a late Raul Tamudo goal at Camp Nou. Would De La Peña's goals lead to another title loss?

Barça certainly looked a long way from their best as the Champions League returned with a game at Olympique Lyon in the last sixteen. The French team overran Barça for most of the first half. Valdés was beaten early on when a Juninho free kick from near the corner flag flew over him and dipped into the top corner, and Karim Benzema came close to a Lyon second when he fired against the post. Thierry Henry snatched an equalizer in the second half, heading in at the far post after Marquez flicked on Xavi's corner, and Barça scraped a draw to take back for the second leg.

February had not ended well and March got off to a bad start as Barça lost a spectacular game 4-3 at Atlético Madrid. Barça had taken a 0-2 lead early on and then after Atlético came back to equalize Barça took the lead again with just fifteen minutes remaining. However, Diego Forlan and Agüero both scored again in the last ten minutes to give Atlético a remarkable victory. Real Madrid's victory at Espanyol meant Barça's lead had been reduced from twelve to four points in little more than two weeks. Did Barça have the strength of character to recover from the setbacks and hold on to their advantage?

The next test was the Copa del Rey semi-final second leg at Mallorca. Guardiola indicated the importance of the game by taking the entire first team squad for the trip including injured players, but then he surprised by leaving Messi, Xavi, Eto'o and Henry on the bench, perhaps believing the 2-0 lead from the first leg was sufficient. There was a boost with the return of Iniesta to the team, however, Barça did not play well and

Mallorca took the lead on the brink of half time. Then early in the second half Caceres, who had come in at left back, was sent off after conceding a penalty. The season might have fallen apart had Marti scored with the penalty but Pinto saved with his legs and ten-man Barça went on to earn a 1-1 draw and a place in the final with Messi coming on for an inspired last half hour and scoring Barça's equalizer with ten minutes to go.

Barça returned to winning ways in La Liga the following Saturday, beating Athletic Club 2-0 at Camp Nou thanks to first half goals from Busquets and Messi. On the same day Real Madrid could only draw 1-1 in the local derby with Atlético at the Bernabéu and Barça's lead at the top of La Liga was increased to six points. Then the following Wednesday it was back to the Champions League with the return game with Lyon at Camp Nou. Guardiola brought back Alves at right back in place of the injured Puyol while Toure returned in place of Busquets in midfield as Barça lined up with Valdés, Alves, Marquez, Piqué, Silvinho, Xavi, Toure, Iniesta, Messi, Eto'o and Henry.

The game started with Barça taking immediate control but without any penetration. Eto'o had the first decent chance after 15 minutes, shooting wide, and then a minute later a great one touch combination between Iniesta, Henry and Xavi ended with the ball coming back to Iniesta who shot over.

Lyon had their first chance in the 19th minute when Ederson shot wide from Benzema's cross, and briefly, for about five minutes, the French team began to venture forward. In the 25th minute a ball aimed towards Benzema was well anticipated by Marquez who then sent a great ball through to Henry who after an excellent first touch found himself clean through with just the keeper Hugo Lloris to beat. As Lloris came out Henry coolly slipped the ball under him to open the scoring. Two minutes later Xavi sent a long ball out to Eto'o on the right, Eto'o then played a long low pass back to Xavi on the edge of the area. Xavi neatly played the ball on towards his left to Henry whose finishing was once again first class.

The double blow hit Lyon hard but there was more to come. Five minutes before half time Piqué played a long ball out to Messi on the right touchline. The little Argentinian controlled the ball with his chest and then set off infield at tremendous pace, beating two defenders before playing a short pass into Eto'o, Messi received Eto'o's wall pass without breaking stride and then picked his spot at the far post perfectly to score an authentic *golazo*.

Barça were now rampant. In the 43rd minute Henry received Sylvinho's throw-in and crossed low towards Eto'o, Boumsong missed his interception, and after controlling with one touch Eto'o powered home a cracking shot to put an end to his mini goal drought. With the score at 4-0 on the night and 5-1 on aggregate Barça relaxed and before the half time break Lyon hit back when Jean Makoun got between Marquez and Alves to head home a corner.

Lyon grabbed another straight after the break. This time César Delgado squirmed free of Iniesta and crossed, Marquez failed to clear, Benzema let the ball run through his legs to Juninho who made the most of his space to fire past Valdés. Lyon tried to keep Barça unsettled but began to resort to foul play to break Barça's rhythm. For a while the ref looked like losing control of the game as he allowed the likes of Makoun, Juninho and Fabio Grosso to hack away without punishment. In the 59th minute Henry had a good chance for his hat-trick after a great break out of defence from Piqué, but his shot was saved by Lloris.

For a while the game looked wide open but this was not really in Barça's interest and the team began to play deeper and take fewer risks. With fifteen minutes to go Keita came on for Henry who had also taken a painful knock from Makoun. And then with ten minutes to go Lyon had a couple of half chances which had they made more of would have led to a very nervous finish for the home crowd. However, Barça regained control and finished the game strongly. In the 90th minute Xavi set up Bojan with a good chance but Lloris saved again. Juninho was then sent off for protesting at Alves for not getting up after a foul. Then in the 94th minute Xavi, who was excellent all night, sent the ball through to Keita who skipped past Lloris and scored into the empty net. The 6-3 aggregate win put Barça through to the quarter finals along with Chelsea, Liverpool, Bayern Munich, Villarreal, Manchester United, Oporto and Arsenal.

Barça: Valdés; Alves, Marquez, Piqué, Sylvinho; Xavi, Toure, Iniesta (Hleb m92); Messi, Eto'o (Bojan m87), Henry (Keita m75).

Lyon: Lloris; Clerc (Bodmer m46), Cris, Boumsong, Grosso; Toulalan, Juninho, Makoun, Delgado (Källstrom m61), Ederson (Keita m85); Benzema.

Goals: m25 Henry 1-0, m27 Henry 2-0, m40 Messi 3-0, m43 Eto'o 4-0, m44 Makoun 4-1, m48 Juninho 4-2, m94 Keita 5-2.

CHAPTER 6 – Barça 4 Bayern Munich 0

The draw for the Champions League quarter finals on Friday 20 March paired Barça with German Champions Bayern Munich with the first leg at Camp Nou. The winners would face either Liverpool or Chelsea in the semi-finals. The other quarter final pairings were Man United against Porto and Villarreal against Arsenal. The weekend before the draw Barça had returned to league action with a 0-2 victory at Almeria. Guardiola surprised by leaving Henry and Eto'o on the bench and giving a rare start to Bojan while restoring Iniesta to the left side of attack. Iniesta had a superb game while Bojan responded by scoring both goals in quick succession early in the second half.

Henry and Eto'o were back for the following game at home to Malaga who had only lost two of their previous thirteen matches. Camp Nou was treated to another wonderfully fluent exhibition as Barça tore their opponents apart, scoring six goals between the 19th and the 57th minute. Xavi was on particularly good form scoring the first goal and setting up two more in a scintillating first half. Guardiola still saw room for improvement, "We played very well in the first half and the first fifteen minutes of the second, but the objective of any team is to improve. I am convinced we can maintain that level for ninety minutes."

Another international break meant that Guardiola left Alves and Messi on the bench for the next game at Valladolid. Barça were below their best but Eto'o scored his 26th goal of the season five minutes before half time to earn a tight 0-1 win. The victory maintained the six-point lead with nine league games remaining but Barça still had to play Sevilla and Valencia before the crunch game with Madrid at the Bernabéu.

First Barça had to deal with Bayern Munich in the Champions League. Bayern arrived to the first leg game on the back of a 5-1 defeat in a top of the Bundesliga clash at Wolfsburg. Defenders Philipp Lahm and Lucio were both injured in that game which with Daniel Van Buyten absent due to a family illness meant coach Jurgen Klinsmann was without three first choice defenders as well as missing striker Miroslav Klose. Martin Demichelis and 19-year-old Breno Borges started in the centre of defence while the experienced Massimo Oddo came in at right back. Klinsmann elected to play a midfield of five with just Luca Toni up front, but perhaps the biggest surprise was his decision to drop goalkeeper Michael Rensing in favour of Hans-Jorg Butt.

Klinsmann had taken Germany to third place in the 2006 World Cup and had taken over at Bayern in July 2008. He was known for his attacking philosophy but there was some suspicion when he introduced 'holistic' training methods including yoga sessions and fitness gurus. He placed emphasis on developing the individual and improving mental quickness but without the necessary results on the field the patience of the Bayern directors and fans was running low. However, a 12-1 aggregate win over Sporting Lisbon in the previous round indicated how dangerous the Germans could be, and with players such as Bastian Schweinsteiger, Ze Roberto and Franck Ribery in their ranks they could not be underestimated.

With Abidal still injured Guardiola preferred to play Puyol rather than Sylvinho at left back which meant Piqué and Marquez continued as the centre back pairing. Thierry Henry returned to form a front three with Eto'o and Messi so Iniesta moved back into midfield alongside Toure and Xavi. Right from the kick off the Barça midfield took control of the game, imposing a high tempo. After just six minutes Alves found Xavi on the edge of the area, Breno didn't get close enough, allowing Xavi to turn and thread a pass into Henry who took the ball past Butt, screwing the ball back towards goal but Demichelis arrived in time to clear off the line. A couple of minutes later Iniesta came forward on the left, after exchanging passes with Henry and under pressure from Hamit Altintop and Van Bommel, he forced the ball through to Eto'o inside the "D". Breno was already close but Christian Lell came across from left back leaving Messi free on the right, Eto'o touched the ball through and Messi's control and finish were typically clinical. In the 12th minute Iniesta found Xavi in space, Xavi moved the ball on to Messi on the right, Messi cut inside before slipping a pass through for Eto'o who was played onside by Oddo, and as Butt came out to close down the angle Eto'o fired through his legs to make it 2-0.

Bayern looked shell-shocked and Barça's constant pressure forced the German defence into constant errors. Barça looked for the kill and should have won a penalty in the 17th minute when Messi went down under Lell's challenge. The English referee Howard Webb saw it otherwise and booked Messi for a dive. Pep Guardiola was furious and protested first with the fourth official and then with the linesman which led to Webb coming over and sending him off.

Barça continued to dominate. Iniesta made a good run and sent a great ball through to Henry, but the Frenchman, clattering into Butt as he shot, sent the ball a yard wide of the far post. Eto'o then fired over after Messi wriggled his way past Lell. There were long periods of Barça possession as the team searched for more openings. The patience paid off as half time approached. Bayern were still struggling to get out of their half and in the 38th minute Barça once again won the ball back in Bayern's half, the ball came to Henry on the left, he sped past right back Oddo and his low cross was met by Messi who slid in front of Lell to poke the ball home. Five minutes later Messi set off on another run inside from the right touchline, he played a quick one-two with Alves before jinking past Demichelis's lunge, Van Bommel brought Messi's run to an end with a crude body check but Messi managed to touch the ball on to Eto'o, Van Bommel spun round to tackle Eto'o but only succeeded in sending the ball straight to

Henry in space on the left, and before Oddo could get across to block, Henry had stroked the ball cleanly past Butt into the far corner.

Four-nil at half time and a display so good that it moved Laporta to say: "Surely we have just seen the best first half in Barça's history". True, Bayern had been poor - Franz Beckenbauer was equally superlative suggesting that Bayern had played their "worst football in the entire history" while Bayern chairman Karl-Heinz Rummenigge claimed he had seen the great Udo Lattek crying at half time - but Barça had been scintillating with quick one-touch passes, excellent off-the-ball movement and tremendous pressure on the Bayern players whenever possession was lost.

With 135 minutes still to play in the tie perhaps it was normal that Barça were more cautious in the second half, perhaps remembering the two goals conceded against Lyon, while Klinsmann brought on Andreas Ottl for Altintop to bolster a midfield that had offered little support to the back four in the first 45 minutes. Barça concentrated on maintaining possession while limiting the risks and there were fewer chances as a consequence. However, Barça came close to a fifth in the 59th minute, Piqué sent a long ball out to Messi who dribbled in from the right and his shot from outside the area was diverted onto the crossbar by Butt's outstretched arm. Bayern's best chance of the night came in the 71st minute as Ze Roberto received the ball inside the area but Barça's defence were alert throughout and Puyol was quick to get across and make an excellent block. Keita came on for Henry and Iniesta moved forward on the left. Soon after Iniesta received a long ball from Messi and dribbled into the area, but after cutting inside Oddo his finishing let him down as he shot over. Barça continued to work hard right to the end as was demonstrated by Eto'o appearing in the Barça penalty area to rob the ball in the 86th minute. With Bojan and Busquets on at the end Barça should have made it five in injury time, Bojan battled the ball through to Iniesta who went outside the hapless Oddo before crossing to find Messi free at the far post but his goal-bound shot hit Keita who could not get out of the way. Before the end Marquez won himself an 'intelligent' yellow card for time-wasting which meant he would miss the second leg in Munich but be available for the semi-finals. Chelsea won 1-3 at Liverpool so a semi-final tie with the Londoners was looking very likely.

Barça: Valdés; Alves, Piqué, Márquez, Puyol; Xavi, Touré (Busquets m81), Iniesta; Messi, Eto'o (Bojan m90), Henry (Keita m74).

Bayern: Butt; Oddo, Demichelis, Breno, Lell; Altintop (Ottl m46), Van Bommel, Zé Roberto (Sosa m77); Schweinsteiger, Ribery; Toni.

Goals: m9 Messi 1-0, m13 Eto'o 2-0, m38 Messi 3-0, m42 Henry 4-0.

CHAPTER 7 – Real Madrid 2 Barça 6

On the Saturday following the tremendous performance against Bayern, Barça faced a relatively simple league game against relegation-threatened Recreativo at Camp Nou. Iniesta continued in fine form, scoring the first and forcing Recre's defender Nasief Morris into conceding an own goal for the second as Barça won 2-0.

There was a boost for the team with the return of Abidal after two months out of action for the Champions League second leg game in Munich. Qualification never looked in danger despite Ribery giving Bayern a 1-0 lead just after half time. Keita drove home a second half equalizer giving Barça a 5-1 win on aggregate and setting up a semi-final against Chelsea who qualified 7-5 on aggregate after a spectacular 4-4 draw with Liverpool at Stamford Bridge. With Manchester United and Arsenal also going through it meant that for the second consecutive season there were three English clubs and Barça in the Champions League semi-finals. As United had beaten Chelsea in the previous seasons final after defeating Barça in the semis there was every reason for the English teams to feel superior.

Back in La Liga Messi scored the only goal of the game in a 0-1 win at Getafe, the victory was more comfortable than the scoreline suggests with Barça looking very solid in defence. Messi was absent for the following game at home to Sevilla due to stomach problems. Iniesta responded with a truly magnificent performance, opening the scoring with a splendid curler over Sevilla's reserve keeper Javi Varas, then setting up the other three goals in a 4-0 win before being subbed off to an ovation after 60 minutes. It was Barça's seventh straight clean sheet in the league but as Madrid kept winning the gap remained at six points.

Messi was back for the always difficult game against Valencia at Mestalla, and he put Barça in front after twice exchanging passes with Iniesta. Then after 675 minutes without conceding a goal in the league Barça conceded twice in three minutes just before half time. Henry came on as a substitute after an hour but it wasn't until the 85th minute that the Frenchman grabbed an equalizer to earn Barça a point. However, the following day Madrid won 2-4 at Sevilla and a week before the *Clásico* the lead at the top was down to four points.

Barça now faced a massive week with the two Champions League semi-final games with Chelsea and the game at Madrid sandwiched in between. Luiz Felipe Scolari had been sacked as Chelsea's coach in February after a run of poor results but Guus Hiddink had taken over and the Londoners had improved in that time. There was still the core of the team that had faced Barça six times under Jose Mourinho between February 2005 and October 2006.and the likes of Petr Cech, John Terry, Frank Lampard, Michael Ballack and Didier Drogba were no strangers to Barça.

For the first leg at Camp Nou Chelsea were without the suspended Ashley Cole so Hiddink switched Jose Bosingwa to left back. Barça had everybody except Milito fit and Guardiola's only surprise was to leave Carles Puyol on the substitutes' bench, playing a back four of Alves, Marquez, Piqué and Abidal. Twelve months previously Man United had come to Camp Nou for a Champions League semi-final first leg and Sir Alex Ferguson's men had frustrated Barça in a 0-0 draw. Now another English team would do the same, as Chelsea generally limited Barça to shots from outside the area which rarely troubled Petr Cech.

Didier Drogba might have given Chelsea a vital away goal shortly before half time after a poor back pass from Marquez but Valdés did splendidly to deny the Ivorian striker twice. Barça looked more dangerous in the second half. Eto'o broke through once but was denied by Cech's outstretched leg, there was a timid penalty appeal as Terry appeared to pull Henry's shoulder, and then in the final five minutes substitutes Bojan and Hleb both missed good chances. It was a disappointing night for culés but the worst news was a knee injury to Marquez that would see him miss the remainder of the season while Puyol picked up a yellow card that meant he was suspended for the second leg at Stamford Bridge.

It was not the best preparation for the *Clásico*. Madrid had suffered their curse of the last 16 in the Champions League, going out at that stage of the competition for the fifth consecutive season after a 4-0 humiliation inflicted by Rafa Benitez's Liverpool, which meant Juande Ramos had the whole week free to work on his *'plan anti-Barça'*. Besides their disappointment in Europe, Madrid had been in excellent form in the league. The defeat to Barça in December had left them 12 points adrift but since then they had taken 52 points from a possible 54 and now if they could beat Barça at the Bernabéu the gap would be down to one point with four games to play. Madrid's captain Raúl felt confident enough before the match to claim that Madrid were favourites to win.

Madrid were without the suspended Pepe and the injured Sneijder and Guti, but Heinze and Robben had recovered from injury in time to play. Ramos selected Casillas, Sergio Ramos, Cannavaro, Metzelder, Heinze, Robben, Gago, Lass Diarra, Marcelo, Higuain and Raul in the coach's habitual 4-4-2 formation. Guardiola made just one change to the team that drew with Chelsea with Puyol returning in place of the injured Marquez as Barça started with a 4-3-3 with Valdés, Alves, Piqué, Puyol, Abidal, Xavi, Toure, Iniesta, Eto'o, Messi and Henry. However, Guardiola made the significant tactical move of asking Eto'o to play out on the right wing while Messi was given the free false nine role that would soon prove to be his most effective position.

Barça took just 24 seconds to force the first save from Iker Casillas when Xavi tried his luck from the edge of the box. Madrid caused some early problems especially from Arjen Robben who started well, twice getting past Eric Abidal. However, Barça were generally looking in control, but then against the run of play Madrid struck with a goal after 13 minutes. Sergio Ramos got past Abidal and crossed to the unmarked Higuain who headed firmly past Valdés. Barça responded magnificently, raising the rhythm and hitting back immediately. Messi sent a beautiful chipped ball through to Henry who gave Ramos all sorts of problems on the left, and the Frenchman ran into the area and coolly side-footed the ball past Casillas.

Then in the 20th minute Henry skipped past Lass, and Cannavaro had to come across to make a clumsy foul. From the free kick Xavi picked out Puyol who powered a header past Casillas to make it 1-2. Madrid tried to come straight back, Robben forcing Valdés to save well with his legs and then Robben sent in Raul whose cross hit Alves but Valdés did well to stop the goal-bound ball. From then on, the rest of the first half was all one-way traffic as Barça cut through Madrid's defence time and again. Messi was working wonders in the free role in the middle and he combined superbly with Xavi and Iniesta on several occasions to create chances. Alves then sent Messi through but his powerful shot was straight at Casillas and soon after Eto'o let fly from the right forcing a tremendous save from Casillas. It didn't matter how hard the Madrid players chased the ball, they were always just too late as Barça moved the ball swiftly on, another great combination from Iniesta and Messi ended with Casillas again saving from Messi.

The pressure from Barça paid off in the 35th minute when Xavi robbed Lass in Madrid's half and sent Messi steaming through, Messi kept his head to slip the ball past Casillas with the outside of his left foot. The writing was on the wall now for Madrid and Barça showed their superiority winning the ball again and again with Toure and Pique both doing a splendid job. Just before half time Alves hit a free kick through a hole in Madrid's defensive wall but Casillas again did well to keep the score down.

Barça continued to dominate in the second half. Iniesta shot wide from 20 yards and then Messi dribbled into the area before shooting across the face of the goal. Madrid could hardly get the ball and needed the help of the referee who twice got in the way of Barça moves to win the ball back for Madrid, the second time led to a Madrid counter attack and a foul by Iniesta on Sergio Ramos. Robben sent in the free kick from the right and Barça's defence left the back post free for Ramos to head past Valdés from close in. At 2-3 Madrid were back in the game.

Once again Barça responded quickly to a Madrid goal and within two minutes the two-goal advantage was restored. Xavi received from Toure just inside the Barça half, spotted Madrid's advanced defence and chipped a pass through for Henry to chase. Despite having Casillas storming out of the area towards him Henry kept his eye on the ball and calmly side-footed the ball past the keeper into the empty net. Madrid had to take risks and Juande Ramos chose to bring on another striker, Jan-Klaas Huntelaar, in place of Marcelo, but it only made things easier for Barça to control the midfield. Eto'o was playing a disciplined game out on the right wing and in the 60th minute he crossed for Messi who missed a relatively simple chance, sending the ball wide of the far post.

Keita came on for Henry and Barça continued to dominate. The difference in class was exemplified by one turn from Iniesta in midfield which left two opponents running in the wrong direction as he slipped between them. Unfortunately Madrid's frustration showed a couple of times with late tackles. Barça were quite simply too good, and despite the fact that Madrid never stopped running they were always behind the ball as Barça continued to move it around at a tremendous speed.

Madrid brought on Van der Vaart for Sergio Ramos in a last attempt to make a comeback but it just left more space for Barça to attack. In the 73rd minute Lass was fortunate that referee Undiano Mallenco waved play on after Iniesta was cut down in the area. Then two minutes later

Messi played the ball on to Xavi who held off Gago, turning 360º to play the ball back into Messi who again beat Casillas in the one-against-one, this time at Casillas's near post. It was Xavi's fourth assist of the game and Barça led 2-5.

The best was still to come. Piqué broke out of defence and found Messi who sent the ball out to Eto'o on the right. Eto'o crossed towards Piqué, who had continued his gallop into the area, and Cannavaro was forced into deflecting the ball towards his own goal. Casillas managed to block the ball but Piqué was quickest to react turning the ball back past the goalkeeper for Barça's 100th league goal of the season.

There was still time for Messi to miss another from Bojan's cross before the referee blew for full time on exactly 90 minutes, perhaps wanting to spare Madrid any more humiliation in injury time. It wasn't important, the blow had been struck, Barça led the Liga by seven points with four games to play and Madrid's 18-match unbeaten league run was looking to count for nothing. Guardiola knew that winning 2-6 at the Bernabéu was something very special. After the match he said, "I am very, very, very happy. It is one of the happiest days of my life, for having come here with a team like Barça, for having played so well and for having won, but above all for having scored so many goals. I am thrilled to have made so many people happy".

Real Madrid: Casillas; Sergio Ramos (Van der Vaart m72), Cannavaro, Metzelder, Heinze; Robben (Javi García m79), Gago, Lass Diarra, Marcelo (Huntelaar m59); Higuaín, Raúl.

Barça: Valdés; Alves, Piqué, Puyol, Abidal; Xavi, Toure (Busquets m85), Iniesta (Bojan m85); Eto'o, Messi, Henry (Keita m61).

Goals: m14 Higuain 1-0, m16 Henry 1-1, m20 Puyol 1-2, m35 Messi 1-3, m56 Sergio Ramos 2-3, m58 Henry 2-4, m75 Messi 2-5, m83 Piqué 2-6.

CHAPTER 8 – Chelsea 1 Barça 1

There was little time for the players to celebrate the historic win in Madrid as the following Wednesday the team was in London for the vital Champions League semi-final second leg at Chelsea. Barça had been frustrated in the goalless draw in the first leg at Camp Nou and now hadn't beaten Chelsea in the last four games between the teams. In four meetings at Stamford Bridge in the previous ten years Chelsea had won three while Barça had won just once in February 2006. However, a score draw would be enough for Barça and the bookmakers made the Catalans slight favourites to go through. On the day before the game Manchester United beat Arsenal to become the first team to reach the final which would be played in Rome's *Stadio Olimpico* on May 27.

With Puyol suspended and Marquez and Milito injured, Guardiola had a problem to form a defence. The logical choice appeared to be to bring in Caceres to partner Piqué in the middle with Alves and Abidal as full backs, but Caceres was a long way from his best and hadn't started a game since the 2-0 win over Recreativo on April 11. The other options involved playing Abidal, Toure or Busquets out of position, while Guardiola's team selection was further complicated by Henry pulling out due to a knee injury picked up against Madrid.

Guardiola opted finally for Toure at the back, presumably feeling his strength would be important against the power of Drogba. Busquets and Keita came into midfield with Iniesta moving forward into Henry's position making a starting XI of Valdés, Alves, Toure, Pique, Abidal, Xavi, Busquets, Keita, Messi, Eto'o and Iniesta.

Chelsea had warmed up well with a 3-1 victory over neighbours Fulham at the weekend. Hiddink had Ashley Cole returning at left back which meant

Bosingwa, who had done so well to contain Messi at Camp Nou, returned to right back. The only other change from the first leg was Nicolas Anelka starting on the right in place of John Mikel Obi as Chelsea lined up in a 4-2-3-1 of Cech, Bosingwa, Terry, Alex, Cole, Essien, Ballack, Anelka, Lampard, Malouda and Drogba.

There was little between the teams in the early exchanges. Then Chelsea took the lead after nine minutes with an absolute corker from Essien. Cole played the ball into Lampard who turned and shot from the edge of the area, the ball hit Toure and flew up in an arc and when it came down it was met by Essien with a stunning left foot volley from 25 yards that flew in off the underside of the crossbar, giving Valdés no chance. Memories of the 2007/08 semi-final between Barça and Man United came flooding back when Paul Scholes scored the only goal of the 180 minutes with a terrific strike from outside the area.

With the goal advantage Chelsea could defend in numbers with Lampard playing deep to support Ballack and Essien in front of the back four. There was little room for Xavi, Iniesta, Eto'o and Messi and Barça were limited to a couple of off-target long range efforts. Chelsea's defenders took few risks in possession, preferring to play quick long balls up towards Drogba rather than risking the possibility of losing possession near Cech's goal. Drogba had more support than at Camp Nou with the speed of Malouda and Anelka testing Barça's makeshift defence.

Chelsea had a first penalty appeal turned down after Malouda fell in the area after tussling for the ball with Alves. The Norweigan referee Tom Henning Øvrebø gave Chelsea the foul but dictated that the foul was just outside the area. From the free kick Drogba fired the ball across goal and Valdés was fortunate to deflect the ball away with his knee. From the resulting corner Terry headed just wide of the far post. Then in the 27th minute Drogba burst into the area before going down as Abidal challenged, for a moment Abidal had grabbed at Drogba's shirt but the striker then seemed to fall too easily and Øvrebø waved play on.

Barça were having little success in penetrating the Chelsea defence, the main stategy seemed to be to get the ball out wide to Alves. However, the Brazilian's crossing was poor as time and again his crosses were too long. Things got worse for Alves when he was booked after 30 minutes for a foul on Cole. The yellow card meant he would be suspended for the final. Messi and Iniesta tried to work passes with Eto'o but Chelsea worked hard and each time closed the space superbly. Messi got away from the man-marking of Ashley Cole a couple of times but it always came to nothing.

After half time Barça showed signs that they might begin to get closer to Cech's goal. But as Barça pushed forward they looked more vulnerable to the Chelsea counter. In the 52nd minute Anelka broke free and fed Drogba in the area, the big striker cut inside Piqué but Valdés came out to make a vital save with his outstretched right leg, the ball flew out to Lampard who drove the ball back in, the ball deflected off Busquets to Malouda who volleyed into the side netting.

Keita and Messi had half chances but both fired well over the bar but the general pattern of Chelsea frustrating Barça continued. Then, in the 66th minute, things got a lot worse for the visitors. Drogba flicked on a long clearance and Anelka got goal side of Abidal, as the Barça defender tried to make up ground he brushed Anelka who then tripped over his own heels and the referee had no hesitation in awarding a foul and showing Abidal the red card.

Chelsea could have gone for the kill. Lampard had a shot from just outside the area which took a slight deflection off Toure that Valdés read well, but then Hiddink brought on Belletti in place of Drogba and Chelsea concentrated on not conceding. As Barça edged forwards, Essien was fortunate only to see a yellow card after an ugly challenge on Iniesta.

Alves fired a free kick over and then in the 80th minute Piqué stormed forward but could only shoot wide from the edge of the area.

Piqué was then extremely fortunate not to concede a penalty. As Anelka tried to nip past, the ball clearly struck Piqué's raised arm though the referee decided it was unintentional. The minutes ticked by, the fourth official signalled four minutes of injury time and Barça made one last push. In the 93rd minute Xavi again sent Alves away on the right, again Alves sent over a cross which went too deep, Samuel Eto'o stretched in an attempt to control the ball but it spun away from him, for once Essien made a mistake with the clearance, slicing the ball to Messi on the edge of the area, the Argentinian looked up and saw Iniesta to his right and played the ball square, Iniesta took one step forward and fired the ball high past Cech's despairing dive into the top corner of the net.

Iniesta tore off his yellow shirt and swung it around his head as he ran to the Barça fans in celebration. Guardiola made an uncharacteristic dash of joy along the touchline as the emotion was impossible to contain. But there was still time for a Chelsea corner with Cech going forward in a last desperate effort, the ball arrived to Ballack who fired in a powerful shot that was charged down by Eto'o, who had turned away from the blast as he ran at Ballack and the ball struck him on the underside of his raised upper arm. Øvrebø was only a few yards away but he waved play on, provoking a spectacular protest from Ballack who ran screaming behind the Norweigian referee but to no avail.

When Øvrebø finally blew for full time the scenes were incredible, as the Barça players celebrated and the Chelsea players surrounded the official. It was a cruel end for Chelsea who had had the better of the game, but they had failed to kill off Barça's ten men and they paid the price in the end. For Barça the dream of the triple was now looking very possible: just five more points were needed from four games in La Liga, and then there were the two cup finals against Bilbao's Athletic Club and Manchester United to look forward to.

Chelsea: Cech; Bosingwa, Alex, Terry, Cole; Ballack, Essien; Anelka, Lampard, Malouda; Drogba (Belletti m72).

Barça: Valdés; Alves, Toure, Piqué, Abidal; Xavi, Busquets (Bojan m85), Keita; Messi, Eto'o (Sylvinho m97), Iniesta (Gudjohnsen m96).

Goals: m9 Essien 1-0, m93 Iniesta 1-1.

CHAPTER 9 - Athletic Club 1 Barça 4

Winning 2-6 in Madrid and then qualifying for the Champions League final had made a very satisfactory week for Barça and things got even better the following Saturday when Madrid, still affected by the previous week's humiliation, lost 3-0 at Valencia. Barça now needed to beat Villarreal at Camp Nou to clinch La Liga ahead of the Copa del Rey final the following Wednesday.

For the football played over the season many critics were claiming that Barça were the best team in the world but the team still hadn't won anything. The stage was set with 95,000 expectant fans hoping to celebrate the league title. Villarreal had slipped down to sixth place in the table but they were still in with a very decent chance of a Champions League top four finish.

With Puyol back in defence and Henry and Marquez still out injured Guardiola picked his strongest possible team with Toure returning to midfield and Iniesta continuing on the left of attack. Barça started well and took the lead when Keita's deflected shot looped over Diego Alves in the Villarreal goal, though ten minutes later Joseba Llorente had equalized with the first league goal that Barça had conceded at Camp Nou since De La Peña's double for Espanyol in February.

Goals from Eto'o and Alves put Barça 3-1 up at half time and everything looked ready for a big party. However, the second half dragged on and Barça may have been guilty of just trying to play out time. The crowd had already been singing: 'campeones campeones oé oé oé' when in the 77th minute Villarreal, who had hardly had an attack in the second half, won a penalty after Abidal used his body to impede Nihat in front of goal. The French defender received his second straight red card in two games meaning he would now miss the Copa del Rey final as well as the Champions League final in Rome. Mati Fernandez fired home Villarreal's penalty and at 3-2 there was everything to play for.

Guardiola brought on Sylvinho and Busquets in place of Eto'o and Xavi and Barça switched to a 4-4-1 formation with just Messi up front. Villarreal failed to threaten as the minutes ticked away, but then in the 92nd minute a long ball from defence was controlled superbly by Llorente inside the area, he held off the challenge of Puyol and smashed the ball in off the top of the post.

The celebration for La Liga would have to wait as attention now turned to the Copa del Rey final with Athletic Club in Valencia. The two clubs were the cup kings in Spain, Barça having won the cup a record 24 times with Athletic just one behind on 23 wins. There had been four previous finals between the two teams. The first was in 1920 when Barça triumphed 2-0, in 1932 Athletic were victorious, winning 1-0, Barça won again in 1943 4-3 after extra time and again in 1953 this time beating the Basques 2-1. The last time the teams had met in the final was in 1984 when Athletic had secured a 1-0 victory in a game remembered more for the tremendous fight after the final whistle with Diego Maradona as the main protagonist. Maradona would later be punished with a three-month ban for his part in the fracas. The win in 1984 was the last time that Athletic had lifted the trophy while Barça's last win was under Louis Van Gaal in 1998 when Dutch keeper Ruud Hesp was the hero of a penalty shoot-out after a 1-1 draw with Mallorca at Mestalla.

There was bad news for Barça as Andres Iniesta finished the Villarreal game with a torn quadriceps muscle, leaving the team's most in-form player facing a race against time to recover for the Champions League final. He was definitely ruled out for the Copa del Rey, and with Abidal suspended and Marquez and Henry still out injured, Guardiola had some important decisions to select the starting XI for his first final. Pinto was expected to continue as the Copa del Rey goalkeeper while players such as Busquets, Bojan and Caceres could all consider themselves as in with a chance of making the team after playing a big part in the cup run.

In the end Guardiola surprised by deploying Toure again as a central defender which was a clear sign that the coach had lost faith with Caceres. Puyol was switched to left back again, meaning no place for Sylvinho as Barça lined up with Pinto, Alves, Toure, Piqué, Puyol, Xavi, Busquets, Keita, Messi, Bojan and Eto'o. Athletic came into the final in good form, having won three and drawn one of their last four league games. This run had put them safe from relegation and coach Joaquín Caparrós, in his second season at the Basque club, could concentrate totally on the cup final, putting out his best team of Gorka Iraizoz, Andoni Iraola, Aitor Ocio, Fernando Amorebieta, Koikili, Francisco Yeste, Pablo Orbaiz, Javi Martínez, David López, Gaizka Toquero and Fernando Llorente.

Barça started the game slowly, with Athletic showing more aggression and winning the midfield battle. In the 8th minute a build up on the right involving Yeste and Lopez ended with Javi Martinez whipping in a shot that Pinto did well to tip round the post. Yeste swung over the corner and Toquero rose at the far post above Xavi and Keita to head firmly past Pinto. Barça struggled to respond, and as in the previous week's game at Stamford Bridge the midfield of Xavi, Busquets and Keita failed to find the necessary creativity to breach the Athletic defence.

Barça's first chance came in the 19th minute when Piqué found Bojan on the right of the penalty area but the youngster held on to the ball too long and ended up being forced to shoot from a tight angle giving Iraizoz no problem. A couple of minutes later Xavi sent a great ball through to Eto'o but ball.again the Barça forward took too long, allowing the defence to get back and hustle him off the ball.

Barça were struggling to find a way through then just after the half hour an equalizer arrived from an unlikely source. Toure was allowed to bring the ball forward from defence and when Athletic's midfield finally tried to close him down he skipped past a couple of weak challenges before firing a low shot from 25 yards which beat Iraizoz at his near post.

Barça grew after the equalizer and Athletic were now getting nowhere near Pinto's goal. In the 33rd minute Messi went on a great run, played a pass inside the full-back to Alves but Alves shot across the face of the goal. Barça were dominating now, knocking the ball around in typical style. On the stroke of half time Alves sent a 30-yard free kick just wide of the post.

Barça began the second half very strongly, with Messi looking particularly keen. In the 48th minute Eto'o found the Argentinian on the right-hand side of the area, he dribbled past a couple of defenders but his shot was blocked. Soon after, Messi combined again with Eto'o but shot just wide with the outside of his left foot. Messi tried again after a splendid move starting with Pinto that involved Pique, Puyol, Busquets, Xavi, Alves and Keita and ended with Messi's low shot from 20 yards being turned round the post by Iraizoz. In the 55th minute Messi's insistence finally paid off, he played in Eto'o on the right, Eto'o's shot was turned out by Iraizoz but the ball came back to Messi who had continued his run and he fired home through a sea of defenders from 12 yards.

Eto'o then had a great chance after Keita's excellent chipped pass forward found him inside the area but he fired over. It mattered little as Barça were now rampant. In the 58th minute Alves won the ball on the edge of Barça's penalty area, starting a one-touch combination out of defence through Xavi, Messi and Alves again, the Brazilian played the ball back to Messi who now had time and space to turn and send Bojan through, and although he had a defender in front of him and Eto'o free to his right, the young striker saw a gap and slotted the ball in off the far post.

Athletic were impotent to stop Barça now. And in the 64th minute Xavi banged the last nail into their coffin, curling home a free-kick from the left-side that went in off the near post. There was nothing more but for Barça to play out time with an exhibition of possession football. The only thing missing was a goal from Samuel Eto'o who missed two more good chances from inside the area. Alves had a free kick saved and there was even time for Hleb to try his luck but the Belarusian seemed destined never to score an official Barça goal.

At the end Puyol collected the cup from King Juan Carlos and the party on the pitch continued for a good half an hour after the final whistle with Guardiola being thrown in the air by the players. It was Guardiola's first trophy as first team coach and Barça's first silverware since 2006. They would not need to wait long for further success.

Athletic: Iraizoz; Iraola, Ocio, Amorebieta, Koikili; Yeste, Orbaiz (Ion Velez m62), Javi Martínez, David López (Susaeta m59); Toquero (Etxeberria m62), Llorente.

Barça: Pinto; Alves, Toure (Sylvinho m89), Piqué, Puyol; Xavi (Pedro m88), Busquets, Keita; Messi, Bojan (Hleb m84), Eto'o.

Goals: m9 Toquero 1-0, m31 Toure 1-1, m55 Messi 1-2. m58 Bojan 1-3, m64 Xavi 1-4.

CHAPTER 10 – Barça 2 Manchester United 0

On the Friday following the Copa del Rey triumph Guardiola fined Messi, Eto'o, Gudjohnsen, Xavi, Toure and Alves €500 each for arriving late for training. The players were only ten minutes late, and a couple of them arrived only a minute or two after the stipulated time, but the coach made it very clear that this was no time for relaxation.

With three league games remaining Barça needed just one more point to clinch the title. Barça were due to play at Mallorca on Sunday 17 May, while Madrid played at Villarreal on the Saturday night needing a win to delay Barça's celebration. Having spoilt Barça's party at Camp Nou the weekend before, Villarreal also frustrated Madrid, and with just minutes remaining in an open entertaining match the home side led 2-1. Then, in the 88th minute, Higuain snatched an equalizer and a glimmer of hope for Madrid. But in the 90th minute Casillas misjudged a corner and Juan Capdevila scored a winner for Villarreal sending the title to Camp Nou for the first time since 2006.

Guardiola could now afford to rest players for the Champions League final. Of the probable starters in Rome only Eto'o was named in the team to face Mallorca. The striker was one goal ahead of Atlético Madrid's Diego Forlan in race for the season's prestigious *Pichichi* top-goalscorer trophy. Forlan had pipped Eto'o to the award with a hat-trick at Camp Nou on the last day of the 2004/05 season, Eto'o won the prize in 05/06 and it was clear he was hungry to win it again now.

Eto'o began the game against Mallorca well, putting Barça ahead with his first chance after ten minutes. However, he then missed countless chances including a last minute penalty as Mallorca came back to win 2-1.

Guardiola took the opportunity to give first team debuts to Oier Olazábal, Xavi Torres, Jeffren Suarez and Thiago Alcantara, while Caceres improved his chances of playing in Rome with a good performance in defence.

The following Saturday, just four days before the Champions League final, Barça played host to Osasuna in La Liga's penultimate week. For Camp Nou it was the chance to celebrate an extraordinary season but the party was dampened a little by Osasuna winning 0-1 and by referee Antonio Rubinos Perez sending off 17-year-old debutant Marc Muniesa just 30 minutes after he came on as a substitute. Eto'o failed to score in the 59 minutes that Guardiola allowed him while Forlan scored three against Athletic Club which put him two goals clear in the race for the *Pichichi*.

Manchester United had to play at Hull on the Sunday giving them one day fewer than Barça to prepare for the final. However, United had already been crowned as the English Premier League champions so Sir Alex Ferguson had the luxury of resting all his key players for the game and Hull were still beaten 0-1. The Red Devils had every reason to be confident of beating Barça, they were current World and European champions and their latest league title success was the third in a row. They also had Cristiano Ronaldo who was the holder of the Ballon d'Or and the FIFA World Player awards.

The view from England was that while Barça had some very good players they had failed to perform when they played Chelsea. In the previous season's semi-final Barça had failed to breach United's defence in 180 minutes and Messi had never scored against an English team. Rio Ferdinand was fit again after missing three weeks with a calf injury and was ready to join Nemanja Vidic to form what many people considered to be the best central defensive pairing around. United had conceded just 24 league goals in 38 matches and they arrived to the final in excellent form having not lost since a 2-0 defeat at Fulham in March though they had been knocked out of the FA Cup semi-finals by Everton on penalties.

Ferguson's only selection problem was deciding who would replace the suspended Darren Fletcher in midfield, though the experienced Ryan Giggs was expected to come into midfield.

Iniesta and Henry recovered in time and were included in the squad that travelled to Rome. With Marquez injured and Abidal and Alves both suspended, Guardiola's main doubt was how to form a defence to cope with Ronaldo and Wayne Rooney. The Barcelona based sports daily *El Sport* predicted an unprecedented back four of Puyol, Toure, Piqué and Keita. There was concern over how the 35-year-old Sylvinho would cope against the energy of Ji-Sun Park and although he had barely played in the position Keita was considered as an option due to his greater stamina. Another option was for Caceres to come in at right back with Puyol switching to the left. Young defenders Alberto Botia and Marc Muniesa were included in the squad as possible back up.

Keita was reported to have told Guardiola not to risk him at left back, and in the end the coach opted for Sylvinho, so the Barça eleven who walked out at the *Stadio Olimpico* were Valdés, Puyol, Toure, Piqué, Sylvinho, Xavi, Busquets, Iniesta, Eto'o, Messi and Henry. There were no surprises from Ferguson as United started with 4-2-3-1 formation of Van der Sar, O'Shea, Ferdinand, Vidic, Evra, Anderson, Carrick, Park, Giggs, Rooney and Ronaldo.

Barça started the game nervously and straight from the kick off sent the ball back to Valdés who kicked the ball directly into touch. United were encouraged, in the second minute Anderson nutmegged Toure and won a free kick 35 yards out. Ronaldo fired in an awkward shot that bounced in front of Valdés who failed to hold on to the ball and Piqué had to be quick to get in front of Park who was storming in for the rebound.

United pressed high up the pitch making it difficult for Barça to bring the ball out from the back and Valdés was forced into long kicks which generally led to United winning back possession. Ronaldo had one hopeful attempt from 40 yards and soon after he tried again with a volley from the left of the area, both efforts went wide but Barça were on the back foot.

Eto'o had been sacrificed again to the right wing, allowing Messi to play the false nine role that had worked so well at the Bernabéu but in the early stages the Argentinian did not manage to link up with Xavi and Iniesta. This would change in the ninth minte, Van der Sar made a long clearance that Busquets headed back over the halfway line, Carrick could only head the ball to Xavi who played a first time ball inside to Iniesta. There seemed little danger at this point but Iniesta exchanged quick passes with Messi and then, spotting the gap between Anderson and Carrick, darted forward before sending the ball right to Eto'o who was running into the area from the wing. Eto'o cut inside Vidic and as Carrick slid in to challenge the Cameroonian toe-poked a shot that Van der Sar touched but couldn't stop at his near post. Eto'o's finishing had been disappointing in the games running up to the final, but when it mattered most he took his first chance decisively.

United were shaken by the set-back. Straight after the restart Vidic mishit a back pass which gifted Barça a corner. Barça began to knock the ball around in typical fashion but Ronaldo continued to pose a threat. In the 16th minute Giggs gave the Portuguese the chance to run at Piqué and the Barça defender was forced into a foul for which he received a yellow card. From the free kick Giggs hit the ball a yard over the bar. Three minutes later Eto'o, who continued to play on the right, played the ball inside to Messi who fired a powerful shot that whistled over Van der Sar's crossbar. Ronaldo had another shot wide and then a header over from Giggs's corner, but Barça were beginning to take control of the game.

United's attempt to push up on the Barça defence meant that Xavi and Iniesta were finding room to dictate things in midfield, with Messi beginning to combine well with the pair. Iniesta won a foul on the left and Xavi hit the free kick just wide. Messi was stopped by a foul after a good run. Ferguson switched Giggs to the left with Rooney coming more central but now it was United who could not find a way through. On the stroke of half time Messi made another good run down the left and Van der Sar fumbled the cross but was rescued by his defence. Then there was still time for Iniesta to chip in a cross which was just too high for Henry.

At half time Ferguson brought on Carlos Tevez for Anderson as United switched to 4-4-2 but the result was to make things easier for Barça's midfield. In the 48th minute Henry skipped outside Ferdinand to create a shooting chance but Van der Sar made a good save. It was all Barça now. In the 51st minute Iniesta made a great run to the edge of the area and was only stopped by a foul inside the "D" of the penalty area. From the free kick Xavi curled one and was unlucky to see the ball bounce out off the bottom of Van der Sar's left hand post.

United had their first chance of the second half in the 56th minute when Rooney crossed from the right, Toure missed the clearance and Barça were fortunate to see the ball bounce over Park's head at the far post. United had a few minutes pinning Barça back but the Barça defence was playing splendidly. Piqué especially against his ex-team mates was superb. Ferguson brought on Berbatov for Park, and Ronaldo switched to the left side where he remained in Puyol's pocket until the end of the game.

Then on 70 minutes Puyol anticipated a clearance from Van der Sar and charged forward, the attack broke down but the ball came out to Xavi 15 yards inside the United half. Spotting Messi unmarked between Ferdinand and Vidic, Xavi sent in a beautiful cross which the little Argentinian met with a great jump and a looping header over Van der Sar into the net. Guardiola brought on Keita for Henry with the intention of protecting the two-goal lead. However, there was a brief loss of concentration in Barça's defence which gave United a chance to pull a goal straight back. Berbatov crossed from the right, the ball arrived to Ronaldo at the far post but Valdés did brilliantly to close the angle and make his only important save of the match.

From then on Barça played out time, frustrating United with stylish possession football. Ronaldo showed his frustration with a couple of fouls on Puyol, and Scholes was lucky to stay on the pitch after a horrendous foul on Busquets. Puyol had a great chance to make it three-nil in the 84th minute but his attempted clip over Van der Sar hit the United keeper. Berbatov had a header over from a corner as United desperately tried to get forward but until the end of the game the English team hardly had the ball again as Barça demonstrated the difference in class.

It was a marvellous end to Guardiola's first season in charge. No Spanish team had ever won the *triplete* of Liga, Copa del Rey and the Champions League in one season and the feat of winning domestic league and cup as well as Europe's top prize had only ever been achieved by Celtic, Ajax, PSV Eindhoven and Manchester United.

Barça still had one final league game to play away at Deportivo. Eto'o scored a late equalizer in a 1-1 draw to take his league tally for the season to 30 goals. However, it was not quite enough to win the *Pichichi* as Atlético's Diego Forlan scored a total of 32.

Barça: Valdés; Puyol, Toure, Piqué, Sylvinho; Xavi, Busquets, Iniesta (Pedro m92); Messi, Eto'o, Henry (Keita m71).

Man United: Van Der Sar; O'Shea, Ferdinand, Vidic, Evra; Anderson (Tevez m45), Carrick, Giggs (Scholes m74); Park (Berbatov m65), Ronaldo, Rooney.

Goals: m10 Eto'o 1-0, m70 Messi 2-0.

CHAPTER 11 – Barça 1 Shakhtar Donetsk 0

After such a successful season, the summer of 2009 was much less eventful than the previous year. There were the usual transfer stories in the press with players such as David Villa, Zlatan Ibrahimovic, Diego Forlan, Karim Benzema, Cesc Fabregas, David Silva and Robinho all rumoured to be possible targets.

However, June passed and while Madrid made the big name signings of Kaka and Cristiano Ronaldo, Barça made no moves. Valdés and Toure signed new contracts but the big doubt was whether or not Eto'o would stay at Camp Nou or move on. Eto'o had a year left on his contract and the club was reluctant to offer him the improved contract he felt he deserved.

On July 15 Barça finally made the first signing of the summer, paying Inter Milan €4.5 million for the defender Maxwell Andrade. At the same time the two clubs negotiated a deal involving Ibrahimovic and Eto'o.

Barça returned to training on Monday 20 July. Some of the international players were given a few extra days holiday, but back to work were Valdés, Hleb, Gudjohnsen, Cáceres, Abidal, Touré, Bojan, Pinto, Jorquera, Márquez, Pedro, Henry, Víctor Sánchez, Keita and Henrique Buss who had rejoined the first team after a year's loan at Bayer Leverkusen. Guardiola also called on ten young players to train with the first team: Martin Montoya, Albert Dalmau, Andreu Fontàs, Marc Muniesa, Victor Espasandín, José Rueda, Jonathan dos Santos, Gai Assulin, Jeffren Suarez and Ruben Rochina.

In his first press conference since the end of the previous season Guardiola was asked about Eto'o's future. Guardiola praised Eto'o highly as a player but said the problem was a question of "feeling". The importance of team spirit and dressing room harmony was fundamental to Guardiola and it seems clear that he felt that Eto'o was not good in this aspect. As the team flew out to London for the first preseason games, reports came through that Eto'o had agreed terms with Inter.

On July 24th Bojan scored Barça's first goal of the 2009/2010 preseason in a 1-1 draw against Tottenham Hotspur at Wembley. Bojan scored again two days later at the same stadium in a 4-1 win over Egyptian side Al-Ahly with the other goals coming from Pedro, Jeffren and Rueda. On the same day Ibrahimovic arrived in Barcelona hoping to complete his move. The next morning he passed his medical and the transfer was finalized in the afternoon with Ibrahimovic signing a five-year contract. While there was no doubting the big Swede's ability, fans found it hard to comprehend that Barça had to pay €43 million plus Eto'o, who had scored 130 goals in 200 games for Barça, to complete the deal.

A broken hand would delay Ibrahimovic's debut for three weeks. Without him, Barça flew to the USA for more preseason games. Pedro and Jeffren continued in good form both scoring in the wins over David Beckham's LA Galaxy (2-1) and Seattle Sounders (4-0), Maxwell made a solid debut against Galaxy and Messi scored his first goals of the season with a double against the Sounders. The US tour finished with a 1-1 draw against the Mexican side Chivas with Bojan grabbing himself another goal.

The first official game of the season was another clash against Athletic Club, this time in the Spanish Supercopa. Barça were without Marquez, Iniesta, Ibrahimovic and Messi for the first leg at San Mames which meant a front three of Henry, who had been doubtful before the game, Pedro and Bojan. Oscar De Marcos gave Athletic the lead just before half time but second half goals from Xavi and a superb 25-yard strike from Pedro gave Barça a deserved 1-2 victory to take into the second leg. Pedro was rewarded a few days later with a first team contract.

Ibrahimovic made his first appearance for Barça, coming on for the second half in the annual Joan Gamper tournament, but he had no luck in front of goal as Barça lost 0-1 to Manchester City. The most positive thing to take from the Gamper match was the exciting second half contribution from Thiago Alcantara and Johnathan Dos Santos. For the Supercopa second leg game with Athletic, Camp Nou had the first chance to see the attacking trio of Messi, Ibrahimovic and Henry in action. The first signs were positive as Barça claimed the first trophy of the season and the fourth of Guardiola's era with a comfortable 3-0 victory thanks to two goals from Messi and one from substitute Bojan.

A few days later, on Friday 28 August, Barça had the chance to add another trophy when they faced Shakhtar Donetsk in the UEFA Super Cup final in Monaco. The Shakhtar defender Dmytro Chygrynskiy was in the curious position of being on the point of signing for Barça as he went into the game. Barça were still without the injured Milito, Marquez and Iniesta, and as the transfer deadline approached there were questions over the depths of Barça's squad. Victor Sanchez, Hleb and Caceres had been loaned out to Xerez, Stuttgart and Juventus, respectively, while Henrique and Gudjohnsen were also negotiating moves. The policy of trusting in homegrown players was emphasized by Guardiola including Jeffren, Muniesa, Fontás and Dos Santos in the squad for the Monaco trip.

Barça were favourites to win the game but Shakhtar had proved to be difficult opponents when the teams met in the previous season's Champions League group stage. The winners of the Champions League had only been victorious twice in the previous five UEFA Super Cup finals while the UEFA Cup champions had won the trophy three times. In 2006 Barça had performed very poorly, losing 3-0 to Sevilla and many blamed that performance on the lack of concentration on the players' part caused by all the fuss surrounding the UEFA player awards ceremony the night before the match. Guardiola pledged there would be no relaxation this time.

The Barça coach made just one change to the team that had beaten Athletic with Abidal returning at left back in place of Maxwell as Barça lined up with Valdés, Alves, Pique, Puyol, Abidal, Xavi, Toure, Keita, Messi, Ibrahimovic and Henry. Before the match there had been talk about the poor condition of the pitch at the Louis II stadium, and the slow rhythm of the game in the early exchanges suggested the players were not comfortable, with nobody wanting to take any risks. There was a slight change to Barça's system with the full backs Alves and Abidal playing further forward and Toure Yaya playing deeper to cover. Barça were dominating possession but were limited to long shots and off-target crosses.

Ibrahimovic was receiving very little service but after half an hour he showed one touch of class with an excellent first time lay off to Messi from a Valdés clearance. The first decent scoring chance didn't arrive until the 34th minute when Messi took a quick free kick to Xavi and sprinted into the area to receive the return before shooting low and forcing the first save of the game from Shakhtar keeper Pyatov. There was little more of note in a disappointing first half apart from a penalty appeal just before half time after a clear hand ball in the Shakhtar defensive wall from Messi's free kick.

The second half continued in much the same way with only one turn and shot wide from Ibrahimovic early on. It wasn't until the last twenty minutes of normal time that Barça began to turn up the rhythm. Henry might have scored a fantastic goal in the 70th minute but he failed to connect when attempting a spectacular overhead kick after Ibrahimovic's flick. Messi then forced a save with a shot from the edge of the area and as play continued the ball came to Henry who nearly surprised Pyatov with a shot from the left wing which the Shakhtar keeper tipped over the bar. A couple of minutes later Xavi robbed the ball in midfield and fed Ibrahimovic who advanced before shooting when he really should have passed to Henry who was in a better position on the left. It was Ibrahimovic's last contribution as Guardiola brought on Pedro in his place with 15 minutes remaining.

As Barça pushed forward, the danger of conceding a breakaway goal increased. Shakhtar had a couple of counter attacks, but it was Barça, and Messi in particular, who looked most likely to score. Messi had a couple of efforts and then in injury time he set off on an incredible run into the area, only to lose the ball as he bore down on goal. Unfortunately immediately after this Messi got involved in a stupid square-up with Srna which earned both players a yellow card. Messi was fortunate as his reaction, with feigned head-butt included, was not worthy of the best player in the world.

As the game moved into extra time the danger of Barça losing increased. Shakhtar, were four games into the league season and they looked fitter and began to cause some problems for Barça's defence. Puyol had to make one great recovering tackle to prevent Vasyl Kobin a chance, and Valdés was forced into his first diving save of the night to deny substitute Julius Aghahowa. The game was much more exciting now and both teams had their chances, Barça's best of the first half of extra time fell to Bojan who made a good run into the area but the keeper saved with his legs to rob the youngster glory on his 19th birthday. Barça showed good spirit by continuing to fight and in the second period of extra time again began to take hold of the game. Pedro and Messi both had attempts on goal but just when it seemed that the game was heading for penalties Pedro played the ball inside from the left to Messi who conjured up a magnificent return pass which Pedro latched onto to shoot low past Pyatov inside the far post. Barça held out for the remaining five minutes with only one shot from Kobin which Valdés saved on the line.

It was far from a convincing display or easy victory for Barça but the team took the game seriously and in the end the win was deserved. It was trophy number five of the Guardiola era and the team had now won five out of five competitions in 2009.

Barça: Valdés; Alves, Pique, Puyol, Abidal; Xavi, Toure (Busquets m100), Keita; Messi, Ibrahimovic (Pedro m81), Henry (Bojan m96).

Shakhtar Donetsk: Pyatov, Srna, Chygrynskiy, Kucher, Rat, Willian (Aghahowa m91), Hubschman, Gai (Kobin m79), Ilsinho, Luiz Adriano y Fernandinho (Jason m79).

Goal: m115 Pedro 1-0.

CHAPTER 12 – Barça 6 Zaragoza 1

Three days after winning the UEFA Super Cup Barça began the 2009/10 league season with a Monday night game at home to Sporting Gijon. It was also the last day of the transfer window and Barça completed the €25 million signing of Chygrynskiy from Shakhtar while Gudjohnsen moved on to Monaco and Henrique, having failed to convince during the preseason, was loaned out to Racing Santander.

Messi was with Argentina preparing for an important World Cup qualifier against Brazil, so with Iniesta still injured and Guardiola preferring to rest Henry, the defence of La Liga began with a front three of Pedro, Ibrahimovic and Bojan. All eyes were on Ibrahimovic but it was Keita who inspired a 3-0 victory, setting up the first for Bojan, scoring the second and also hitting the post. However, the biggest cheer of the night came near the end when Ibrahimovic scored his first goal for the club with a diving header.

There was then an international break so it was two weeks before Barça returned to action with a game at Getafe. Iniesta appeared to have recovered from his thigh injury but it was considered more prudent for him to start as a substitute along with Messi who was just back from Argentina where the pressure was mounting as defeat to Brazil had left qualification for the 2010 World Cup far from certain. Guardiola also rested Alves and Henry, giving a debut to Chygrynskiy and a start on the left wing to Jeffren. Barça were slow to get started and Getafe twice hit the woodwork in a goalless first half. Guardiola brought on Messi and Iniesta with just over half an hour remaining and Barça came to life with goals from Ibrahimovic and the Argentinian to seal a 0-2 victory.

The defence of the Champions League could not have begun with a bigger game as Barça travelled to Milan to take on Inter at the San Siro. The build-up to the match quite logically focused on Eto'o and Ibrahimovic as both players faced an early reencounter with their ex-teammates. However, more importantly, it would be the first clash between Guardiola and José Mourinho in what would become an epic battle between the two coaches over the following three years. Barça had slightly the better of a disappointing 0-0 draw and neither Ibrahimovic nor Eto'o came close to scoring against their ex-teammates as both defences dominated.

Barça had no problem finding the net back in La Liga. Atlético Madrid (5-2) and Racing (1-4) were comfortably dealt with, Messi and Ibrahimovic scoring in both games. However, there was some criticism, notably from Johan Cruyff, saying that the team was not playing so well. There were still some teething problems with the new players, though more noticeably with Chygrynskiy and Maxwell than with Ibrahimovic, while there were questions over the defensive midfield position as Toure had been a bit below form. Busquets was preferred for the games against Atlético and Racing though he was at fault in Atlético's second goal when his header back to Valdés was intercepted by Kun Agüero.

Toure was back for following game at Malaga which turned into a bruising bad tempered game mainly due to the referee, Carlos Delgado Ferreiro, who allowed Malaga to get away with some highly unsporting behaviour particularly from defender Weligton who escaped without punishment after stamping on Messi's leg. Henry and Chygrynskiy both had to go off with injuries but curiously their substitutes, Ibrahimovic and Pîqué both scored soon after coming on as Barça won 0-2. Barça had maximum points from five matches and Ibrahimovic had scored in each of those games. However, Madrid had also won all their games and were top of La Liga on goal difference.

Iniesta had still not started a game since the Champions League final in Rome and had only accumulated 96 minutes in four appearances as substitute. Guardiola finally included him in the starting line-up for the Champions League game with Dynamo Kiev. Iniesta showed signs of his class, setting up Messi for the opening goal, but he was substituted at half time as a precaution. Pedro came on in his place and scored the second in a comfortable 2-0 win.

Pedro was rewarded with a start against Almeria and he repaid Guardiola's growing confidence in him with a terrific strike to give Barça a narrow victory, though the team lacked fluidity as Xavi suffered the obsessive man-marking of Almeria's Chico. Madrid's defeat at Sevilla the following day left Barça with a three-point lead going into another international break. Henry and Ibrahimovic both returned with slight injuries after playing for their countries which left Barça lacking punch up front for the visit to Valencia. A defeat would not have been unjust but an excellent performance from Valdés earned Barça a point from a goalless draw. Madrid beat Valladolid and Barça's lead was back down to a point.

Qualification for the Champions League last 16 was put in danger after the Russian champions Rubin Kazan made their first ever visit to Camp Nou on October 20. Barça were expected to win comfortably but after just two minutes the Russians took the lead when Aleksandr Ryazantsev made the most of a poor control from Marquez to send a tremendous 35-yard strike past Valdés. Despite an equalizer from Ibrahimovic at the start of the second half Barça were unable to recover after a second Rubin goal in the 73rd minute. Ibrahimovic and Toure hitting the woodwork near the end and a shots ratio of 24-3 counted for nothing. To make things worse Alves was injured in the final minutes of the game which would see him out of action until the return game with Rubin two weeks later.

With just two goals scored in the last three matches, questions began to be asked about goal-scoring ability and the lack of back up to cover for injuries. Henry, Iniesta and Marquez had all begun the season with problems, and since then, Bojan, Chygrynskiy, Ibrahimovic, Maxwell and Alves had all suffered slight injuries while Xavi and Piqué played on despite not being at 100%. Ibrahimovic had generally done well, fitting in quickly and scoring, but Messi seemed to be suffering from the pressure from Argentina over World Cup qualification. Pedro had been asked to fill in for the injured Thierry Henry, and despite his excellent work rate he had begun to frustrate some fans a little.

The pressure was on for a positive result as newly-promoted Zaragoza arrived at Camp Nou, though there was a boost the night before when Madrid could only draw at Sporting which meant a victory would send Barça three points clear at the top. With Alves out injured, Guardiola moved Puyol to right back while preferring the more attack-minded Maxwell over Abidal on the left. The fit-again Chygrynskiy came in to partner Piqué in the middle, Busquets and Keita returned to the midfield alongside Xavi while Iniesta was again played further forward supporting Ibrahimovic and Messi. Zaragoza's coach Marcelino Garcia left his most creative player, Angel Lafita, on the bench with the intention of stifling Barça with a solid five-man midfield.

The doubts about Barça's attacking strength were mainly concerned with the left side but the game with Zaragoza began with Maxwell, Keita and Iniesta combining well. In the fifth minute Keita crossed low to Xavi who laid the ball on to Messi in an excellent position but the little Argentinian put the ball disappointingly wide. Barça's other main route of attack in the first twenty minutes was the long ball into Ibrahimovic. After seven minutes he made a good control before turning and shooting straight at keeper Juan Carrizo. In the 12th minute he headed down Xavi's chip to Messi whose shot was saved. Then after 20 minutes the big Swede controlled well with his chest before sending in a wicked shot that forced a good save from Carrizo. In between Zaragoza managed one chance after a mistake from Piqué but Valdés was there to save Javier Arizmendi's shot.

Barça were creating chances but the finish was lacking. Then in the 24th minute Xavi took a corner short to Messi who had time to turn and cross for Keita who dived to head past Carrizo. The first goal was followed soon after by the second. Ibrahimovic had shown the potential of his free kick ability against Rubin and in the 29th minute he hit a free kick from nearly 35 yards out at such a velocity that Carrizo could only flap at the ball as it flew into the net. The keeper might have done more to stop the ball but it would still be remembered as a tremendous strike from the Swede. Barça made it 3-0 five minutes before the break, Xavi played a great ball through to Ibrahimovic on the left and his low cross was met by Keita making a superb run into the area to slide in and touch the ball home.

With a three-goal advantage at half time perhaps it was normal that the rhythm dropped a little in the second half though Barça continued to create chances. In the 54th minute Messi went on another superb burst through the middle and as he reached the edge of the area he tried a delicate chip over the keeper which would have been one of the goals of the season except that Carrizo managed to get a hand to the ball. Ibrahimovic, following up, was called offside after knocking in the rebound. Two minutes later Iniesta did well to battle past two opponents and force the ball wide to Keita who crossed low from the left and Ibrahimovic stuck his foot out at the near post to turn the ball past the keeper for his second of the game and Barça's fourth.

Despite the comfortable lead Barça continued to play a high pressing game and in the 69th minute this forced an error from Zaragoza close to their penalty area, Messi quickly played the ball forward to Busquets who returned the ball with a delightful back-heel but Messi's final shot hit the keeper's foot and went wide. A bit of carelessness began to creep into Barça's play and Zaragoza scored a consolation after 78 minutes following a mistake from Maxwell, Valdés made a good save from the first effort from Ewerton but the ball came out to Jorge Lopez who fired the ball back in and this time Valdés might have done better to keep the ball out.

The Zaragoza goal seemed to spark Barça back into action and the game finished with two more goals for the home team. First, Iniesta collected a poor pass out of defence, accelerated through the middle before touching the ball to Messi on the right and this time Messi's flick over the keeper found the net. It was an important boost for the Argentinian after his recent below-par performances. Keita made it 6-1 near the end, heading Iniesta's corner firmly into the corner from 12 yards out. It was Keita's first ever hat-trick and thoroughly deserved after his run of good form.

One game can do a lot to change the mood at a club, from being in a so-called 'mini-crisis' everything seemed rosy as Barça went three points clear at the top. Ibrahimovic was not only scoring, he was also showing some excellent touches and good movement up front while Keita was playing his best football since arriving. If there was a negative point for some fans it was Chygrynskiy's lack of pace at the back, despite showing good distribution he had been exposed a couple of times by Arizmendi. With Marquez struggling to regain his form and Milito suffering setbacks in his rehabilitation process, only Piqué and Puyol seemed to offer a central-defensive pairing capable of stopping the best.

Barça: Valdés; Puyol, Piqué (Marquez m72), Chygrynskiy, Maxwell; Xavi (Jeffren m82), Busquets, Keita; Messi, Ibrahimovic (Bojan m72), Iniesta.

Zaragoza: Carrizo; Pulido, Pablo Amo, Pavón, Paredes; Gabi, Abel Aguilar; Jorge López, Ander Herrera (Songo'o m77), Pennant (Lafita m61); Arizmendi (Ewerthon m68).

Goals: m24 Keita 1-0, m29 Ibrahimovic 2-0, m41 Keita 3-0, m56 Ibrahimovic 4-0, m78 Jorge Lopez 4-1, m80 Messi 5-1, m85 Keita 6-1.

CHAPTER 13 – Barça 1 Real Madrid 0

Barça began their defence of the Copa del Rey with a tie against the Segunda División B team Cultural Leonesa. The night before the first leg, another Segunda B team, Alcorcon, proved that anything can happen in the Copa by humiliating Real Madrid 4-0. However, Barça secured a comfortable 0-2 win in Leon with two goals from Pedro who had now scored in the league, the cup, the Champions League and both supercups all in one season. The promising 18-year-old Gai Assulin was given a debut on the left wing though the 57 minutes played by the youngster would prove to be his only official first-team game for the club.

Back in La Liga Barça faced a tough away game at Osasuna. Alves was still injured which meant Puyol continued at right back with Chygrynskiy alongside Piqué. However, Chygrynskiy struggled against Carlos Aranda, leading to Guardiola putting on Marquez in his place after an hour. Barça took the lead with 15 minutes remaining when Keita converted Puyol's cross but Barça then missed chances to seal the three points. A mistake from Marquez late in injury time led to Javier Camuñas getting the chance to cross from the left and the unfortunate Piqué, trying to clear, sliced the ball into his own goal via Valdés's face. The 1-1 draw meant Barça lead over Madrid was down to one point.

A long trip to Kazan followed for the return match with Rubin. Alves returned at right back but temperatures of -5ºC made things difficult. Ibrahimovic hit the post early on but it was the closest Barça came to a goal while Valdés had to make a magnificent save from Ryanzantev to salvage a point. After four games there was still everything to play for in Champions League Group F, Inter led on six points followed by Barça and Rubin on five with Dynamo on four. Barça needed to take four points from the remaining fixtures at home to Inter and away to Dynamo to reach the last sixteen.

Messi, Xavi and Iniesta had all been below form for a while but it was still a big surprise when Guardiola left all three of them, along with Alves on the bench for Mallorca's visit to Camp Nou. Pedro took Messi's place on the right and he responded with a brace while Henry, making his first start since September, scored his first goal of the season. Barça were also awarded their first penalty of the season which substitute Messi converted near the end as Barça won 4-2. However, there were more doubts about the defence with Chygrynskiy again failing to convince.

Five second half goals including two from Bojan saw Cultural comprehensively beaten in the Copa del Rey second leg as Barça progressed to the last 16. There then followed an international break which would see Abidal and Ibrahimovic return with injuries but there was an encouraging piece of news for the club when Gabi Milito completed 45 minutes of his first friendly training match, though he was still a long way from full fitness. Then on Friday 20th November there was the worrying announcement that Abidal and Toure had been diagnosed as having the H1N1 virus, commonly known as swine flu.

Defending a one-point advantage at the top of La Liga, the depleted squad travelled to Bilbao for the game with Athletic Club. Despite taking the lead early in the second half when Alves coolly finished from Xavi's excellent pass, the team couldn't hold on and a lack of concentration from Alves allowed Toquero in to equalize. A week before the *Clásico* and Madrid went a point ahead after a narrow home win over Racing. However, there was worse news for Barça as Messi had picked up a slight thigh strain.

Barça were not in the best condition at the beginning of a crucial week with the visits of Inter and Madrid to Camp Nou. On the day before the Inter match Toure, Chygrynskiy, Abidal and Milito were considered definite non-starters while the possibilities of playing for Messi, Ibrahimovic and Marquez seemed to be very low. When the teams were announced these last three were among the substitutes – more for the psychological effect than anything else as none of them were used - but there was a huge surprise with Abidal named at left back. When the player injured his thigh playing for France it was said he would need three weeks to recover yet just ten days later he was fit to play again. Added to this was his remarkable recovery after going down with swine flu just a few days before. The evening before the game he had trained in solitary while still wearing a facemask and he hadn't received the all clear to play until two hours before kick-off.

Abidal's return was a boost to the team and right from the start Barça took control, playing a high tempo with the ball and suffocating Inter with an aggressive pressing game whenever the Italians had the ball. Piqué gave Barça an early lead, stabbing home a volley after Henry flicked on Xavi's corner and Inter never recovered from the early blow. Guardiola made an interesting tactical decision to play Iniesta on the right where he could be closer to Xavi and the move paid off when a fine combination between the two led to Barça's second after 26 minutes. Busquets played the ball forward to Iniesta and then with two quick-fire first time passes, one from Iniesta and one from Xavi the ball came wide to Alves who sent in a cross for Pedro to finish. After the second goal Barça controlled the game with few problems, concentrating more on keeping possession than on scoring a third. The game was a magnificent response from the players to the critics and doubters. Perhaps the most satisfying thing was the performances of the six home grown outfield players. Besides the two goals coming from Piqué and Pedro, Busquets was magnificent in the holding role in midfield winning back possession and always finding a team mate with a simple quick pass. Xavi and Iniesta were back to being themselves, proving once more that there were no better midfield players in the world at this time, while Piqué and Puyol dominated completely at the back which made it impossible for Eto'o on his return to Camp Nou to get a chance to score against his ex-team.

At the end Camp Nou sang "Mourinho, go to the theatre" in reference to the Portuguese coach's accusations that Messi had acted to get Asier Del Horno sent off in the game between Chelsea and Barça at Stamford Bridge in 2006. However, after the game Mourinho was unusually magnanimous saying "Barcelona have a squad of players who play genuinely well. They play a high intensity game, pressing high and very quickly. And when they have the ball they use it with high-speed passing. That is a real speciality. It is easy to say that they are a better team than we are". The victory put Barça two points clear at the top of Group F and on the verge of qualifying. Only a defeat by more than one goal in the final game at Dynamo Kiev could put Barça out.

With confidence firmly restored Barça prepared for Madrid's visit with the intention of recuperating top spot in La Liga. Messi, Ibrahimovic and Toure faced a race to be fit in time while Alves was nursing a bruised ankle from the Inter game though there was little doubt that he would be fine for the *Clásico*. Having spent over €200 million in the summer to sign Cristiano Ronaldo, Kaká, Karim Benzema and Xabi Alonso, a lot was expected of Madrid and their new coach Manuel Pelligrini. Madrid had started the season very strongly before suffering a dip in October when they suffered defeats at the hands of Sevilla, AC Milan and Alcorcon, but since the 4-0 humiliation against the Second Division B team, a run of 6 wins and a draw at Milan suggested they would prove to be a bigger test for Barça than Inter had been.

Madrid were without the injured Metzelder, Guti and Van Nistlerooy but their starting lineup of Casillas, Sergio Ramos, Pepe, Albiol, Arbeloa, Lass Diarra, Xabi Alonso, Kaká, Marcelo, Cristiano Ronaldo and Higuaín looked considerably stronger than their eleven for the corresponding fixture 12 months before. Guardiola left Toure and Ibrahimovic on the bench and started with Valdés, Alves, Puyol, Piqué, Abidal, Xavi, Busquets, Keita, Messi, Henry and Iniesta.

In the first half Madrid managed to suffocate Barça in midfield by playing an advanced defence which left little space in the zone where Xavi and Iniesta usually work their magic. Faced with such tactics Barça tried to find the ball over the top, but the few times this was tried the linesman's flag was raised every time. Barça also tried to get out wide but when the crosses came in they were off target and there were few Barça players getting into the area to aim at.

Madrid were content to try and counterattack and in the 20th minute they created the first real goal-scoring chance. Kaka got past Piqué, Abidal had to come across to cover, leaving Ronaldo open on the right, Kaka slipped the ball through but Ronaldo's shot was hit too close to Valdés who made a vital save with his outstretched right foot. Six minutes later Ronaldo dribbled in from the right, fed Kaka who laid the ball on to Marcelo in an excellent position but Carles Puyol got across superbly to make an excellent block.

It was Madrid's best period of the game but they had no more chances in the first half except for a hopeful shot from Marcelo that gave Valdés no problem. However, Barça also failed to get anywhere near Casillas's goal and the Madrid keeper's only work was to deal with a low cross from Andres Iniesta.

Early in the second half Ibrahimovic came on for the ineffective Henry. Soon after Xavi had a chance after a great build up but his shot was blocked. Then in the 53rd minute Madrid broke away, Ronaldo cut inside Abidal but when he looked likely to score Puyol made another great block. Three minutes later, another Madrid attack broke down when Piqué robbed Ronaldo. The defender brought the ball out of defence and fed Xavi. After an exchange of passes with Ibrahimovic, Xavi played the ball square to Keita who swept the ball out to the right to Alves. In the first half Alves's crossing had been well off target but this time he sent in a beauty that found Ibrahimovic steaming in at the far post to volley left-footed past Casillas.

Madrid were stunned. However, when Busquets was sent off in the 62nd minute for his second yellow card after an unnecessary handball in midfield it seemed likely that Madrid would salvage something, but Barça rose to the occasion with a heroic last 30 minutes. Pep Guardiola brought on Toure Yaya for Keita but there was no intention of sitting back and defending as Barça stuck to the principle of keeping possession. In this aspect Iniesta and Messi were brilliant, and despite being down to ten men Barça continued to look for another goal. Piqué had a header just wide from Xavi's free kick when Ibrahimovic was in a better position to score. Eric Abidal came close to his first Barça goal after being put through by an excellent ball from Xavi, and near the end Alves played a fantastic pass into Messi who was denied by Casillas's legs.

At the other end Madrid had their chances. Ronaldo had a header over shortly before being subbed off for Benzema. Then, in the 70th minute, Puyol, in magnificent form, made his third vital block, this time on Benzema as he shaped to shoot from close in. There were three corners near the end which put Barça under pressure but the ten men defended bravely and deserved to hold on. Near the end Lass lost his patience as Xavi, Iniesta and Messi played keep-ball and he was also sent off for a hack on Xavi.

After some of the doubts during November, beating Inter and Madrid in a week was an excellent response from the players. Against Inter there was some delightful football but the victory over Madrid was more to do with great courage and it demonstrated the character of Guardiola's team. The three points put Barça back to the top of La Liga which was a fitting way for the club to celebrate its 110th anniversary.

Barça: Valdés; Alves, Puyol, Piqué, Abidal; Xavi, Busquets, Keita (Toure m66); Messi, Henry (Ibrahimovic m51), Iniesta.

Real Madrid: Casillas; Sergio Ramos, Pepe, Albiol, Arbeloa (Raúl m74); Lass Diarra, Xabi Alonso, Kaká, Marcelo; Cristiano Ronaldo (Benzema m66), Higuaín.

Goal: m56 Ibrahimovic.

CHAPTER 14 – Barça 2 Estudiantes 1

December began with Leo Messi being confirmed as the 2009 Ballon d'Or winner. Having come third in 2007 and second in 2008, Messi's continued development in the 2008/09 season was reflected in the 38 goals scored and Barça's success in winning La Liga, La Copa and the Champions League. Since the change in the Ballon d'Or voting system Kaka had achieved 444 votes to win the award in 2007, while Cristiano Ronaldo won in 2008 with 446 votes, Messi's dominance in 2009 saw him earn a record 473 votes which left second place Ronaldo with 233. Barça's success was also reflected with Xavi Hernandez coming in third with 170 votes, Andres Iniesta was fourth with 149 votes, ex-blaugrana Samuel Eto'o finished fifth with 75 votes while Zlatan Ibrahimovic was seventh with 50. There were also seven votes for Thierry Henry who came 15th.

Due to the FIFA Club World Cup the league game away to newly promoted Xerez was brought forward to the first Wednesday night of December. With no other teams in action it was a chance for Barça to go five points clear at the top. However, with Messi, Ibrahimovic and Iniesta starting on the bench Barça were far from convincing. The front three of Pedro, Bojan and Henry were below par though Henry redeemed himself by opening the scoring just after the break. Guardiola deemed it necessary to bring on Messi, Ibrahimovic and Iniesta, but it wasn't until injury time that Ibrahimovic scored to seal a 0-2 win.

There followed a difficult trip to La Coruña where Barça had only beaten Deportivo three times in the seventeen previous visits. Before the game Guardiola told the press, "We will not accept just winning, it is necessary to continue trying to do things better because that is how we have won respect, and respect is something we need to continue to earn." The team responded well with a strong performance led by Messi who was back to his brilliant best with two goals in a 1-3 victory. However, Valdés was guilty of a lack of concentration when he allowed Adrian Lopez's soft header to sneak in for Depor's goal.

Barça still needed to qualify for the last 16 of the Champions League. Despite only needing to avoid a big defeat in the final group match in Kiev – Barça would still go through with a 1-0 or 3-1 defeat - sporting director Txiki Begiristain rightly described the match as "our most important game of the season." The game could not have got off to a worse start when in the second minute Valdés, who had started the season so well, made his second mistake in a week, misjudging Artem Milevskiy glanced header. The goal put Barça's qualification in serious danger and there were some nervous minutes. However, the team recovered its composure and Xavi, playing his 100th Champions League game, scored an equalizer after half an hour. Dynamo now needed three goals to put Barça out but they rarely threatened Valdés's goal again. Messi curled in a free-kick to clinch the victory near the end as Barça finished top of Group F with Inter Milan qualifying in second place.

Messi was injured at the end of the Kiev match which forced him to miss the local derby with Espanyol at Camp Nou. Barça won a heated and scrappy game thanks to a disputed first-half penalty after Xavi went down after a slight brush with Raúl Baena. Ibrahimovic blasted the spot kick into the roof of the net for the only goal of the game. Barça had not beaten Espanyol at Camp Nou in La Liga since May 2006 and the victory meant it was Barça's best ever start to a league season with 12 wins and 3 draws from 15 games.

On December 13 Barça flew out to Abu Dhabi to take part in the FIFA Club World Cup as champions of Europe. The tournament, which had developed from the Intercontinental Cup, was the one competition that Barça had never won, having lost the final twice against Brazilian opponents, São Paulo in 1992 and Internacional in 2006. There were many reasons to consider that the FIFA Club World Cup was not the most important tournament in the calendar. It broke up the league season, it was played in a place that was hardly known for its footballing history, and FIFA seemed to organize the tournament with an eye to making a quick buck rather than anything else. However, for Barça there was the added incentive of becoming the first team ever to win six out of six competitions entered in one year. To reach the final Barça first had to face the Mexican team Atlante who had qualified as CONCACAF champions.

There was concern that the eight-hour journey combined with the recent long trips to Kazan and Kiev could take its toll on the players, while the warmer climate was also likely to have an effect. Pep Guardiola surprised with his team selection for the semi-final, playing both Toure and Busquets in midfield and bringing in Marquez in place of Piqué in defence. After just four minutes Marquez misjudged a long free kick from Atlante goalkeeper Federico Vilar and Dani Alves failed to pick up Guillermo Rojas who flicked the ball over Valdés to score into the empty net. It was a nightmare start for Barça and proved once again that one of the biggest weaknesses in defence was dealing with long balls down the middle. Despite a couple of quick chances to equalize Barça were looking somewhat sluggish but then in the 35th minute Toure flicked on Xavi's corner and Busquets equalized with a side-foot volley. Eight minutes into the second half Guardiola brought on Piqué and Messi, who had not been expected to play, and the Argentinian responded by putting Barça in front with his first touch after being put through by Ibrahimovic. Pedro put the result beyond doubt ten minutes later when he finished from Iniesta's assist. The goal gave Pedro the unique record of being the first player ever to score in six official club competitions in one year.

Three days later, on Saturday 19 December, Barça faced Estudiantes from the Argentine city of La Plata in the big final at Abu Dhabi's Zayed City Sports stadium. Estudiantes were known as a tactical and aggressive team led by the 34-year-old Juan Sebastian Veron who had been voted South

American Player of the Year in 2008. They were expected to be much tougher opponents than Atlante.

Barça were without Iniesta who had suffered another thigh injury at the end of the semi-final, this time in his left leg, so Henry started on the left side of the attack while Messi returned on the right in place of Pedro. Busquets and Keita were preferred over Toure in midfield while Piqué was back in defence in place of Marquez.

Both teams began the game strongly. Estudiantes had the first half chance when Veron put Enzo Perez through but Valdés was out well to reach the ball first. Estudiantes were playing a high pressing game but the Barça defence was finding ways to pass the ball out. In the eighth minute, Alves played a long vertical pass to Ibrahimovic who, after controlling the ball, played a splendid back-heel for Xavi to run on to. With just the goalkeeper Damián Albil to beat, Xavi decided to pass the ball across the goal but the pass was too long for Henry to arrive. It was a great shame because the back-heel from Ibrahimovic meritted a goal.

Estudiantes continued to press, giving Barça's players little time to think but Barça were looking slightly the better team showing a good level of concentration to keep possession. However, Messi was struggling to get involved and when he did have a run after 22 minutes his final attempt was blocked. Some of the challenges from Estudiantes, particularly on Busquets, were a bit late but the Mexican referee Benito Archundia decided to give the first yellow card to Messi, presumably for diving though Messi seemed to be just jumping out of the way as Veron shaped to kick him.

Barça began to look a bit rattled by the referee's decisions and were struggling to find the forwards. Estudiantes managed the next attempt on goal when Veron chested down a clearance from a corner but his shot went well wide. Then in the 32nd minute Barça had a big penalty appeal after Messi played in Xavi who was brought down after touching the ball past the goalkeeper but the referee pointed for a goal kick.

Having been robbed of a golden opportunity to take the lead Barça went behind five minutes later. Veron headed the ball out left to Juan Manuel Diaz who sent in a perfect cross to Mauro Boselli who got between Puyol and Abidal to head firmly past Valdes. There had been talk before the game of how it would be much more difficult to come back from a goal behind than it had been in the semi-final against Atlante, and that proved to be true. The Argentinian team made no effort to look for another goal after they took the lead and it was clear that Barça would not find chances easy to come by. Before half time there was just one but Ibrahimovic failed to make contact with a spectacular leap to try an overhead kick.

At half time Guardiola brought on Pedro for Keita and Messi moved into a free role in midfield, and with 45 minutes to go it still looked very likely that Barça could find a goal. Estudiantes could not keep up the same level of pressure and Barça began to create the odd occasion. In the 48th minute Henry sent the ball out left to Ibrahimovic who went outside a defender but shot just wide of the far post. Barça were dominating the game now but the crosses were always to the keeper or just out of reach of the forward. In the 59th minute Henry managed to get a good cross over which Albil misjudged but the goalkeeper did enough to distract Pedro who failed to make contact with the goal gaping.

Barça increased the tempo but the goal wouldn't come. In the 69th minute Xavi played a ball into Pedro who let the ball run past one defender before skipping past another but his shot was from a tight angle and Albil managed to stick out a foot to save. Estudiantes continued to only think about defending and it began to look as if they would hold out. In the 79th minute Xavi crossed to Ibrahimovic in space but the big man's header was poor and went well wide.

Guardiola brought on Jeffren for Henry with seven minutes to go and in the 87th minute the young substitute got past right back Clemente Rodriguez and crossed but it was just out of Ibrahimovic's reach. It seemed as if fate was going to deny Barça, but then in the 89th minute Xavi played another ball towards the area, the ball ballooned up off a defender's head and Piqué battled well to chase the ball and win the header, flicking it on for Pedro, the smallest man on the pitch, to loop a header over the goalkeeper and in for the equalizer.

Barça looked physically stronger going into extra time and Estudiantes must have been affected by being so close only to have victory snatched away. The game continued with the same pattern of Barça domination and Estudiantes defending, clearly hoping they could hold out for penalties. There was little goalmouth action. Messi had a chance in the 97th minute after Ibrahimovic laid the ball back for him, but his shot went disappointingly wide. Jeffren on the left wing was causing Rodríguez problems, and in the 102nd minute he laid the ball onto Ibrahimovic who shot wide.

Barça's insistence finally paid off five minutes into the second half of extra time. There was not the same level of pressing from Estudiantes now, and when Alves received the ball from Xavi he had time to look up and see Messi running into the area. The Brazilian's cross found its target and Messi dived forward and stuck out his chest to meet the ball and deflect it past Albil. Scoring with his chest, or with his heart or with the club badge on his shirt as many fans liked to remember it, was a fitting manner for Messi to end a remarkable year. There were a couple of scares for Barça in the last ten minutes, one was called incorrectly offside but Valdés made an excellent save all the same and then in the last minute central defender Leandro Desábato got forward for a free kick but he sent his header inches wide. It would not have done justice if Estudiantes had equalized but it was a moment when all of Catalunya held its breath. Barça had completed the most incredible year winning six trophies out of six. Guardiola's tears at the end demonstrated just how much the achievement meant to him.

Barça: Valdés; Alves, Piqué, Puyol, Abidal; Xavi, Busquets (Toure m79,), Keita (Pedro m45); Messi, Ibrahomivic, Henry (Jeffren m83).

Estudiantes: Damián Albil; Clemente Rodríguez, Cristian Cellay, Leandro Desábato, Germán Ré (Marcos Rojo m90+1); Enzo Pérez (Maximiliano Núñez m79), Juan Sebastián Verón, Rodrigo Braña, Leandro Benítez (Matías Sánchez m75), Juan Manuel Díaz; Mauro Boselli.

Goals: m37 Boselli 0-1, m89 Pedro 1-1, m110 Messi 2-1.

CHAPTER 15 – Barça 4 Sevilla 0

The year 2010 began with a Saturday night fixture at home to Villarreal. Messi would miss the game as he'd been allowed a couple of extra days Christmas holiday, while Toure and Keita were on international duty preparing for the African Cup which gave Johnathan dos Santos the chance to make a first league start in midfield. Before the game the first team squad came out to present the six cups of 2009 to the fans but Villarreal once again spoilt the Camp Nou party by holding Barça to a 1-1 draw. Pedro put Barça into an early lead but David Fuster equalized for Villarreal early in the second half. Ibrahimovic missed two chances near the end and showed his frustration by getting another booking which would see him miss the following league game at Tenerife.

There was a first leg Copa del Rey game with Sevilla to deal with first. After an absence of over 20 months Gabi Milito made his first start in an official game alongside Chygrinskiy in defence. Messi was also back, forming a front three with Pedro and Bojan while Guardiola experimented with a midfield of Marquez, Iniesta and Thiago Alcántara, who made his first start for the first team. Milito showed encouraging form for just over an hour before coming off while Thiago gave a good showing too before Xavi replaced him on 70 minutes. However, with so many changes to the team and with Chygrynskiy, Marquez and Bojan all disappointing it wasn't to be Barça's night. Diego Capel put Sevilla ahead on the hour and despite Ibrahimovic slotting in an equalizer with fifteen minutes remaining, an Alvaro Negredo penalty a minute later after Chygrinskiy brought down Capel, gave Sevilla a 1-2 win on the night to take back for the second leg at the Sánchez Pizjuán.

Back in La Liga Barça dished out a humiliating 0-5 thrashing at Tenerife though the game might have been very different had Tenerife taken their early chances. Until the opening goal from Leo Messi Tenerife had the better of the game but Barça scored twice more before half time to put the game out of Tenerife's reach. Messi completed his hat-trick with a beautiful chip fifteen minutes from the end and an own goal from Luna completed Tenerife's humiliation. Despite the scoreline it was not a good performance from Barça.

Guardiola had rested Piqué and Abidal for the Tenerife match with the intention of putting out his strongest team at Sevilla for the Copa del Rey second leg. The only concession was to continue with Pinto in goal; even Bojan, who had nearly always started in cup games, was on the bench as Ibrahimovic and Henry started up front with Messi. Xavi gave Barça hope in a close-fought game when he put Barça level on aggregate midway through the second half. However, despite Barça pouring on the pressure near the end Sevilla keeper Andres Palop played a blinder and Sevilla hung on to go through on away goals. It was the first trophy that Barça had lost since Guardiola took over as first team coach in 2008. The disappointment and ambition of the players was made evident by Messi's tears in the dressing room after the game.

There was an immediate chance for revenge as Sevilla visited Camp Nou three days later in the league. Sevilla may have won the previous week at Camp Nou but they hadn't taken a point in their last five league visits. The last time they had managed to grab a point was in 2003 in Ronaldinho's home debut for Barça. Guardiola put out the same team that had played in the cup at Sevilla with the exception of Victor Valdés who came into the team in place of Pinto, while Sevilla put out a weaker team with an eye on the Copa del Rey quarter finals. The game was due to start at 10pm and just before kick off Barça were boosted by news that Athletic Club had beaten Madrid 1-0 at San Mames which gave Barça the chance to go five points clear at the top.

Barça took control of the game right from the start. After just two minutes Alves had the first attempt but his 30-yard drive went well wide. Then in the 6th minute Iniesta played the ball forward to Henry on the left, Henry's cross evaded a couple of defenders and came to Ibrahimovic who seemed sure to score from six yards out, but he momentarily took his eye off the ball and glanced his shot wide. Barça's next chance came in the 13th minute when Xavi slipped a pass through to Henry but Palop came out of his area and managed to block the shot with his knee.

Barça continued to control the game, with few defensive worries as Sevilla struggled to put an attack together. In the 20th minute Iniesta, who seemed finally to be getting back to the form of the 2008/09 season, went on a fantastic run which ended with a pass into Alves who fired his shot into the side netting. After this the intensity of Barça's game began to drop a bit but there were two Puyol headers from corners, the first he hit wide and the second he was unlucky to see his effort hit Palop on the leg. Soon after Messi tried his luck from outside the area, his shot taking a deflection before looping towards the top corner but Palop made a spectacular one-handed save to push the ball over. Sevilla's first chance didn't come until the 38th minute when Kone wriggled free of Puyol but Abidal managed to get in the way and deflect the shot wide for a corner.

Marquez came on for Puyol at half time with the score still at 0-0 and just a couple of minutes into the second half Kone dribbled past both Marquez and Piqué inside the left side of the penalty area and Valdés had to be alert to cut out the cross. If this was a bad moment from Barça's two centre backs a couple of minutes later they combined in attack to make up for it. Messi fed Marquez on the right and his low cross was touched on by Piqué and Sevilla's centre back Julien Escude could do no more than divert the ball into his own goal. Barça nearly made it 2-0 straight after when Alves broke quickly down the right, he played the ball inside to Messi who sped into the area but his shot was denied by Palop's outstretched leg.

There was one dicey moment for Barça when Alves's misdirected back header almost beat Valdés but for the rest of the game it was one-way traffic towards Palop's goal. Ibrahimovic brilliantly set up a chance for Henry but again Palop saved with his legs and soon after Ibrahimovic had the ball in the net only to be called offside. Henry tried again from outside the area but Palop got down quickly to save again. Then in the 67th minute Abidal did well to keep the ball from going out of play, pulling the ball back to Xavi who played a quick pass to Messi on the right of the area. A goal seemed certain but Palop made yet another excellent save from Messi's shot and then when Ibrahimovic tried to stab home the rebound Ivica Dragutinovic appeared on the line to clear. Pedro, who was on for Henry, had another chance saved in the 70th minute but within a minute he got Barça's second. Alves cut out a pass and the ball came to Xavi who spotted Pedro's run and sent a fantastic defence-splitting pass which Pedro controlled before flicking the ball over Palop and into the net.

After the second goal Barça continued to dominate the game with some lovely one-touch football. The icing on the cake came in the last five minutes when Messi finally found a way past Palop. First Xavi played the ball out wide to another surge forward from Alves whose cross was controlled by Messi who finished coolly for his 100th official goal for Barça, which at the age of 22 made him the youngest player in the club's history to achieve this feat. Then in injury time Abidal, who had a fantastic game at left back, robbed the ball and sent a pass through to Messi who beat Palop with a clinical finish. The win gave Barça a five-point advantage over Real Madrid , but with 20 games still to play, La Liga was far from over.

Barça: Valdés; Alves, Piqué, Puyol (Marquez m45), Abidal; Xavi, Busquets, Iniesta (Bojan m87); Messi, Ibrahimovic, Henry (Pedro m63).

Sevilla: Palop; Konko (Adriano, m60), Dragutinovic, Escudé, Fernando Navarro; Marc Valiente (Duscher m46), Lolo; Stankevicus, José Carlos (Capel m46), Navas; Koné.

Goals: m48 Escudé (o.g.) 1-0, m70 Pedro 2-0, m85 Messi 3-0, m93 Messi 4-0.

CHAPTER 16 – Zaragoza 2 Barça 4

The early exit from the Copa del Rey at least allowed Barça a few weeks with only one game per week. On Wednesday 20 January Guardiola confirmed that he would continue as Barça's coach in the 2010/11 season, dispelling rumours of a possible move to England, and the players responded the following Saturday with a comfortable 0-3 win at Valladolid. Xavi scored a fine opener after 20 minutes, taking part in the build-up before hooking in a volley from Alves's cross, and Alves added a second a minute later though it wasn't clear he had intended to shoot. Alves ended an excellent game sending in Ibrahimovic to set up Messi with an easy finish for the third. Valdés had another fine game in goal, making three good stops that denied Valladolid the chance to get back in the game, and Barça ended the first half of the league season with a record of only four goals conceded in ten away games. It was also only the fifth time in the history of La Liga that a team had remained unbeaten at the halfway stage.

Valdés kept another clean sheet as Barça notched up three more points with a 0-1 win at Sporting Gijón. Pedro was preferred over Henry in the starting XI and the youngster responded with the only goal of the match after being put through by Iniesta's excellent pass. Later, some parts of the press would use a photo from a deceptive angle to try and suggest Pedro had been offside but the goal was perfectly legal. Abidal gave another good performance at left back but there was growing concern about the form of Ibrahimovic who had now scored only once in his last eight appearances.

February began with the visit of Getafe to Camp Nou. With Puyol suspended, Guardiola chose Milito, over Chygrynskiy and Marquez, to partner Piqué at the back. Alves was injured in the warm-up before the game which gave Maxwell the chance to give a good performance at right-back. Barça seemed to be on the way to an easy victory when Messi curled in a beauty from 25 yards after just seven minutes, but the sending off of Piqué for a clumsy lunge after 25 minutes complicated matters. However, Barça adapted superbly to the circumstances and had the better chances during the rest of the game. Xavi added a second midway through the second half and Getafe had to wait until injury time to pull a goal back after Marquez gave away a penalty. Marquez was also sent off for this foul and Barça finished the game with nine men though there was no time for Getafe to look for the equalizer.

Barça now faced the complicated visit to Atlético Madrid with both Piqué and Marquez suspended. Toure had picked up an injury against Getafe and he joined Alves on the injured list and then Abidal pulled a thigh muscle in training which would sideline him for six weeks. With only three recognized first-team defenders available, Guardiola gave the right back spot to Jeffren, though Marc Bartra would get a league debut, replacing Jeffren for the last 30 minutes. To add to the injury problems at the back, Seydou Keita had to go off after pulling a muscle in the second minute. It was not to be Barça's day, early goals from Forlan and Simao gave Atlético a two-goal advantage and despite Ibrahimovic pulling one back and a brief revival before half time Barca failed to match Atlético's commitment and rarely looked like finding the equalizer. The 2-1 defeat brought an end to Barça's unbeaten start to the league season and Real Madrid were now only two points behind.

The defeat at Atlético brought doubts. A 4-0 win over Racing the following Saturday – Barça's 71st victory in Guardiola's first 100 games in charge – may have satisfied some, but Johan Cruyff described the game as Barça's worst in the Guardiola era. There were some positives as Iniesta slotted home his first goal since the Stamford Bridge stunner, and after Henry and Marquez had made it 3-0 Thiago came on for promising last 15 minutes in which he scored his first goal for the club with the help of a deflection off Henrique.

Barça had been drawn against VfB Stuttgart in the Champions League last 16 with the first leg in Germany. As against Lyon at the same stage of the competition twelve months previously Barça were overrun in the first half. The Brazilian striker Cacau opened the scoring for Stuttgart after 25 minutes, leaping above Puyol to head home Stefano Celozzi's cross. A second half goal from Ibrahimovic, pouncing on the rebound after Jens Lehmann had saved his first shot, earned a 1-1 draw which was a good result but didn't change the fact that Barça's form was below the usual high standard. Players such as Marquez, Busquets, Toure, Ibrahimovic and Henry had come under critism but the team's drop in form also coincided with some below par performances from 'match-winners' such as Messi and Xavi.

Guardiola needed a reaction, and against Malaga at Camp Nou he surprised with a new tactical formation. Pedro, who had started only one of the previous nine games, started on the right side of attack with Iniesta on the left with Messi given a completely free role behind Ibrahimovic. Busquets played the holding role with Xavi a little further forward in what could be described either as 4-2-4 or 4-2-3-1. The players reacted well with an overall improved performance. With Alves back, there were more attacking options on the flanks and in the first half Alves, Pedro, Maxwell and Iniesta bombarded Malaga with crosses though Barça had no luck with finishing. Pedro proved once again his valuable knack for scoring important goals, blasting Barça in front from 25 yards midway through the second half. The goal had taken a long time to come but it seemed as if the hard work was now done. Then, in the 80th minute, Piqué and Puyol failed to cut out a pass through to Valdo who ran on to beat Valdés for Malaga's equalizer. However, Barça kept playing patient football, keeping the ball and waiting for the right moment to pounce. In the 84th minute there was a build up on the left involving Ibrahimovic, Maxwell and Pedro but with no way through Pedro played the ball inside to Xavi, Alves made a tremendous run from deep on the right and Xavi timed his pass to perfection, slotting the ball through the gap for Alves who unselfishly squared to give Messi a simple finish. Barça wouldn't let the lead slip again and some sensible possession football made sure of holding on at the end for three hard-earned points.

Guardiola kept the same 4-2-3-1 shape for the visit to Almeria the following week. Almeria had shown a great improvement in the previous weeks since Juanma Lillo took over from Hugo Sanchez as first team coach and Barça were shocked early on when Domingo Cisma headed in a corner. Messi responded just before half time floating a free-kick over the wall, but Barça looked in serious trouble when Puyol put through his own goal in the second half followed soon after by Ibrahimovic earning a stupid red card for retaliation. However, the ten men reacted well with Messi popping up for an equalizer in the 66th minute and with a little more luck Barça might have stolen a winner in the last 20 minutes. It wasn't to be and Barça had to settle for a point. Two hours later Madrid moved top of the league on goal difference after coming back from 0-2 down to beat Sevilla with a 92nd minute winner.

With Ibrahimovic suspended for Valencia's visit to Camp Nou, Guardiola reverted to Barça's classic 4-3-3 with Bojan coming in on the left to partner Messi and Pedro in attack. Barça struggled against strong opponents and with David Albelda and Ever Banega controlling the midfield Valencia began to create danger on the flanks through Pablo Hernandez on the right and Jordi Alba on the left. Valencia lost Albelda just before half time with an injury and then at half time Henry came on for Bojan and the game changed completely. The second half was completely dominated by Barça with Messi netting a stunning hat-trick in a 3-0 victory.

Ibrahimovic was available again for the Champions League return leg with Stuttgart but Guardiola surprised by leaving the Swede on the bench. The team began with an attacking 4-2-3-1 formation with Henry at centre forward, Pedro on the right, Iniesta on the left and Messi in behind Henry. In midfield Toure came in for the injured Xavi to play alongside Busquets, and the Ivorian had his best game of the season – with Busquets playing the holding role he was allowed the freedom to surge forward, causing Stuttgart plenty of probems. Messi was flourishing in the free role and he responded with two more goals and a fantastic pass to Toure to set up Pedro for another. Ibrahimovic came on for the last 25 minutes, showing a better attitude and setting up Bojan to make it 4-0 with his first touch.

Xavi was still injured for the following game at Zaragoza and Guardiola also saw fit to rest Iniesta, Puyol and Henry which meant a return to the starting XI for Keita, Milito and Ibrahimovic. The most noticeable thing about the team selection was the physical midfield of Busquets, Toure and Keita as Barça returned to the classic 4-3-3 formation. Messi overcame a dental infection to start the game on the right.

Barça got off to a fantastic start, taking the lead in the fifth minute. Messi's poor pass went straight to Carlos Diogo but the Uruguayan defender made an awful clearance straight at Ibrahimovic who sent the ball quickly out to Pedro on the left, Pedro made a neat stepover before zipping past Diogo and crossing to the far post where Messi headed comfortably past Zaragosa keeper Roberto.

Soon after, another defensive mistake gave Keita the chance to get into the area but his cross was cut out. From the resulting corner Piqué's backheel flick went straight at Roberto. Zaragosa were struggling to get into the game and were restricted to a couple of hopeful long shots that went wide. It wasn't until the 17th minute that Eliseu looked to have a decent shooting chance but Alves did brilliantly to get back quickly and block. Barça continued to dominate and in the 23rd minute Pedro, Keita and Maxwell combined well on the left and Maxwell's cross found Toure stretching at the far post but he was only able to hook the ball back over the crossbar. In the 30th minute Messi's corner from the right cleared the defenders but Ibrahimovic saw it late and his header from 5 yards went just wide of the far post. Zaragosa began to come into the game in the last 15 minutes of the first half but Barça's defence was solid with Alves and Milito playing particularly well and Valdés did not have a save to make.

Zaragoza came out in the second half searching for the equalizer. They won three corners in quick succession but Barça defended solidly. From the third corner Valdés caught the ball cleanly and threw out quickly to Pedro to start a counter attack, Pedro brought the ball forward before freeing Busquets to his left. Busquets pushed the ball into the area to Ibrahimovic who backheeled to Toure but unfortunately the final shot from Toure went over from a tight angle. Barça continued to search for a second goal, in the 61st minute Alves crossed to the far post but Messi had to stretch and could only turn his volley over.

Barça finally scored the second goal five minutes later and it would be an absolutely amazing goal from Messi. Busquets forced Ander Herrera to turn towards his own goal and Messi robbed the ball 45 yards out. With typical lightning speed he broke away, skipping past Jiri Jarosik as though he wasn't there. Then as the Argentinian reached the area he cut first inside and then outside of Matteo Contini before firing low past Roberto into the far corner. It was a goal that brought back memories of Ronaldo's incredible goal against Compestela in 1996.

Roberto had to make an excellent save to keep the score down when Contini nearly turned Pedro's cross into his own goal, and then Ibrahimovic had a couple of good chances in quick succession. The Swede's poor finishing was made more evident by Messi completing his hat-trick soon after, curling in from the edge of the area after receiving a short pass from Iniesta.

In the 84th minute Messi might have made it 0-4 but he unselfishly set up Ibrahimovic who was obviously in need of a goal but the Swede again fired wide from a good position. Barça might have paid dearly for the miss as Zaragosa found substitute central defenders Marquez and Puyol sleeping. First Marquez allowed Adrián Colunga to get away from him for speed to receive a long pass and arrive unchallenged into the box to fire past Valdés. Then in the 89th minute it was Puyol who failed to mark Colunga after a quick free kick and the Zaragoza striker made it 2-3 to set up a nervous finish. However, Messi hadn't finished his exhibition and he again turned Jarosik and Contini inside out. Jarosik could take no more humiliation and pulled Messi back to deny him another spectacular goal. Messi allowed Ibrahimovic to take the resulting penalty and the Swede finally got on the scoresheet, sending Roberto the wrong way.

With Messi in such exhilarating form it seemed unlikely that anybody could stop Barça. However, Madrid were still top on goal difference after a run of nine straight wins in La Liga, and having been knocked out of the Champions League by Lyon, Barça's greatest rival could concentrate solely on the one competition. Both teams had a remarkable 68 points from 27 games but Barça still had to go to the Bernabéu and also worry about a Champions League quarter final with Arsenal.

Barça: Valdés; Alves, Piqué (Puyol m69), Milito (Marquez m73), Maxwell; Toure (Iniesta m63), Busquets, Keita; Messi, Ibrahimovic, Pedro.

Zaragoza: Roberto; Diogo, Jarosik, Contini, Ponzio; Edmilson (Lafita m46), Gabi; Arizmendi (Colunga m62), Ander Herrera, Eliseu; Suazo (Penant m80).

Goals: m5 Messi 0-1, m66 Messi 0-2, m77 Messi 0-3, m85 Colunga 1-3, m89 Colunga 2-3, m91 Ibrahimovic (pen) 2-4.

CHAPTER 17 – Barça 4 Arsenal 1

Barça had two leagues games before facing Arsenal, against Osasuna at Camp Nou and then away at Mallorca. Abidal and Xavi were still out injured for the Wednesday night Osasuna game while Piqué also missed out, having bruised a knee against Zaragoza, which meant Milito partnered Puyol at the back. Guardiola experimented with a 4-3-1-2 formation in the first half with Leo Messi playing behind a front two of Thierry Henry and Ibrahimovic. The experiment didn't work as Barça gave possibly the worst first half performance at Camp Nou since Guardiola took over as first team coach. In the second half Pedro came on for Henry and Iniesta moved to the left wing as Barça reverted to 4-2-3-1. Ibrahimovic finally broke the deadlock in the 73rd minute, stabbing home Maxwell's low cross. Then near the end substitute Bojan made it 2-0, turning in Iniesta's cross to score his second goal in two brief appearances.

With an eye on the Champions League, Guardiola left both Messi and Xavi on the bench for the game at Mallorca while neither Piqué nor Henry was even included on the bench. The coach went back to Barça's classic 4-3-3 formation with Pedro on the right wing and a surprise place for Jeffren on the left. Mallorca had won 12 out of 13 home games in the league and in the first half Barça were put under pressure with Valdés making one excellent early save and Mallorca twice being denied by the woodwork. However, Barça improved in the second half, especially after Messi and Xavi were brought on, and it was from Xavi's corner that Ibrahimovic pounced to score the only goal of the game after Mallorca's keeper Aouate had failed to hold Puyol's shot. It was Ibrahimovic's third goal in three games and a welcome return to form before the first leg of the Champions League quarter-final in London.

The price for the victory in Mallorca was another thigh injury for Iniesta which would rule him out for The Emirates and cause him problems for the remainder of the season. Guardiola switched back to 4-2-3-1 with Pedro on the right and Keita on the left, Xavi and Busquets in midfield while Piqué returned to partner Puyol. Henry, on his return to the club where he scored 226 goals, started on the bench. Arsenal had a very talented young squad and their attacking prowess had been clear to see when they thrashed Porto 5-0 in the previous round. However, Barça began the game in scintillating form, pinning Arsenal back and creating countless chances in the first 20 minutes. A remarkable mixture of luck, last-gasp defending, poor finishing and brilliant goalkeeping from Manuel Almunia kept the score goalless until half time. Ibrahimovic struck twice early in the second half, latching onto balls over the top, first from Piqué and then from Xavi, to give Barça a deserved 0-2 lead. With 20 minutes left Busquets made his one mistake in an otherwise excellent performance, giving the ball away to Samir Nasri, and Theo Walcott sped away from Maxwell to beat Valdés. The goal inspired Arsenal and rattled Barça, Henry came on for an ineffective fifteen minutes at the end, and with just six minutes remaining Puyol impeded Cesc Fabregas as he shaped to shoot and Arsenal won a penalty while Puyol was sent off. Fabregas blasted home from the spot to make it 2-2 but Barça's ten men managed to play out the last five minutes without conceding again.

Before the return game with Arsenal, Barça first had to face Athletic Club in the league at Camp Nou. There were quite a few surprises in the starting lineup with Chygrynskiy returning to the team after a lengthy absence, Puyol moving to right back in place of the suspended Alves, and Abidal coming in at left back after his injury. Toure and Busquets played as a double midfield pivot while Maxwell started on the left wing and there was another chance for Jeffren on the right. Ibrahimovic was injured during the pre-match warm-up which gave a chance to Bojan to start as centre forward with Messi in the space behind him. Jeffren opened the scoring early on, sliding in at the far post to meet Abidal's cross for his first goal for the club, and then Bojan notched up two more to continue his good run in front of goal. Messi added a fourth before Markel Susaeta grabbed a consolation for Athletic near the end.

Ibrahimovic's injury would see him sidelined for two weeks, giving Bojan another chance to show his worth, but for the second leg with Arsenal the main problem for Guardiola was in defence. First choice centre backs Puyol and Piqué were both suspended while Chygrynskiy was illegible to play having appeared for Shakhtar at the start of the season. This left Guardiola with just Marquez, who was a long way off his best form, and Milito, unless he wanted to play Toure or Abidal at centre back. In the end he opted for Marquez and Milito and Barça lined up with Valdés, Alves, Marquez, Milito, Abidal, Xavi, Busquets, Pedro, Messi, Keita and Bojan in a 4-2-3-1 formation. Arsenal coach Arsene Wenger had problems of his own. Fabregas, Andrey Arshavin and William Gallas were all injured in the first leg at the Emirates, while Alex Song was left out after picking up a knee injury in Arsenal's 1-0 win over Wolverhampton Wanderers the previous weekend. Robin Van Persie and Aaron Ramsey were both absent with long term injuries, while there were doubts over whether 35-year-old Sol Campbell would be ready to play his second game in a week. In the end Wenger opted for Mikael Silvestre rather than Cambell in central defence, and with the need to go after the game Arsenal started with a 4-3-3 with Almunia, Bacary Sagna, Thomas Vermaelen, Silvestre, Gaël Clichy, Denilson, Nasri, Abou Diaby, Walcott, Nicklas Bendtner and Tomás Rosický.

Before the game both Guardiola and Wenger talked about the importance of keeping the ball, but it was Barça who dominated in the first 15 minutes with 73% of possession. Xavi, Pedro and Messi twice had attempts on goal but none of the shots were on target. Then, after 18 minutes, Diaby robbed Milito on the half way line before sending Walcott away on the right. Walcott played the ball in low to Bendtner who resisted a challenge from Alves to force a shot which Valdés saved well but the ball went straight back to Bendtner who fired home with his second attempt.

It was the first time in the tie that Arsenal had been in front and it was hard to believe after the dominance Barça had shown up until then. However, it took only three minutes to pull the goal back. Messi tried to slip a pass through to Xavi, the defence cut the pass out but only succeeded in giving the ball back to Messi who controlled the ball before whiplashing a tremendous shot into the top corner from 20 yards.

It was just the beginning of the Messi show. In the 32nd minute Milito sent a long clearance out of defence which Messi controlled brilliantly on the right touchline before setting off again towards goal, he turned Silvestre inside out but this time his final shot could only find the side netting. Then in the 37th minute Messi played a ball inside the full back for Abidal to run on to, Abidal's cross was cut out but not cleared and Pedro recovered the ball to lay it back to Messi who skipped past Silvestre before shooting over Almunia into the net.

With Messi in such form there was little that Arsenal could do to stop him. Five minutes later Keita was quick to spot Messi's run and he played him in past the defence with an intelligent header from inside his own half. Messi galloped away with electric speed and as Almunia came out to close him down Messi made it 3-1 with a delightful scooped chip over the Arsenal keeper to complete a first half hat-trick. Two minutes later Messi had another run at goal but for once his touch let him down, allowing Vermaelen the chance to get across to intercept.

With the two-goal advantage Barça adopted a more cagey game in the second half. Arsenal gained more possession and found more chances to come forward. Abidal came off injured, and Toure came on for Bojan to bolster the midfield, but Arsenal began to create the odd chance. In the 60th minute Milito had to make an excellent last-ditch tackle to deny

Bendtner an opportunity, and soon after, Rosicky had a shot from just outside the area but it went well wide.

Barça were now practically non-existent in attack apart from one chance when the quick-thinking Messi sent Pedro through with a rapidly taken free kick, but Pedro's chip over Almunia went wide of the far post. However, Barça concentrated on keeping things safe and keeping Arsenal out, and in the second half Marquez and particularly Milito were very solid to keep tracks on Bendtner. The Arsenal striker and Walcott gave Barça a scare when they both hit the post in quick succession but neither would have counted as the linesman had given offside.

As Arsenal pushed men forward Barça began to find spaces behind them and as the game neared its end Maxwell forced a save from Almunia. Messi completed his fantastic performance in the 88th minute with a fourth goal after another mazy run into the area, Almunia saved his first shot but Messi fired home the rebound through the keeper's legs.

Barça had not played nearly as well as a team as in the first leg at The Emirates but it didn't matter with Messi in such astonishing form. At the post-match press conference Wenger said of Messi, "He is the best player in the world by some distance. He's a *PlayStation*. He can take advantage of every mistake we make." Messi's performance would be remembered for many years by those fortunate enough to witness it.

Messi had now scored four hat-tricks in three months. He was top scorer in the Champions League with 8 goals and also top scorer in La Liga with 26 goals, which added to goals from other competitions took his season's total to 39. The 6-3 aggregate win set up another battle with Inter Milan in the semi-finals, but first it was back to the league with the long-awaited top-of-the-table clash with Real Madrid.

Barça: (4-2-3-1) Valdés; Alves, Marquez, Milito, Abidal (Maxwell m53); Xavi, Busquets; Pedro (Iniesta m86), Messi, Keita; Bojan (Toure m56).

Arsenal: (4-3-3) Almunia; Sagna, Vermaelen, Sylvestre (Eboue m64), Clichy; Denilson, Nasri, Diaby; Walcott, Bendtner, Rosicky (Eduardo m73).

Goals: m18 Bendtner 0-1, m21 Messi 1-1, m37 Messi 2-1, m42 Messi 3-1, m88 Messi 4-1.

CHAPTER 18 – Real Madrid 0 Barça 2

Barça and Madrid had been neck-and-neck at the top of La Liga since the beginning of March. The *Clásico* on April 10 2010, with just seven league games remaining, seemed sure to play a major part in the final outcome of the 2009/10 title race. Madrid were in impressive form, since losing 1-0 to Athletic Club back in January they had won 12 straight league games, scoring 41 goals in the process. They could boast a 100% record in 15 league games at the Bernabéu where they had scored 50 and only conceded 13. They also had the whole week to prepare for the *Clásico* having been knocked out of the Champions League by Lyon in the last 16.

Madrid had home advantage but they were under more pressure to win as they would finish the season without a trophy for the second year running if they didn't reclaim the league. Kaka, Pepe and Drenthe were all out injured but Xabi Alonso passed a fitness test and Sergio Ramos was also available again after suspension. There were no surprises from Manuel Pelligrini as Madrid lined up with Casillas, Ramos, Garay, Albiol, Arboloa, Van der Vaart, Alonso, Gago, Marcelo, Higuian and Ronaldo in a 4-4-2 formation.

Barça were without Eric Abidal and Zlatan Ibrahimovic but Gerard Piqué was fit again and ready to return to defence. Guardiola's main doubt was who to play in attack with Messi and Pedro. Bojan could continue at centre forward or there was the option of playing Pedro on the right, Messi in the middle and then a choice of Henry or Iniesta, or even Jeffren or Maxwell, on the left. Henry had a good record at the Bernabéu but his form had not been great while there were doubts about Iniesta's fitness as he had only played five minutes as a substitute against Arsenal. When the Barça eleven was announced an hour before the kick off there was still some doubts about Guardiola's intentions as five defenders (Alves,

Piqué, Puyol, Milito and Maxwell) were named in the team. Guardiola's surprise was to place Alves on the right wing with Puyol moving to right back, the idea being to control the threat from Marcelo and Ronaldo on Madrid's left.

The game began at a very high speed but neither side had time to settle on the ball and there were no shots in the first 15 minutes. The main talking point was a possible penalty for a foul by Albiol on Messi in the 12th minute but the referee, Mejuto Gonzalez, was not impressed. Barça had more of the ball but failed to get into any decent scoring positions as Madrid harried and pressed, conceding a number of fouls which was reflected in the total fouls of Madrid 8 Barça 1 after 20 minutes. From one of the free kicks Dani Alves had the first shot of the game but it went well over Casillas's crossbar.

Madrid's first effort came with a Xabi Alonso shot going wide after 23 minutes, and three minutes later Puyol did well to rob Cristiano Ronaldo denying him a run at goal. At this point the game was still wide open but Barça got the breakthrough a few minutes later. Messi received a quickly taken free kick from Maxwell 30 yards out, he played the ball square to Xavi and ran into space on the left of the area where he received Xavi's lofted return, jumping to control the ball with his chest, he slipped inside past Albiol before slotting the ball right-footed inside Casillas's near post. It was Messi's 7th goal in 8 games against Madrid, his 27th league goal of the season, and his 40th in all competitions.

Madrid tried to hit back but they lacked precision near goal, Xabi Alonso had the best chance, heading just over from a corner. Then Higuian got goal side of Piqué from a long ball from Ramos but the Argentinian striker fired well over. That was it from Madrid for the first half, and Barça went in with a goal advantage at the break, having taken their only real chance of the half. Victor Valdés had nothing to deal with other than one high ball and a few back passes in the first 45 minutes.

In the second half Alves moved back to right back with Puyol switching to the left, which meant Maxwell moved forward and Pedro moved to the right wing. Madrid had to push forward in search of an equalizer and they managed their first shot on target in the 52nd minute but Valdés saved easily from Marcelo's effort from just outside the area. Barça began to look more comfortable in possession and Madrid sometimes went for more than a minute without touching the ball. However, after one such spell, Madrid broke quickly with Higuain freeing Ronaldo on the left but Valdés was alert to save Ronaldo's shot. Almost immediately Barça hit Madrid for a second. Again it was the brilliant Xavi who made the difference with a defence splitting pass to Pedro who sprinted away from Arbeloa before picking his spot left-footed inside Casillas's far post.

Madrid fought back, firing three shots in the next three minutes. First Valdés had no problem with Gago's long shot, then Higuian shot wide, but the best chance was for Van der Vaart, put through by substitute Guti, but Valdés held his ground superbly to save. Madrid continued to try shots from distance but Valdés dealt well with everything that came near him, with one other notable save with his legs to deny Ronaldo in the 69th minute. Despite the shots on goal total reading 7-2 in Madrid's favour, it was Barça who were still looking the better team. Puyol, Milito and Piqué were dominating at the back while Xavi was masterful in midfield. Twice in the last twenty minutes Xavi set up Messi with clear chances but on both occasions Casillas managed to divert the ball wide for a corner. Barça ended the game strongly with an impressive work-rate to prevent Madrid chances from close in. Raul finally got the ball in the net after 86 minutes but the goal was disallowed for a previous handball by Benzema.

The victory was a massive step towards repeating the league title. Barça now had a three-point lead with the added advantage of the head-to-head goal difference with just seven games to go. Barça's four home games, Deportivo, Xerez, Tenerife and Valladolid, did not look too difficult on paper, but there were also three difficult away games at Español, Villarreal and Sevilla which suggested that the title race was far from over.

Real Madrid: Casillas; Ramos, Albiol, Garay, Arbeloa; Van der Vaart (Raul m68), Gago, Alonso, Marcelo (Guti m57); Higuian (Benzema m79), Ronaldo.

Barça: Valdés; Puyol, Piqué, Milito (Marquez m79), Maxwell (Iniesta m63); Xavi, Busquets, Keita; Alves, Messi, Pedro.

Goals: m33 Messi 0-1, m56 Pedro 0-2.

CHAPTER 19 – Barça 1 Inter Milan 0

Halfway through April 2010 and Barça were still in with a very good chance of retaining both Liga and Champions League. However, there was little room for error, and with two games a week throughout the month the pressure was growing. Abidal and Ibrahimovic were still recovering from injury. Then the day before the Wednesday night league game with Deportivo de La Coruña Iniesta tore a thigh muscle in training that would see him sidelined for a month.

Guardiola decided to rest Puyol against Depor, bringing Marquez back into defence while restoring Toure to midfield. Jeffren and Bojan both got another chance up front which, with Pedro and Messi also starting, gave the team a 100% homegrown attack. Pedro hit the post early on, then after 16 minutes Bojan put Barça ahead, sliding the ball under Depor keeper Daniel Aranzubia after Xavi's assist. However, despite an excellent first half including a spectacular overhead kick against the bar from Alves the score remained at 1-0 at half time. There was always the danger that Depor could sneak a goal against the run of play but Barça finally added a second with one of the goals of the season. Valdés came out to catch a high free kick and he quickly spotted Alves making an excellent sprint forward. Valdés sent a long kick down the middle, Alves was neck-and-neck with Depor's right back Manuel Pablo in the chase for the ball when Aranzubia came darting out of his area to clear. Aranzubia's clearance went at pace to Pedro who was only ten yards inside the Depor half, but he didn't hesitate to hit the ball first time for the open goal. The ball came to him very quickly but Pedro's contact was perfect and the ball flew in a beautiful arc into the empty net. Toure capped a fine performance in midfield by cracking in Barça's third soon after to seal the victory, and the lead at the top of the table remained at three points.

The following Saturday was the first local derby at the new Cornellà-Prat stadium where Espanyol had been unbeaten in their previous nine matches. Abidal and Ibrahimovic were both declared fit again though neither made the starting XI. Guardiola surprised by using Maxwell again on the left wing with Puyol moving to left-back, while Toure continued in midfield despite Busquets returning to the team. The defensive looking 4-3-3 meant there were few chances in an intensely fought game. Just when Barça looked to be getting on top after the introduction of Keita and Henry early in the second half Alves received a second yellow card after bringing down José Callejón and Barça were left with ten men for the last half hour. Despite the numerical disadvantage Barça managed a late push in search of a winner but Espanyol fought doggedly until the final whistle and held out for a goalless draw. The following day Madrid beat third-placed Valencia and reduced the gap to just one point with five games to go.

The eruption of the Islandic volcano Eyjafjallajökull provoked an unexpected problem for Barça's travel plans to Milan for the Champions League semi-final first leg, as the volcanic ash in the atmosphere caused havoc to European air traffic. With the possibility of there being no flights available, and with UEFA insisting that the game must go ahead at the scheduled time on Tuesday evening, Barça took the decision to travel the 985 km to Milan by coach. Leaving on Sunday lunchtime the team spent the night in Cannes before continuing the journey and arriving in Milan at 2.30 pm on the Monday.

Mourinho's Inter were looking very solid and certainly seemed stronger than when the two sides met in the group stage. Like Barça, Inter were involved in a tight battle for their domestic league, but it was their performances in Europe, knocking Chelsea out in the last 16 before going on to beat CSKA Moscow in the quarter-finals, that impressed most.

The game at the San Siro began with Barça looking more comfortable in possession than they had against Espanyol. However, it was soon clear that when Inter did win the ball their intention was to get the ball forward as quickly as possible, looking to get Diego Milito in behind the Barça back four. Barça had created very little going forward until in the 19th minute Xavi sent Maxwell away on the left. The full back got into the area before pulling the ball back to Pedro who struck his shot into the far corner from 16 yards. With the away goal Barça wanted to control the game but the speed of Milito and Eto'o was a constant threat. Inter got a deserved equalizer after half an hour when Alves left Wesley Sneijder free to score from Milito's pass.

Whether it had anything to do with the journey or not, Barça were looking pedestrian going forward. Ibrahimovic was ineffective, Messi could find no way through with his runs, and the crossing, especially from Alves was poor. It looked like a disaster waiting to happen and early in the second half the Brazilian full back Maicon got ahead of Keita to score Inter's second after a quick break from Sneijder and Milito. Then, in the 61st minute, Xavi, of all people, lost the ball 35 yards out. Thiago Motta played the ball to Eto'o' on the right and his cross found Sneijder who headed the ball back across the goal to Milito who, despite being half a yard offside, headed the ball past Valdés. Guardiola's only answer was to bring on Abidal for the ineffective Ibrahimovic but it really didn't change much. Inter seemed content to defend the 3-1 lead and the closest Barça came to another goal was when Lucio cleared off the line from Piqué. It would be an uphill battle in the second leg at Camp Nou and Puyol would be suspended for the game after picking up a booking.

Before the return match with Inter, Barça faced bottom-of-the-league Xerez in their first ever visit to Camp Nou. It may have appeared to be one of the easier games of the season but Barça could not afford any slip-ups. Even so, Guardiola rested Piqué, Milito, Busquets, Messi and Pedro, while Alves was suspended. Despite early goals from Jeffren, with a fine shot from a tight angle, and Henry, after Ibrahimovic unselfishly set him up, the team was somewhat disjointed with the centre back pairing of Marquez and Chygrynskiy looking short on match practice. Bermujo struck a magnificent shot past Valdés to pull a goal back for Xerez and it wasn't until Guardiola brought on Messi and Piqué in place of Jeffren and Marquez early in the second half that Barça began to look more comfortable. Ibrahimovic put Barça 3-1 up after a strong surge from Toure into the area. With the two-goal advantage restored there was little more threat from Xerez, and Barça held out for three more vital points.

With a place in the 2009/10 Champions League final at Madrid's Santiago Bernabéu stadium at stake, Barça needed a repeat of the 2-0 victory over Inter in the group stage back in November to overturn the 3-1 defeat from the first leg. On the two previous occasions that Barça had lost 3-1 in the first leg of a Champions League tie the team had responded with memorable comebacks. In March 2000, extra time was needed before finally beating Chelsea 5-1, and in September 1993, in a match that many remember as the best performance in Johan Cruyff's eight years as first team coach, Barça's Dream Team beat Dynamo Kiev 4-1.

Barça were without the suspended Puyol, while Abidal had again joined Iniesta on the injured list. As in the previous season's final in Rome and semi-final second leg at Stamford Bridge, Guardiola opted for Toure at centre back. Gabi Milito was preferred over Maxwell at left back, setting up an interesting contest against his brother Diego, as Barça started with a 4-3-3 of Valdés, Alves, Toure, Piqué, Milito, Xavi, Busquets, Keita, Messi, Ibrahimovic and Pedro. Mourinho made only one change to his first leg XI, with the defensive Cristian Chivu coming in on the left wing in place of Goran Pandev, with the intention of stopping Alves.

Barça started promisingly, pinning Inter back in their half. After three minutes, Pedro cut inside from the left and shot just wide of the far post. However, Inter defended superbly, concentrating on cutting off the final pass so that even Xavi couldn't find a gap, while Messi was well marked by Cambiasso and found it difficult to start any runs. Barça failed to get past the full backs and Inter's central defenders Lucio and Samuel had few problems dealing with crosses from deep. However, in the 22nd minute Alves's cross found Ibrahimovic who knocked the ball down to Xavi but the defence were quick to respond before Xavi could shoot. A minute later Alves crossed again to the edge of the box and Pedro met the ball with a half volley that went just wide.

The game changed in the 28th minute when Motta, who'd already been booked early on, stuck his arm up to keep Busquets at bay, Motta's hand went into Busquets throat and Busquets went down dramatically in a heap. The Belgian referee Frank de Bleeckere didn't hesitate to send off the furious Motta. With over an hour still to play, the Italians reorganized with an extremely defensive 4-4-1 and basically renounced any form of attack. Soon after, Barça created the best chance of the first half when Messi, cutting across the edge of the area, finally found a gap to shoot through. The ball was heading for the bottom corner but Inter keeper Julio Cesar made a tremendous save, diving to his right to tip the ball round the post.

Barça failed to build on this chance and for the remainder of the first half Inter continued to close all spaces. Ibrahimovic hardly had a sniff of goal and his only involvement was in giving away a series of free kicks. He did have one chance after Alves knocked down Xavi's cross but he was immediately shut down by Samuel. Then just before half time the big Swede tried a free kick from over 30 yards which whistled just wide of the post.

Despite the lack of scoring opportunities for Barça in the first half there was still a feeling of optimism around Camp Nou that the chances would come after the interval. Maxwell replaced Gabi Milito at left back but Barça began to look anxious as the minutes passed as Inter continued to close down all routes into the penalty area. There were long shots off target from Alves, Toure and Pedro, and it was beginning to look worrying for the defending champions. Guardiola decided it was time for some drastic action and he brought on Bojan and Jeffren for Ibrahimovic and Busquets. However, the game continued to follow the same pattern with Inter defending deep and Barça struggling to penetrate. It wasn't until the 78th minute that Jeffren put in a dangerous low cross that was just out of Bojan's reach.

Piqué had had an excellent game at the back, recovering the ball whenever it came into the Barça half. As a final resort Guardiola pushed the young defender up into attack and the cracks began to appear in Inter's defence. In the 82nd minute Messi sent in a fine cross to the far post but Bojan missed a great chance, glancing his header wide. Then in the 84th minute Messi squared to Xavi 25 yards out, Xavi slipped a pass into the area to Piqué who controlled in front of Julio Cesar, turned 360º to get away from the keeper and Maicon, before sweeping the ball into the empty net.

The goal was only Barça's second shot on target of the game, but with just one more goal needed to reach the final Barça piled players forward into the packed Inter penalty area. Xavi and Messi both forced saves from Julio Cesar. There was a penalty appeal from Alves when he appeared to be held back by Muntari. Then, in the 92nd minute, Toure charged down a clearance and the ball broke through to Bojan who fired into the top of the net a split second after De Bleeckere had blown for a handball against Toure. The replay showed the ball had hit Toure's hand but his arm was across his body and it didn't look deliberate. However, it wasn't to be Barça's night. Inter won 3-2 on aggregate and reached the final without managing one shot at goal in the second leg. At the final whistle Mourinho celebrated on the Camp Nou pitch, provoking an angry reaction from Victor Valdés, and the Barça fans were left to reflect on what might have been.

Barça: Valdés; Alves, Toure, Piqué, G.Milito (Maxwell m45); Xavi, Busquets (Jeffren m63), Keita; Messi, Ibrahimovic (Bojan m63), Pedro.

Inter: Julio Cesar; Maicon, Lucio, Samuel, Zanetti; Motta, Cambiasso; Eto'o (Mariga m86), Sneijder (Muntari m67), Chivu; D.Milito (Cordoba m81).

Goal: m84 Piqué 1-0.

CHAPTER 20 – Sevilla 2 Barça 3

There was little time to dwell on the disappointment of missing out on the Champions League final as the following Saturday Barça travelled to Villarreal for a vital league fixture. With just four games to play and a slender one-point advantage over rivals Madrid there was no room for slip-ups.

Villarreal had moved up from 10th place to 6th in the table since Juan Carlos Garrido took over from Ernesto Valverde as their coach at the start of February and they were still in with a very realistic chance of clinching a Champions League spot. They had won all six league games at their El Madrigal stadium with Garrido in charge, and despite a low budget their squad boasted talents such as Marcus Senna, Santi Cazorla, Giuseppe Rossi, Diego Lopez, Diego Godin, Joan Capdevila and Cani.

Xavi and Busquets both overcame knocks to play, but the big surprise was Guardiola's decision to leave Ibrahimovic on the bench, starting with a front three of Pedro, Messi and Bojan. The pint-sized trio ran Villareal's defence ragged in the first half with the brilliant Xavi directing from midfield. Messi put Barça ahead after 19 minutes, turning and shooting low past Diego Lopez after receiving Xavi's assist. Xavi then turned goalscorer, curling a beautiful free kick over the wall and into the top corner. Barça made it 0-3 just before half time with a brilliant goal from Bojan. The youngster was 35 yards out with his back to goal when he received a pass from Xavi. He turned and flicked the ball one side of Gonzalo Rodriguez while sprinting past the Villarreal defender on the other side to speed into the area and fire low into the far corner past the advancing Diego Lopez. Llorente pulled a goal back for Villarreal midway through the second half and with more than 20 minutes to go there was still a chance for Villarreal to make a comeback. Memories came back of the 3-3 draw at Camp Nou at the end of the previous season when Barça were 3-1 up with 15 minutes to go. However, Barça ended the game strongly, having looked serious all night with Piqué impressing at the back. Near the end, Xavi played a superb ball through for Alves to cross to Messi who clipped the ball over Diego Lopez to seal a 1-4 victory.

The following day Madrid came from behind twice to beat Osasuna 3-2 at the Bernabéu with an 89th minute winner from Ronaldo to stay just one point behind. There was then a midweek fixture with Barça playing relegation candidates Tenerife at Camp Nou on the Tuesday while on the Wednesday Madrid had a tough away game at fourth-placed Mallorca. Tenerife had taken nine points from their previous four games and they made Barça suffer. Messi opened the scoring after 17 minutes but Tenerife's Román Martinez equalized before half time after a poor pass from Puyol was intercepted by Daniel Kome. Barça were looking anxious with the score at 1-1 and it wasn't until the 63rd minute that Alves got past a defender before slipping a ball into Bojan who shot low under the keeper into the far corner. With time running out, there was still the threat of a Tenerife equalizer until Pedro made it 3-1 after Messi's pass in the 77th minute. Then right at the end, man-of-the-match Alves crossed into Messi who made the control and flick over the keeper look easy. Barça went four points clear and there was a lot of hope in Mallorca's ability to upset Madrid the following night. A hat-trick from Ronaldo put an end to that hope as Madrid won comfortably 1-4 and the gap remained at just one point with two games to play.

As Barça's final game of the season was a relatively easy game at home to Valladolid, the away match at Sevilla on Saturday 8 May was considered by most to be the deciding game of the 2009/10 league season. It was a vital game for Sevilla too as they had just moved a point above Mallorca into fourth place with a Champions League spot at stake. Barça had won on the previous two visits to the Sánchez Pizjuán, but Sevilla, under coach Antonio Alvarez, had only lost two out of eighteen home league games and they had, of course, knocked Barça out of the Copa del Rey back in January.

Iniesta had still not quite recovered from his injury though he travelled with the squad to Seville, while Abidal and Piqué faced late fitness tests before the game. Piqué was passed as fit and started alongside Puyol in defence. Abidal began on the bench as did Ibrahimovic who was again left out as Barça lined up with a 4-3-3 of Valdés, Alves, Piqué, Puyol, Maxwell, Xavi, Busquets, Keita, Pedro, Messi and Bojan.

From the start of the game it was clear that Barça were well tuned in for the challenge. In the fourth minute, Messi found Alves running into the area but the full-back had to stretch to reach the ball and only managed a soft shot straight at Sevilla's keeper Palop. A minute later, Busquets made an excellent tackle to deny Luis Fabiano a run at goal, Barça maintained possession until the ball came out to Maxwell on the left and he lofted a ball into Messi who controlled on his chest, made one touch to turn before firing a low left-footed shot across Palop into the far corner.

After the early goal Barça continued to look the better team, playing a quick-tempo passing game with an excellent work-rate to win the ball back. Xavi sent in one through ball that Keita failed to control, and not long after, Palop had to come racing out of his goal to deny Pedro. The ball only came out as far as Alves who drove the ball back in but Bojan couldn't jump high enough and his header went over.

Barça's dominance was rewarded again in the 28th minute. Alves played the ball inside towards Xavi, the ball clipped off the top of a Sevilla player's head and Xavi adjusted brilliantly to meet the ball on the half volley and send a swift pass into Bojan who held off the challenge of Konko and fired low past Palop for the second goal. Sevilla still hadn't had a shot on goal. Then, in the 34th minute, Capel finally managed a header from 15 yards but it was easy for Valdés. Soon after, Xavi put Alves away on the right but from just four yards out Messi put the cross over the bar. Sevilla's best chance of the half came just before the break when Piqué failed to close down Luis Fabiano who received a long ball into the box but Valdés did well to save the Brazilian striker's shot from close range. It was Barça's only real lapse in an otherwise superb first half.

The second half began with Barça showing the same level of excellence, though Sevilla were trying to press further up the field. Freddie Kanoute had a header wide from a corner. Then, in the 56th minute, Abdoulay Konko saw his second yellow card after pulling back Bojan and with the score at 0-2 the game looked to be all over. Barça had chances to increase their advantage in the next five minutes. First Messi shot wide from Maxwell's cross. Then the Argentinian had another chance from close in that hit Palop before going for a corner. Soon after, Bojan was given a good chance from Messi's assist but his shot was saved by Palop's outstretched leg.

However, the third goal did not elude Barça for much longer. Alves was having an exceptional game and in the 62nd minute he played a good ball through to Messi who cut inside to shoot, the shot hit a defender but came straight to Pedro who controlled before shooting hard and low past Palop from 25 yards. Three-nil up against ten men with just over 25 minutes remaining and of course it should have been all over. Barça could easily have had a fourth but Bojan incredibly missed a sitter at the far post after a fantastic run into the area from Messi.

What happened next was really not to be expected. Abidal had just come on for the injured Maxwell but that didn't explain Barça's lack of concentration. In the 69th minute, Puyol failed to cut out a pass through to Kanoute who tucked the ball past Valdés to make it 1-3. Then, just two minutes later, the entire Barça defence was caught sleeping as Zokora took a quick free kick which found Luis Fabiano in acres of space and Valdés again had no chance with the shot.

Barça had seemed completely in control before the Sevilla goals, but with an electric atmosphere inside the Sánchez Pizjuán stadium Sevilla gave their all in the search for an equalizer. It was a terribly nervous time for Barça, especially as news came through that Madrid were beating Athletic Club at the Bernabéu. Despite the pressure Barça's players kept their heads and more or less restored order. The referee, Undiano Mallenco, should have given Luis Fabiano a second yellow card after some clear shirt pulling but then he also ignored a small push by Piqué on Kanoute in the area. It was a moment when all Barça fans held their breath but Kanoute's exaggerated fall may have influenced the referee's decision to wave play on.

The tension was unbearable as Sevilla pushed men forward. Kanoute headed a free kick over the bar but generally Barça did a good job of keeping Sevilla away from the penalty area. Pedro and Bojan both went close to a fourth for Barça. Then, well into injury time, Sevilla sent a long throw into the area, but Piqué and Jeffren managed to clear the danger and much to Barça's relief and joy the referee blew the final whistle.

Madrid had beaten Athletic to stay just one point behind going into the final game of the season but nobody gave Valladolid much chance of causing an upset at Camp Nou. Javier Clemente had taken over as Valladolid's coach in an attempt to survive relegation but Barça were showing no mercy. After resisting for 27 minutes Valladolid conceded the first through an own goal from Luis Prieto. Pedro added a second soon after, and two second half goals from Messi completed a comfortable 4-0 victory. Barça clinched their 20th Liga with an incredible 99 points, three points above Madrid who drew at Malaga on the final day. Particularly sweet for culés was the fact that Madrid, who had spent over €250 million the previous summer to bring in Ronaldo, Kaká, Benzema and Alonso, had finished the season with nothing.

Sevilla: Palop; Konko, Fazio (Squillaci m27), Escudé, Adriano (Lolo m67); Jesús Navas, Zokora, Renato (Stankevicius m61), Capel; Luis Fabiano, Kanouté

Barça: Valdés; Alves, Piqué, Puyol, Maxwell (Abidal m66); Xavi (Toure m87), Busquets, Keita; Pedro, Messi, Bojan (Jeffren m92).

Goals: m5 Messi 0-1, m27 Bojan 0-2, m62 Pedro 0-3, m68 Kanouté 1-3, m70 Luis Fabiano 2-3.

CHAPTER 21 – Barça 4 Sevilla 0

The summer of 2010 marked the end of Joan Laporta's seven-year mandate as Barça's president. As a last act Laporta secured the signing of the 28-year-old David Villa from Valencia for €40 million. Villa was Spain's most prolific striker in years and he had just been named in Spain's squad for the 2010 World Cup in South Africa along with Xavi, Iniesta, Busquets, Piqué, Puyol, Pedro and Valdés.

In contrast with Barça's previous presidential elections there was little the candidates could offer Barça's members in the way of change. Nobody wanted to remove Guardiola and there were no promises of big signings as was usually the case. The fact that the four candidates had all worked with the Laporta at some point meant the campaign was more about accusations of what one or the other had tried to do in the past.

The big favourite was Sandro Rosell who had resigned from Laporta's board back in 2005 after the two fell out. In part of the slur campaign in the run-up to the elections Laporta had accused Rosell of wanting to sell Ronaldinho to Chelsea in 2004 in order to pocket a 10% fee. Rosell's election promises included the shelving of the Norman Foster plan for the renovation of Camp Nou while he also wanted to make it more difficult to become a club member with the intention of keeping to the club's Catalan roots (the explanation behind this was that 200,000 foreigners could become members and thus change the identity of the club). Rosell also believed that Johan Cruyff had too much influence over what went on at the club. In a controversial decision in March 2010 Laporta had made Cruyff the club's *President d'honor*. Some argued that constitutionally Laporta did not have the power to make such a decision while the timing (just before elections) was considered by most to be inopportune.

The other presidential candidates, ex-vice-president Marc Ingla, Laporta's 'successor' Jaume Ferrer, and the outsider Augustí Benedito who had supported Laporta's successful 2003 campaign, either lacked Rosell's charisma or were simply not well known enough. In a runaway victory Rosell received more than any other candidate in the history of Barça's presidential elections, over 35,000 votes (61.5%), with Benedito making a late surge to finish second with 14.09%. Three important decisions were taken very quickly: Cruyff's title of Honorary President was removed, under the argument that the position was not stipulated in the club's statutes, Andoni Zubizaretta was brought in as the club's sporting director after Txiki Begiristain's departure, and Guillermo Amor replaced José Ramón Alexanco as director of youth football.

With such a high presence of Barça players in the Spanish team it is impossible to look at the 2010 World Cup without recognizing the importance of this presence in Spain's eventual triumph. Of the eight Barça players in the Spanish squad Valdés was the only one who didn't play at all. Piqué and Puyol's excellence as the centre back pairing was reflected by Spain's defensive record of only conceding two goals in seven games. Busquets, Xavi and Iniesta were instrumental in Spain's midfield while Villa led the attack, scoring five goals to end the tournament as joint top scorer. Pedro was seen more sparingly at first but after three good performances as substitute he broke into the team to start in both the semi-final and final, meaning Spain started both these games with seven blaugranas in the starting XI. There was a proud boast for culés in the fact that Spain's eight goals scored in winning the tournament all came from Barça players, including Puyol's header in the semi-final against Germany and Iniesta's extra-time winner to beat Holland in the final.

Back in Barcelona the new board was overseeing business in the transfer market. At the start of July, Toure Yaya became the first player to leave, moving to Manchester City for €32 million. Toure had been at the club for three seasons and his performances, especially in the first two seasons, made him a favourite with fans. He was heroic in the 2007/08 season when he continued playing despite suffering from a painful back injury, and despite the team's below-par performances in Frank Rijkaard's last season he was one of the few who played at an excellent level. The following season under Pep Guardiola, Toure continued to impress, proving his versatility by filling in at centre back in the Champions League semi-final and final victories and also in the Copa del Rey final when he also scored the vital equalizer on the road to beating Athletic Club. However, his last season was not his best which led to Guardiola preferring Busquets for the defensive midfield position. Toure was understandably unhappy at not getting more playing time and decided to move on.

Later in July, Henry, Marquez and Chygrynskiy also left the club. Henry and Marquez were both nearing the end of their careers and both took the chance to play Major League Soccer with the New York Red Bulls. The case of Chygrynskiy was a little strange. In an interview after moving back to Shakhtar Donetsk for €15 million, Chygrynskiy claimed that Guardiola had called him at the end of June indicating that he was counting on him for the coming season. It seems a decision was taken by the board of directors that Barça needed the money, and despite receiving €10 million less than the original fee paid for the player the previous summer, the deal was accepted as a way of cutting losses on a player who had generally disappointed in his year at the club.

With reinforcements needed, Adriano Correia became Barça's first signing of Sandro Rosell's presidency when he arrived from Sevilla for a fee of €9.5 million. When Adriano joined the first training session of the new season on July 19 there were many faces missing as the World Cup players remained on holiday. Guardiola included 14 non-first team players including Cristian Tello, Sergi Roberto, Sergi Gomez, Ilie Sanchez and Johnathan dos Santos for the trip to Norway where Barça beat Valerenga 2-4 in the first preseason friendly.

The squad then flew out to Asia for two friendlies at the start of August. First, in South Korea, Barça won 2-5 against a selection of the best players from the Korean K-League. Messi played 15 minutes, having just joined the group after his holidays, but he still managed to show his quality chipping in with two goals. Then in China Barça beat local side Guoan 0-3 with Guardiola trying out Abidal at centre back for the first time.

The team returned home to prepare for the Spanish Supercopa against Copa del Rey winners Sevilla, a preparation that was not helped at all by the Spanish Football Federation's decision to play a friendly for Mexico's bicentennial just three days before the first leg in Seville. Barça's World Cup winners only returned from their holidays on August 9 and the following day Valdés, Piqué, Puyol, Busquets, Xavi, Pedro and Villa flew out to Mexico with the Spanish squad – only Iniesta was spared the trip.

None of the World Cup winners made the list for the first game at Sevilla, so for Barça's first official game of the 2010/11 season three youngsters Ruben Miño, Sergio Gomez and Oriol Romeu were thrown in at the deep end while Messi began on the bench. Ibrahimovic put Barça in front after 20 minutes, poking the ball past Palop at the near post after an excellent ball from Maxwell on the left. However, in the second half, even with Messi coming on as a substitute, Barça wilted and Sevilla took advantage with a goal from Luis Fabiano and two from Kanoute to finish 3-1 winners. Adriano came on as a late substitute to make his Barça debut against the club that had sold him.

For the return game a week later at Camp Nou Guardiola had his eight World Cup winners available again and was able to put out a much stronger starting XI with Valdés, Piqué, Xavi, Busquets and Pedro all returning to the team. Ibrahimovic was left on the bench which led to renewed rumours of a possible move before the transfer window closed at the end of the month. Abidal started at centre back, a position he had played in for France but very rarely for Barça, something that would change in the 2010/11 season.

If Barça had been weakened for the first leg, now it was Sevilla with the disadvantage as the game took place just three days before Sevilla faced a vital Champions League second leg qualifying match against Sporting Braga, having lost the first leg in Portugal 1-0. Sevilla's coach Antonio Álvarez opted to leave Federico Fazio, Luis Fabiano, Kanoute and Diego Perotti out of the starting line-up, but still fielded a competitive XI that looked to defend the 3-1 lead from the first game.

Right from the kick off Barça took control of the game with the trademark style of high-tempo passing in possession and asphyxiating pressure on the opponent whenever the ball was lost. Messi fired well over with the first shot of the game in the 6th minute, but it didn't take long for Barça's dominance to reap its first reward when in the 14th minute Pedro dribbled past two players to break into the right side of the area and his low hard cross hit Konko and ricocheted into the net. Four minutes later Maxwell fired in a similar cross from the left but it was just too fast for Bojan to react in time. Bojan then had two low efforts from outside the area that both went wide.

Xavi was dominating in midfield and in the 25th minute he was quick to spot Messi's run through the middle. The through ball was perfectly timed and Messi ran clear into the area before dummying a shot to create a better angle and firing low under Palop for Barça's second. With the away goal from the first leg Barça were now in front over the two legs and the team concentrated on keeping the ball and wearing down Sevilla. Valdés was not troubled once and just before half time Barça scored a third. Pedro laid the ball on to Alves on the right, Alves played a low cross into the near post where Messi had again found space, as the ball reached him Messi span and fired a right foot shot first time over Palop and into the roof of the net. Another superb finish to complete an excellent first half.

Barça continued to dominate in the second half. The first chance came in the 50th minute when Messi dribbled into the area but he pulled his shot wide of the far post. There was a tremendous ovation in the 57th minute when Iniesta and Villa for his debut came on in place of Pedro and Bojan, and with such talent on the field there were some great combinations. In the 60th minute Messi played the ball inside to Iniesta who flicked a pass back to Messi who crossed first time from the right but Iniesta, who'd continued his run, could only manage to poke the ball just wide.

Alvarez brought on Luis Fabiano and Perotti, and Sevilla began to look a little more dangerous. However, Barça's defence kept excellent concentration, with Piqué in particularly good form, and Valdés remained untroubled. At the other end Villa began to demonstrate his abilities: one dangerous pass into Messi that was cut out by Palop, another shot deflected for a corner, and then he fired a volley which was beaten away by Palop. Sevilla caused one scare near the end when Luis Fabiano and Navas beat the offside trap but they both left the ball for the other, allowing Abidal to sprint back and intervene. It was a worrying moment for Barça as a Sevilla goal at this point would have meant extra time. However, Barça put the contest beyond doubt in the 90th minute after a fine ball from Villa into Iniesta who, instead of shooting, cut the ball back across goal for Messi to complete his hat-trick and clinch trophy number eight of Guardiola's era.

Barça: Valdés; Alves, Piqué, Abidal, Maxwell; Xavi (Adriano m88 --), Busquets, Keita; Pedro (Villa m57), Messi, Bojan (Iniesta m57).

Sevilla: Palop; Dabo, Konko, Escudé, Fernando Navarro; Alfaro (Perotti, m62), Zokora, Romaric (Cigarini, m62), Capel (Luis Fabiano, m62); Navas, Negredo.

Goals: m14 Konko (o.g.) 1-0, m25 Messi 2-0, m44 Messi 3-0, m90 Messi 4-0.

CHAPTER 22 – Barça 5 Panathinaikos 1

Following the triumph in the Spanish Supercopa Barça had one more preparation game before the start of the 2010/11 Liga, against AC Milan in the Joan Gamper tournament. Milan arrived with Ronaldinho who returned to a hero's welcome from the Camp Nou crowd though the main talking point was the ongoing behind-the-scenes negotiations between the two clubs for the sale of Zlatan Ibrahimovic. The Swede played the first 45 minutes of the game and had one spectacular effort disallowed. Early in the second half Villa scored his first goal for the club, converting Adriano's low cross to the near post, but Milan hit back through a magnificent volley from Filippo Inzhagi to take the game to penalties. Pinto demonstrated his expertise at penalties, stopping three of the four Milan kicks and Barça lifted the trophy.

While negotiations continued for Ibrahimovic, Barça made a final reinforcement to the squad by signing the 26-year-old Argentinian, Javier Mascherano, from Liverpool for €22 million. Mascherano had played in England for four seasons, generally as a ball-winning midfielder, and his signing was seen chiefly as being cover for Busquets after the sale of Toure Yaya.

The Ibrahimovic move to Milan went through on the eve of the first league game of the season at Racing Santander. The deal was a strange one with the player signing on loan for the Italians with the obligation that they would have to complete the purchase at the end of the year for a fee of €24 million. It was a big loss on the €43 million + Samuel Eto'o paid the previous summer to Inter but it was felt that Barça were cutting their losses and that the savings made on the player's wages made the deal worthwhile. It also meant that Guardiola now had a first team squad with no difficult characters. However, without Ibrahimovic Barça were left to start the season with just five first team forwards, Messi, Pedro, Villa, Bojan and Jeffren.

The other position that seemed to lack strength in depth was centre back. Following the departure of Marquez and Chygrynskiy the only recognized central defenders were Puyol, Piqué and Milito. Guardiola showed he trusted in the versatility of other players such as Abidal or Busquets. Abidal was paired with Piqué for the game at Racing, allowing the in-form Maxwell to continue at left back.

Barça's league campaign got off to a perfect start in Santander with an early goal. Iniesta played in Messi who showed speed to get away from a defender and then subtlety to lift the ball over Racing's keeper Toño with a neat little flick of his right foot. Messi had scored 47 goals in the 2009/10 season and he had started 2010/11 with a bang: a hat trick against Sevilla in the Supercopa and now his first league goal with just 2 minutes 35 seconds on the clock. Iniesta added a brilliant second after half an hour, volleying Toño's punched clearance back over the stranded keeper from 30 yards. Villa completed the 0-3 victory in the second half with his first league goal for Barça, heading home from Alves's cross. The victory was even sweeter a couple of hours later when the news came in that Madrid had only managed a goalless draw in Mallorca.

An international break followed during which Argentina beat world champions Spain 4-1 in a friendly with a goal from Messi included. The return to league action on September 11 saw Barça take on newly-promoted Hercules at Camp Nou. The last time Hercules had been in the top flight, in the 1996/97 season, they had surprisingly beaten Bobby Robson's Barça in both league games, being instrumental in stopping Barça from winning the title that year. However, with the first Champions League group game against Panathinaikos coming up the following Tuesday, Guardiola opted to leave Xavi, Busquets, Alves and Pedro on the bench while giving a debut to Mascherano in the defensive midfield role. It was not to be a happy first game for the Argentinian who was booked early on and might have seen a second yellow card before being subbed off at half time. The whole team struggled to click and Hercules again upset the big boys, winning 0-2 with two goals from the Paraguayan striker Nelson Valdez.

In the Champions League Barça had been drawn against Panathinaikos, FC Copenhagen and Rubin Kazan in what appeared to be a relatively easy group. The first opponents, Greek champions Panathinaikos, returned to Camp Nou for the first time since 2005 when they had been beaten 5-0 with Messi scoring his first ever Champions League goal. Following the defeat against Hercules, Guardiola opted for his strongest XI sending out Valdés, Alves, Piqué, Puyol, Abidal, Xavi, Busquets, Iniesta, Pedro, Messi and Villa. In the 2009/10 season Barça had perhaps lacked a clearly defined 'best XI', mainly because nobody claimed the left wing position for himself. This had changed now with Villa on the left and this was the first time this classic XI had played together.

Right from the kick off it was clear that the connections between the players were infinitely better than they had been against Hercules, and Barça began to create danger very quickly. After just two minutes Messi twisted and dived to head Pedro's cross goalwards forcing the first save from Panathinaikos goalkeeper Alexandro Tzorvas. Then in the 6th minute Messi played a swift pass into the area to Iniesta who played a delightful touch to set up a chance for Xavi but Tzorvas did well to save again.

Barça continued to push forward. Messi had a powerful shot that went straight at the keeper, and then Villa and Iniesta both had chances in the space of a minute but failed to get shots in. It seemed just a matter of time before Barça would break the deadlock but then in the 20th minute Panathinaikos scored with their first attack. Tzorvas punted a long ball forward, Puyol failed to get close on Djibril Cisse who flicked on a hopeful backheel which fell perfectly for Sydney Govou who outsprinted Abidal and found his spot past Valdés.

It was a blow for the home team and memories of Hercules came back. However, Barça found an equalizer almost immediately when Xavi slipped a trademark pass through to Messi who advanced into the right of the area before touching the ball past Tzorvas. It wasn't long before Barça took the lead. Panathinaikos gave away a corner, Xavi sent in the cross, Busquets flicked on at the near post and Villa was on hand at the far post to hook the ball in from six yards. Not long after Pedro came close with a header from Alves's cross, and then in the 43rd minute Messi was unlucky to see his sidefoot shot bounce out off the crossbar. However, Messi made it 3-1 shortly before half-time. Receiving the ball from Alves on the right the Argentinian played two 1-2s, first with Xavi and then with Pedro to burst through and fire low past Tzorvas. Yet another sensational Messi goal to add to an ever-growing list.

The second half was disappointing in comparison as Barça slowed the pace a little and concentrated on keeping possession. Messi should have completed his hat-trick after he won a penalty after a neat exchange with Villa, but his spot-kick was weak and easy for Tzorvas to save. Pedro then missed a good chance when instead of shooting he dribbled round the keeper but was forced too wide to get in a shot, and not long after Villa failed to get good contact on Abidal's dangerous cross.

Panathinaikos were failing to get anywhere near Valdés's goal, but Barça were lacking the intensity to take more advantage of possession. However, there were two more late goals to give the scoreline a more realistic look. In the 77th minute Bojan played in Messi whose shot from an impossible angle hit both posts before Pedro forced the ball over the line. Then deep into injury time Messi exchanged passes with Alves before sending a delightful chip for the Brazilian to flick a header over Tzorvas to make it 5-1 at the final whistle.

The game could have been won by an even bigger margin and despite the fact that Barça's three forwards all scored they were also all guilty of missing good chances. Messi's two goals made him Barça's top scorer in the Champions League with 27 goals, two more than Rivaldo, while the victory put Barça top of Group D where in the other game FC Copenhagen beat Rubin Kazan 1-0.

Barça: Valdés; Alves, Puyol, Piqué (Milito m75), Abidal; Xavi (Mascherano m79), Busquets, Iniesta; Pedro, Messi, Villa (Bojan m69).

Panathinaikos: Tzorvas; Vyntra, Kante, Boumsong, Marinos; Katsouranis (Karagounis m64), Gilberto Silva, Simao; Govou (Luis Garcia m70), Cissé, Leto (Ninis m81).

Goals: m20 Govou 0-1, m22 Messi 1-1, m35 Villa 2-1, m45 Messi 3-1, m78 Pedro 4-1, m93 Alves 5-1.

CHAPTER 23 – Barça 5 Sevilla 0

Barça returned to La Liga with a trip to Madrid to take on Atlético at the Vicente Calderón. Guardiola was without Abidal who was allowed time off to spend with his family due to his grandfather being seriously ill, so Maxwell came in at left back in an otherwise unchanged XI. Barça began the game strongly with Messi looking particularly lively. In the 13th minute an attack continued after Villa had hit the post and ended with Pedro picking out a defence splitting pass which found Messi who nicked the ball past David De Gea with a delightful flick with the outside of his left foot. Raul Garcia equalized for Atlético midway through the first half heading in Simao Sabrosa's corner after Valdés came but didn't arrive and Piqué forgot to jump. Piqué made up for his mistake soon after, chesting down Messi's corner before firing low through a pack of defenders to restore Barça's lead. With Iniesta in mesmerizing form Barça should have built on the lead in the second half but a series of saves from the 19-year-old De Gea kept Atlético in the game. It was a nervous finish but Barça held on to win 1-2 though there was a heavy price as Messi would miss the next two games with a ligament injury caused by an ugly tackle from Tomás Ujfalusi for which the Atlético defender was sent off.

The first game without Messi was the following Wednesday at home to Sporting Gijon. Guardiola went with a front three of Bojan, Villa and Iniesta in the go-anywhere Messi role, while Milito and Keita both came into the team. Barça struggled more than usual against an unambitious opponent but just after half time Alves played a perfectly weighted pass with the outside of his right foot through to Villa who hit the ball on the turn past Sporting keeper Iván Cuéllar to earn Barça a 1-0 win and three more points.

Still without Messi and Abidal Barça travelled to Bilbao to play Athletic. Piqué and Pedro returned to the side in place of Milito and Bojan while Adriano was preferred over Maxwell at left back. Iniesta continued in the free role and he caused problems for Athletic from early on, sending one great ball into Villa who hit the post from eight yards, and later in the first half he was on the receiving end of Amorebieta's foul which saw Athletic reduced to ten men. Keita gave an excellent display in midfield supporting both the attack and the defence and he broke the deadlock early in the second half latching on to Villa's pass and skillfully slotting the ball under Gorka Iraizoz. Xavi made it 0-2 with a deflected drive from outside the area and with the numerical advantage there seemed little danger for Barça. However, with three minutes left on the clock Villa got himself sent off for stupidly lashing out at Carlos Gurpegi, and when Igor Gabilondo pulled a goal back a couple of minutes later there were some worries for Barça as San Mames roared the home team on. As Athletic pushed up in injury time Barça broke away and Busquets capped a fine performance with a goal to make it 1-3 at the end.

Messi and Abidal both returned to the squad for the second game of Champions League Group D, away to Russian champions Rubin Kazan, though neither was included in the starting lineup. Busquets was rested which gave Mascherano the opportunity to give a very decent performance in the midfield holding role, often moving back between the two centre backs when the full backs pushed up. Despite dominating the game for long periods Barça fell behind after 30 minutes when Alves conceded a penalty. David Villa equalized after an hour, also from a penalty after a foul on Iniesta, but Rubin's packed defence made things very difficult for Barça even after Leo Messi came on for the last half an hour. Barça could be satisfied with the 1-1 draw in the end especially after Obafemi Martins almost won it for Rubin in the 87th minute with a header that hit the post.

Barça started October with a league game against Michael Laudrup's Mallorca at Camp Nou. Bojan came in for the suspended Villa while Xavi was given a rest due to an Achilles tendon problem which made Guardiola's decision to also leave Busquets on the bench again seem a little strange. Perhaps Busquets was not at 100% or perhaps Guardiola wanted to give Mascherano continuity after his good performance in Kazan. Either way, it didn't appear to be affecting Barça much, as after 15 minutes possession was 90-10% in Barça's favour and after 20 minutes Barça had 6 corners to nil. Then Messi put Barça in front with a perfectly placed shot from the edge of the area and a home victory was looking a certainty. However, just before half time Barça were caught sleeping at a corner and Emilio Nsue got between Piqué, Milito and Keita to head firmly past Valdés for the equalizer. Anxiety seemed to get the better of the team in the second half with Bojan particularly disappointing with his finishing. Guardiola's only response was to bring on youngsters Thiago, Jeffren and Nolito, though it was a difficult game for inexperienced players to turn round and Mallorca held on for a 1-1 draw. There were definitely some alarm bells now as Barça had already dropped five points at Camp Nou in games where Guardiola had rested players.

Following a break for internationals Barça returned to action with another home game against early league leaders Valencia. There could be no more slip-ups at home as a defeat for Barça would see Valencia open a gap of six points at the top. The first half, however, was dominated by the visitors. For once, Barça were outplayed, with Valencia having slightly more of the possession while causing Barça problems with high-intensity pressing. Pablo Hernandez deservedly put Valencia ahead before the break and Barça were looking in trouble. However, two minutes into the second half Iniesta dribbled forward, played a neat square ball to Xavi and ran on to receive the return and slip the ball under Cesar for the equalizer. The goal turned things round and Barça began to dominate. Fifteen minutes later Xavi sent in a delightfully weighted cross which Puyol met at the near post with a superb bullet header that flew past Cesar into the top corner. Barça held on to win 2-1 and move above Valencia into third place. After seven games Madrid were now leaders on 17 points with Villarreal, Barça and Valencia all a point behind on 16.

Barça were not top of their Champions League group either. Leaders FC Copenhagen had beaten both Rubin Kazan and Panathanaikos without conceding a goal and they arrived at Camp Nou for the third group game with a two-point advantage. With Valdés suffering with fever after a night of vomiting and Xavi again rested due to his ongoing Achilles tendon problem, Guardiola opted to change things around by bringing in Pinto in goal, Maxwell and Mascherano into midfield and Barça played with a very flexible 4-4-2 but with Alves getting forward all the time which allowed Iniesta the freedom to go all over the place to try and assist Messi and Villa. However, the formation failed to click and despite Messi putting Barça in front with a splendid shot from 25 yards after 20 minutes Barça failed to build on the lead and suffered a couple of anxious moments at the back. Pinto was guilty of imitating the referee's whistle to fool Copenhagen's forward Cesar Santin who, believing he had been called offside, stopped running for a through ball. Pinto's unsportsmanlike action was later punished by UEFA with a two-match suspension. It wasn't until injury time at the end of the game that Messi secured the three points, forcing the ball in after Abidal's mishit volley.

Messi grabbed another brace the following Saturday at Zaragoza. Guardiola continued to experiment, this time with only three at the back with Alves pushed into a midfield line with Busquets and Keita. There was then another line of three with Pedro and Iniesta given wide attacking roles with Messi in the hole behind Villa. Messi's first goal came shortly before half time when Villa's pass put him clean through to slip the ball under the advancing keeper Toni Doblas. Just after the break Zaragoza were reduced to ten men when Leonardo Ponzio was sent off for hitting Alves, and Messi completed the 0-2 victory halfway through the second half.

The Copa del Rey campaign began with an away game at Ceuta on the north coast of Africa. Guardiola took the opportunity to pair Bartra and Fontás in central defence while also starting with Thiago in midfield. There were also appearances from Nolito (after Jeffren injured an arm) and Dos Santos as Barça earned a comfortable 0-2 victory to take to the second leg thanks to goals from Maxwell and Pedro.

October ended with another game with Sevilla, this time in La Liga at Camp Nou. The teams had already met six times in 2010, on Sevilla's two previous visits to Barcelona the games had ended in 4-0 wins for Barça but Sevilla had won 1-2 in the Copa del Rey back in January, going on to win on away goals. Sevilla were without the suspended Fernando Navarro and the injured Jesus Navas and keeper Palop which meant Javi Varas, with only eight previous appearances in the top division, came in between the posts.

Guardiola started with his strongest possible XI, with the eight Spanish World Cup heroes plus Alves, Abidal and Messi, and Barça began brilliantly. In the first minute Messi put in a dangerous cross after a good combination with Villa and as play continued the ball came to Xavi who shot wide. It was immediately evident that Barça were on song and it took just four minutes to break the deadlock. Pedro was playing on the left and a neat dribble got him past Konko, his cross was palmed away by the diving Varas but the ball fell to Messi who skipped past a Caceres's lunge before shooting home. Antonio Luna partially stopped the ball on the line and Villa showed great intelligence by not forcing the ball home as he would probably have been given offside if he had touched the ball in. Considering the fact that Villa hadn't scored for a month and was clearly in need of a goal, this action showed great restraint.

Villa's parents had come to watch him at Camp Nou for the first time, as had a coachload of 50 from his hometown of Tuilla in Asturias, and Villa didn't take much longer to give them a goal. In the 24th minute Messi brilliantly skipped between two before slipping the ball out to Villa on the right, the Asturian cut inside before curling a superb left foot shot that crept inside the far post to make it 2-0.

The intensity of Barça's pressing game gave Sevilla problems to get out of their own half and their frustration was evident with a number of fouls being committed. Romaric was fortunate to escape punishment for a cowardly kick at Xavi's heel and then for swinging an elbow at Busquets, but Konko was not so fortunate, receiving two yellow cards for fouls on Busquets and Pedro which saw him sent off just before half time.

Perhaps it was fitting that it was Romaric who sent an awful back header towards his own goal that was intercepted by Alves, jumping spectacularly to flick the ball over Varas with an outstretched right leg for Barça's third goal in the 52nd minute. Alves remembered his past at Sevilla by not celebrating the goal. With the points in the bag Guardiola gave Xavi and Pedro a rest, bringing on Mascherano and Bojan. The intensity of the game dropped but there was never any danger of Sevilla getting back into it. In the 64th minute Messi robbed the ball just inside the Sevilla half and showed great acceleration to spurt towards the edge of the area before shooting low past Varas into the corner of the net. On 80 minutes, Villa came close after dribbling round Varas but his shot was from a tight angle and Dabo got back to clear off the line. However, Villa got his second just before the end after good work from Messi and Busquets. After receiving the ball on the edge of the area the striker fired another splendid finish just inside the post.

Madrid were still top of the league by one point but the 5-0 win over Sevilla certainly did a lot to silence some of Barça's doubters. When Guardiola's team played with the intensity shown in the first 45 minutes it would be very difficult for anybody to stop them. There were still concerns about the strength in depth of the first team squad but it was difficult to deny that the first choice XI was one of the best seen anywhere for quite some time.

Barça: Valdés; Alves, Piqué, Puyol (Adriano m66), Abidal; Xavi (Mascherano m60), Busquets, Iniesta; Pedro (Bojan m60), Messi, Villa.

Sevilla: Javi Varas; Konko, Cáceres, Alexis, Luna; Perotti (Zokora m46), Renato, Romaric, Capel; Luis Fabiano (Dabo m46), Kanoute (Negredo m69).

Goals: m4 Messi 1-0, m24 Villa 2-0, m52 Alves 3-0, m64 Messi 4-0, m90 Villa 5-0.

CHAPTER 24 – Barça 3 Villarreal 1

Barça began November with the return Champions League game against FC Copenhagen. Having beaten the Danes 2-0 at Camp Nou Barça now had a point advantage over their opponents at the top of Group D. Barça's 21-year-old goalkeeper, Ruben Miño, got his first taste of Champions League football, starting on the bench in place of the suspended Pinto, while Keita came into the starting line-up in place of Pedro.

Barça had won only one of their last ten away games in Europe while Copenhagen had won nine of their last ten Champions League matches at the Parken stadium which made Barça's condition as clear favourite to win seem slightly optimistic. From the start it was a closely fought contest with both sides hitting the woodwork in the first 25 minutes. Then just after the half hour Busquets sent a good ball forward to Keita who headed down to Villa, and when a defender knocked the ball away from the Asturian, Messi was following up to fire a right foot shot that went in via the keeper's hand and the post. Barça's lead only lasted a minute as Claudemir de Souza's volley deflected off Abidal past Valdés. The score remained at 1-1 until the final whistle though substitute Pedro was close to snatching a last-minute winner when his shot bounced out off the far post. The point kept Barça on top of the group with 8 points followed by Copenhagen on 7, Rubin Kazan on 3 and Panathanaikos on 2.

The following Sunday Barça faced an away game at Getafe with the intention of keeping up the pressure on leaders Madrid. Getafe were not in their best moment having lost 0-3 at home to Stuttgart in the Europa League the previous Thursday. Guardiola brought back Pedro, with Iniesta moving back to midfield in place of Keita, while giving a rest to Abidal and Busquets who were replaced by Maxwell and Mascherano. Barça completely controlled the game from the beginning, moving into a comfortable three goal lead by the 65th minutes thanks to strikes from Messi, Villa and Pedro. However, with twenty minutes remaining Piqué was unfortunate to handball in the area and the ref awarded Getafe a penalty while sending Piqué off for his second bookable offence. After Manu del Moral converted the penalty there were a couple of nervous moments for Barça's ten men. In the 76th minute Valdés made an excellent save from Juan Angel Albin's powerful shot, and three minutes later Maxwell headed off the line from Javier Arizmendi's header. At this point a second Getafe goal would have set up a nail-biting last ten minutes. Fortunately for Barça the goal didn't come and in the 80th minute Derek Boateng fouled Mascherano and got his second yellow card. With numerical equality restored, Barça held on comfortably to win 1-3.

The second leg of the Copa del Rey tie with Ceuta was pretty much a foregone conclusion with Barça holding a two-goal advantage from the first game. Guardiola rested his most important players and gave starts to Marc Bartra, Thiago and Nolito from the B team, while the 18-year-old Sergi Roberto made his official first team debut, coming on in the second half. Barça ran out easy 5-1 winners on the night with goals from Nolito, Milito, Pedro, Bojan and Messi who came on for the last 30 minutes as a reward to the 39,000 who attended the game. However, the victory had a price as Milito tore the femoral biceps muscle in his right leg which would see him sidelined for 7 weeks.

Back in the league Barça played hosts to Villarreal on Saturday 13 November. Villarreal were in excellent form and hadn't lost in La Liga since the opening day of the season back in August. They started the game in third place in the table, two points behind Barça and three behind leaders Madrid. They had always been a tough opponent for Barça and in eleven league games at Camp Nou they had taken an impressive three wins and four draws, and it was four years since Barça's last victory.

With Milito injured and Piqué suspended Guardiola had to choose between switching Abidal to central defence or bringing in the 19-year-old Bartra. In the end Abidal was given the job of filling in next to Puyol and he generally had a very good game, showing concentration and anticipation to deny both the dangerous front pairing of Nilmar Honorato da Silva and Giuseppe Rossi in the first 15 minutes. With Cani and Santi Cazorla supporting the forwards well, Barça's defenders had to be on their toes.

The game began at a tremendous pace with both teams playing a pressing game. The technique of Barça's quick-passing players gave them the edge but Villarreal were always snapping at heels. Barça were also winning the ball back quickly and often in the Villarreal half and this led to several occasions. In the first five minutes Iniesta was involved in three attacks, first he just failed to control Alves's long pass, then he shot wide under pressure, and then in the fifth minute he produced a fantastic turn in the area but failed to find a finish. Messi also had an exciting run into the area but the Argentinian defender Mateo Musacchio held his ground well.

Barça came very close to taking the lead in the 14th minute when Alves got to the byline to cross to the far post where Messi headed firmly down and Diego Lopez made a difficult save as the ball bounced just in front of his dive. The game was already looking great but it got even better after the 20th minute. First Abidal had to make a last ditch lunge on Nilmar after Maxwell failed to get a good clearance. Then Barça's pressing game was rewarded when Villa stole the ball and found Xavi, the ball came forward to Iniesta who put it through to Villa who skipped past one challenge, managed to keep control when the ball seemed to be under his feet, and slid the ball past Diego Lopez.

In the 26th minute there was a decision that could easily have cost Barça the points. Xavi played a vertical pass through for Messi to get a clear run on goal, Pedro finished the move but it counted for nothing as the linesman had flagged a non-existant offside on Messi who was more than a metre onside. The Barça players complained about the decision to referee Delgado Ferreiro and this may have been the moment when their concentration went. Moments later, Nilmar ran past Puyol, Rossi dragged Abidal away with a good decoy run and Nilmar went through the gap and snuck the ball in off the far post.

So from a possible 2-0 the score went to 1-1 with more than an hour to go. Barça took a while to react and Villarreal tried to take advantage of the home team's stunned state. Rossi started causing havoc, with one pass he gave a chance for Cazorla to shoot over, then he took advantage of Alves being too fancy at the back and Abidal got a yellow card for bringing him down on the edge of the area, then from the free kick Valdés had to get down by the post to stop his curler. However, Barça's lull only lasted about ten minutes and the half ended with Pedro nearly getting a shot in but just being denied by Musacchio, and Messi firing a free kick just over.

The game continued with great intensity in the second half and Barça had to find their quickest passing game to keep possession as Villarreal continued to press. Xavi and Iniesta took a lot of punishment with Villarreal's aggressive game, in particular from Cani and Angel who were allowed to get away with a lot by Delgado Ferreiro's leniency. However, whether it was a great cross field pass from Iniesta or a dangerous dribble inside the area from Villa, Barça were the side creating the danger. Barça's intensity paid off in the 58th minute when Villarreal were caught out by a quick free kick and a 1-2-3-4 between Messi and Pedro which ended with Messi's sublimely subtle clip over the keeper with his right foot. A splendid goal to put Barça 2-1 up.

The tackles continued to fly in as Villarreal attempted to unsettle Barça, but the aggression was matched with Messi leading the way by chasing down defenders at every opportunity. Guardiola brought on Keita for Villa to strengthen the midfield and Barça began to look as though the game was under control. Iniesta and Xavi gave another masterclass of quick simple movement and maintaining possession while at the back Abidal proved a lot of doubters wrong with a very strong game at centre back.

Messi put the result beyond doubt in the 83rd minute, being alert, after Pedro's shot hit Capdevila, to jump in and once again find a classy finish with a deft twist of his foot to turn the ball inside the post. The 3-1 victory maintained Barça's title challenge, two weeks before the first *Clásico* of the season. Madrid were still a point in front of Barça, but with Villarreal now five points behind Guardiola's men in third place it was beginning to look like another two-horse title race again.

Barça: Valdés; Alves, Puyol, Abidal, Maxwell (Adriano m85); Xavi (Mascherano m89), Busquets, Iniesta, Pedro, Messi, Villa (Keita m72).

Villarreal: Diego Lopez; Masacchio, Marchena, Angel Lopez, Capdevila; Bruno, Borja Valero (Jefferson Montero m78), Cani (Senna m70), Cazorla; Rossi (Marco Ruben m89), Nilmar.

Goals: m22 Villa 1-0, m26 Nilmar 1-1, m58 Messi 2-1, m83 Messi 3-1.

CHAPTER 25 – Barça 5 Real Madrid 0

Barça faced two away games at Almeria and Panathinaikos before the eagerly-awaited *Clásico*. Guardiola decided not to risk Piqué, who was one yellow card away from suspension, for the Almeria game, and with Milito and Abidal both out he brought in Fontás to the defence while Mascherano replaced Busquets in midfield. Barça continued in exhilarating form and poor Almeria found themselves on the end of a historic thrashing. The 0-8 scoreline equalling a fifty year old record set by Barça at Las Palmas as the highest away win by any team in the history of La Liga. Messi led the way with a hat-trick while substitute Bojan did his confidence some good, adding a late brace. There was one from Iniesta and an own goal from Almeria's Santi Acasiete but the best goal of the lot was the fourth when Fontás sent a terrific long ball out of defence which found Pedro speeding in to prod the ball past the unfortunate Diego Alves.

Pedro grabbed another two as Barça clinched top spot in Champions League Group D with a game to spare after a 0-3 win over Panathinaikos in Athens. Adriano was given a chance at left back and he responded with an very strong performance while also setting up Messi for Barça's second after a beautiful flowing move involving Messi, Alves, Xavi and Iniesta before Adriano's overlap and quick first time pass gave Messi the chance to steer the ball home at the near post.

Barça were certainly hitting form at the right time. The following Monday, November 29 2010, José Mourinho brought the unbeaten league leaders Real Madrid to Camp Nou for his first *Clásico*. Madrid were also in excellent form, having won their last five games with a goal difference of 17-2, while Cristiano Ronaldo had scored five in the last two games, a 5-1 league win over Athletic Club and a 0-4 victory at Ajax in the Champions

League. Mourinho got up to his usual tricks of trying to wind up the opposition by saying a few days before the game, "If it was fun going to Camp Nou with Chelsea or with Inter, it will be even more fun going there with Real Madrid."

For many years the press had been in the habit of building up every *Clásico* as 'the match of the century'. However, given the extraordinary form being shown by both teams in the run up to the first *Clásico* of the 2010/11 season, there were plenty of ingredients to indicate a top quality game. Mourinho and Guardiola were the last two winning coaches in the Champions League and on the pitch at kick off there were ten of the eleven players who started in Spain's World Cup Final victory against Holland plus the two previous winners of the Ballon' d'Or.

Guardiola decided on his strongest eleven of Valdés, Alves, Piqué, Puyol, Abidal, Xavi, Busquets, Iniesta, Pedro, Messi and Villa. Mourinho was denied the chance to do the same by a late injury to Higuain who was replaced by Benzema. The Madrid coach stuck with a 4-2-3-1 formation, starting with Casillas, Ramos, Pepe, Carvalho, Marcelo, Khedira, Alonso, Di Maria, Ozil, Ronaldo and Benzema.

The Madrid forwards were not so used to chasing and harrying which gave Barça's defenders more time to bring the ball out comfortably. With Madrid playing a very high defence Barça would find plenty of opportunities to look for the killer pass into space, though Villa would be somewhat guilty of getting caught offside too often early on.

Barça didn't take long to start creating chances. In the 6th minute the ball came to Puyol in the area after a short corner, he played the ball out to Messi in the right wing position and the Argentinian sent in a delightful floated chip from a very tight angle that bounced out off the far post. Then in the 10th minute Iniesta cut inside from the left and tried his luck from 25 yards, his shot touched Ricardo Carvalho before catching

Xavi on the back of the leg, the ball looped nicely forward and Xavi reacted quickly to flip the ball past Casillas to open the scoring.

Madrid tried to hit straight back and Valdés had to be alert to tip over an effort from Di Maria. However, this turned out to be the closest Madrid came all night and after just 18 minutes Barça went further ahead. Xavi played a long crossfield ball that found Villa on the left, Villa got past Ramos to get in a cross which Casillas failed to cut out and Pedro was quicker than Marcelo to sprint in at the far post and knock the ball home.

With the score at 2-0 the game was looking very comfortable for Barça. Then, in the 30th minute, Ronaldo provoked an incident by pushing a surprised Guardiola after the ball went out for a Madrid throw and the Barça coach had taken a moment longer than he should have to give the ball back. The reaction of some of Barça's players was not too clever and Valdés went into the book, along with Ronaldo, for running out of his goal to get involved in the pushing and gestering. Barça looked a little unnerved by the incident. Soon after, Villa also got a card, giving away a free kick which was wasted by Ronaldo. The Portuguese forward then had a fair shout for a penalty when Valdés slid into him but the Basque referee Iturralde González awarded a goal kick to Barça. This proved to be just a brief interruption of Barça's dominance and the Catalans were soon back on top with a couple of typically exciting runs from Messi before half time.

Mourinho brought on the more defensive Lass Diarra in place of Ozil for the second half but if anything the game swung even more into Barça's control. In the 48th minute Villa was denied by Casillas, then in the 52nd minute Messi sent a sweet pass into Xavi who looked to have got round Casillas but from an angle he could only screw his shot back into the side-netting. Messi continued to show his vision to find the pass, slipping a superb ball through to Villa, who this time was just level with the last defender, and the Asturian striker's run took him away from Pepe before shooting low past Casillas into the far corner.

The joy for the crowd increased even more just three minutes later when Messi, this time from much deeper, played another sublime pass through to Villa who beat Casillas to the ball on the edge of the area, prodding the ball past the Madrid keeper and into the net. It was very tough for Madrid's players to keep their heads up after this. They kept running but could generally never get close to the ball and the ref was kept busy as more yellows came out for late challenges. The few times Madrid tried coming forward Barça's defence was always alert with Puyol, in particular, putting in a typically heroic performance, getting stuck into every single challenge as though his life depended on it even with the score at 4-0.

Guardiola showed it was his day and not Mourinho's by getting some effect from his substitutions with Bojan sending in the cross for Jeffren to get the historic fifth goal in injury time. All around Camp Nou hands were raised with five figures stretched out to signify the *manita*. There was still time for Sergio Ramos to receieve a straight red card for a cynical scythe on Messi, and the Madrid defender showed his frustration by pushing both Puyol and Xavi in the face before leaving the pitch.

Madrid had arrived at Camp Nou as leaders of La Liga, unbeaten all season, with the supposed tactical genius of Mourinho to organise the players who had cost millions of euros. Yet at the end of 90 minutes Barça had outclassed their old rival so comprehensively that it did not seem unfair to suggest that Madrid could easily have lost by more than five goals.

In the past, Mourinho had always found an excuse, usually to do with controversial refereeing, when his team had lost to Barça. This time he accepted the defeat as "easy to take" because "one team had played to their maximum potential and one team played very badly". It could not be denied that the difference between the sides on the pitch was enormous but Madrid would not have to play Barça every week. Barça now had a two-point advantage over their rivals at the top of La Liga but there was still a very long way to go to the finishing line.

Barça: Valdés; Alves, Piqué, Puyol, Abidal; Xavi (Keita m87), Busquets, Iniesta; Pedro (Jeffren m87), Messi, Villa (Bojan m76).

Real Madrid: Casillas; Ramos, Pepe, Carvalho, Marcelo (Arbeloa m60); Khedira, Alonso; Di Maria, Ozil (Lass Diarra m45), Ronaldo; Benzema.

Goals: m10 Xavi 1-0, m18 Pedro 2-0, m55 Villa 3-0, m58 Villa 4-0, m91 Jeffren 5-0.

CHAPTER 26 – Espanyol 1 Barça 5

On the Saturday following the 5-0 victory over Madrid, Barça were due to play Osasuna in Pamplona. Since Guardiola had been first team coach Barça had taken to travelling to away games on the day of the game rather than making the trip a day earlier and staying in a hotel. There was a solid logic behind this decision as it gave the players more time to spend with their families.

Unfortunately, on the day of the Osasuna game the air traffic controllers in Spain decided to go on strike. Of course, Barça could easily have travelled the 352 km to Pamplona by land but on the morning of the game there was still hope that the trip could be made by air. Barça later claimed that the Spanish Football Federation (RFEF) had assured them that the game would be postponed until the following day if there were no flights.

All morning Barça negotiated with the RFEF and with the airports in the hope of travelling by air. However, at 1.30 pm there were still no available flights so the Barça players, who had been at Camp Nou all morning waiting on developments, were sent home, convinced they would be playing the following day. Then at 3 pm Barça received a call from the RFEF. Osasuna, who would claim they had not been informed of any possible postponement, had refused to change the day of the match and the game would go ahead as originally scheduled on the Saturday.

This led to a mad rush to Barcelona's Sants train station to catch a 4 pm train to Zaragoza. Pedro needed to sprint through the station in order to catch the train a minute before its departure time. From Zaragoza the team took a coach to travel the 144 km to Pamplona, arriving just minutes before the 8 pm kick off. The lateness of Barça's arrival meant that the kick off was eventually delayed by nearly 50 minutes and there was a hostile atmosphere from the home crowd who obviously blamed Barça for delay. However, Barça reacted well, possibly fired up by the feeling that powers in Madrid were conspiring against them. Pedro, playing mainly on the left, put Barça in front after fifteen minutes and Messi added two more to earn a comfortable 0-3 win.

The final game in Champions League Group D saw Barça play host to Rubin Kazan who in the three previous games between the clubs had taken a win and two draws. The game was of little importance for Barça, having already clinched top spot in the group, and Guardiola experimented, bringing in several youngsters and playing Busquets as the free man in defence in a 3-4-3 formation. Rubin's ultra defensive game frustrated Barça until half time but second half goals from Fontás and Victor Vazquez gave Barça a 2-0 win to finish the group with 14 points.

The following Saturday, December 11, Barça announced a new five-and-a-half-year shirt deal worth €30 million a year with The Qatar Foundation. It was the first time that Barça would wear a sponsor on the chest of the shirt, though the ground had been prepared four years earlier when the club paid €1.5 million to UNICEF for the privilege of wearing the charity's name on the shirt. Sandro Rosell was quick to point out that the deal was "not with a brand but with a foundation" while insisting "we still have a charitable shirt". However, critics of the deal pointed out that The Qatar Foundation was just an extension of the Qatar royal family who ruled in a state with a poor standard of politic rights and civil liberties.

The controversy over the shirt deal didn't seem to affect the team. Back in the league Barça continued in exhilarating form with another 5-0 win at Camp Nou, this time over Real Sociedad. The players were clicking brilliantly with some beautiful combinations for the goals. For the first, Xavi and Messi played in Pedro on the right and his low first time cross was finished by Villa at the far post. For the second, Pedro received from Iniesta before knocking the ball on for Iniesta who had continued his run to fire low past Real's keeper Claudio Bravo at his near post. However, the best combination of all came at the start of the second half as Messi and Alves exchanged six passes to dissect Real's defence with Messi sidefooting past Bravo into the far corner to finish the move. Near the end Messi scored a brilliant individual effort, dribbling horizontally across the area before cutting the ball back past Bravo into the far corner. Substitute Bojan scored the fifth, firing home after Bravo had stopped his first shot. Since Nilmar's goal for Villarreal at the end of October Barça had now scored twenty-eight goals without conceding.

It was an imposing statistic to take into the following weekend's derby at Espanyol, though Barça's local rival had begun the season with an impressive seven league wins out of seven at the Cornella-El Prat stadium. In the week before the game it was mentioned in the press that the one thing that Barça hadn't done under Guardiola was to give local rivals Espanyol a good stuffing.

The game began at a typical high local-derby tempo with Espanyol hoping to surprise Barça early on. In the first minute Valdés had to get down low at his near post to gather a cross-shot from Pablo Osvaldo, but Barça reacted soon after with a cheeky overhead effort from Busquets that went just wide.

Guardiola had chosen his strongest XI, playing in the typical 4-3-3 shape with the only variant being that Puyol played on the right of Piqué rather than to the left. Both teams were playing with very high defensive lines which meant that the 20 outfield players were often all found in a thin band near the halfway line. There was not much room for Barça's short passing game but there was the tactical option of playing the ball into space behind the Espanyol back four to make the most of the pace of Pedro and Villa. As the game went on Barça began to find these two players with more and more frequency.

Messi forced the first save from Carlos Kameni in the 9th minute and a minute later Alves robbed the ball high up the pitch and got a run at goal, however, he hesitated and squared back to Messi who only succeeded in firing over the bar. The warning signs were there for Espanyol, and Barça took a deserved lead after 19 minutes. Puyol broke down an Espanyol attack and Busquets was on hand to clear up, lobbing the ball forward to Pedro on the half way line, Pedro laid the ball off first time to Messi who pushed the ball through the middle and Pedro sprinted away from Francisco Chica and Victor Ruiz before sliding the ball under Kameni.

Barça went further ahead in the 30th minute, Messi, Villa and Pedro combined on the left with Messi sending in a chip to the far post where Xavi fired in a cross which hit Alves, the ball bouncing back to Xavi who smacked a shot back which found a space inside the far post.

Espanyol had few moments near Barça's goal but Valdés had to make a tremendous save from Callejon in the 35th minute. Barça's passing game was usually too good despite Espanyol's high pressing though some of the short passes to play the ball out from the back would have given many coaches a heart attack.

Espanyol continued to work hard to try and close Barça down in the second half but the visitors were on top of their game and their patient approach eventually led to more chances. In the 60th minute Messi made a great run in from the right, bounced a pass off Pedro and took the return before sending in a powerful shot that Kameni failed to hold, Pedro was quickest to pounce on the rebound and Barça were three goals up. A couple of minutes later Iniesta unselfishly squared to Pedro who was looking for his hat-trick but Kameni was out fast to close the angles. From a possible 0-4 Espanyol went straight up the other end and made it 1-3 when Osvaldo got away from Puyol to shoot low past Valdés from 15 yards. The goal brought to an end Valdés's run of 576 minutes without conceding which beat his previous record of 570 minutes set at the start of the 2009/10 season.

For about ten minutes the result looked like it could be in danger but apart from one weak header over from Osvaldo, Valdés's goal was not threatened. Instead Barça took advantage of the tiring Espanyol defence to find passes into space. In the 76th minute Messi held the ball up and waited for the right moment to slip a pass through to Villa who ran on to beat Kameni easily. Then eight minutes later it was Xavi who found the pass for Villa to race through and make the final score 1-5.

Barça were really looking quite invincible. After 16 league games the team had taken a record 43 points, scoring 51 with just 9 conceded. However, there could be no letting up as Real Madrid had also taken full points since the 5-0 defeat at Camp Nou and remained just two points behind in the title race.

Espanyol: Kameni; Chica (Amat m64), Forlin, Victor Ruiz, Didac (David Garcia m81); Baena, Javi Marquez; Luis Garcia (Dátolo m62), Verdu, Jose Callejon; Osvaldo.

Barça: Valdés; Alves, Piqué, Puyol, Abidal; Xavi, Busquets (Mascherano m78), Iniesta (Keita m85); Pedro (Bojan m88), Messi, Villa.

Goals: m19 Pedro 0-1, m30 Xavi 0-2, m60 Pedro 0-3, m63 Osvaldo 1-3, m76 Villa 1-4, m84 Villa 1-5.

CHAPTER 27 – Valencia 0 Barça 1

Four days before Christmas Barça played their last match of 2010, a Copa del Rey 1st leg game at home to Athletic Club. Guardiola made changes with Valdés, Puyol, Busquets, Villa and Messi all starting on the bench while Pinto, Maxwell, Mascherano, Keita and Bojan came into the team. Despite a reasonably good game from Iniesta playing in the false nine role, there was a lack of punch in front of goal and even after Messi and Villa came on for the last half hour Barça couldn't find a way through. The 0-0 final score brought a ten-game winning streak to an end and left Barça with a difficult trip to San Mames in the second leg.

Following the Christmas break the team was back in action on January 2nd with a league game at home to Levante which would see Xavi equal Migueli's club record of 549 first team games. Messi had been allowed extra Christmas holiday and therefore missed the game though Barça's problems were in defence. Puyol had been injured playing for Catalunya and Piqué was suspended, which with Milito only just given medical clearance after seven weeks out led to Guardiola pairing Busquets and Abidal in central defence. Levante were 16th in the table but they frustrated Barça with a packed defence and it wasn't until the second half that Pedro continued his excellent form with two goals. However, a splendid volley from Christian Stuani in the 80th minute pulled one back for Levante which left a nervous finish which even saw Levante's keeper Manolo Reina going up for an injury time free kick though Barça held on to win 2-1.

There were more tense moments the following Tuesday when Barça went to Bilbao for the return Copa del Rey game with Athletic. Xavi became the first player to reach 550 first team games for Barça though it wasn't to be his best game. As in the first leg the defences had the better of the game but the deadlock was finally broken in the 75th minute when Messi drew the Athletic defence towards him before slipping a pass through for Abidal to sidefoot the ball past Iraola for his first goal for the club. Perhaps the surprise of seeing Abidal score affected his team mates' concentration as Barça allowed Fernando Llorente to grab an equalizer with five minutes to go. However, Athletic couldn't find a winner and Barça went through thanks to Abidal's away goal. The 24-year-old Dutch international, Ibrahim Afellay, who had signed for €3.4 million from PSV Eindhoven during the winter transfer window, came on for his Barça debut right at the end.

With games coming twice a week it was perhaps normal that Guardiola should decide to rotate his players. For the league visit to Deportivo the following Sunday the coach rested Alves, Xavi and Busquets which meant a rare start for Adriano at right back while Mascherano and Keita came into midfield. The result was that Barça were a bit slow to get moving and Adrian Lopez missed a great chance to put Depor ahead early on. However, once Villa had squeezed the ball past Aranzubia after Messi's assist on 26 minutes, Barça took control. Messi curled in a splendid 30-yard free kick early in the second half and then late goals from Iniesta and Pedro earned a handsome 0-4 victory.

The day after beating Depor was a historic day for the club with the top three places for the 2010 Ballon d'Or (now the FIFA Ballon d'Or) going to Barça players who had all been produced by La Masia. Messi won the trophy for the second time with 22.65% of the total points, Iniesta was second with 17.36% followed by Xavi in third with 16.48%, leaving Inter's Wesley Sneijder in fourth place with 14.48%. There were also votes for Carles Puyol (1.43%) who came 11th and for Dani Alves who came equal 22nd with 0.05%.

Messi celebrated his award two days later by scoring a hat-trick in the Copa del Rey quarter final 1st leg against second division Betis. Guardiola showed he meant business by selecting a very strong side for the game with only Valdés and Abidal left out of the theoretical strongest eleven. Betis played bravely and tried to attack and until Messi's opener just before half time they pretty much held their own. However, in the second half the visitors were swept aside, Messi completed his hat-trick by the 73rd minute, and late goals from Pedro and substitute Keita left Betis with a 5-0 deficit for the second leg.

Barça's good form continued back in the league with the visit of Malaga, now owned by billionaire businessman Sheikh Abdullah Al Thani. Just before the kick off there was a boost when news came in that Madrid had only managed a 1-1 draw at Almeria. Guardiola was able to play his best eleven of Valdés, Alves, Piqué, Puyol, Abidal, Xavi, Busquets, Iniesta, Pedro, Messi and Villa, and right from the start the passing was spot-on and the gaps in Malaga's defence began to appear. Iniesta opened the scoring in the eighth minute with a perfectly timed sidefoot shot from Alves's centre that flew past Malaga's keeper Sergio Asenjo and in off the far post. Villa fired through Asenjo's legs after Messi's killer pass for the second and before half time Pedro had made it 3-0, pouncing on the rebound after Asenjo blocked Iniesta's shot. Malaga's Duda curled in a free kick midway through a disappointing second half but Villa got his second of the game soon after, skipping round Asenjo's lunge before tucking the ball in the empty net to leave the final score at 4-1. Since losing to Hercules at the start of September Barça had now gone 28 games unbeaten.

The run came to an end the following Wednesday in the return Copa del Rey quarter final at Betis. With the five goal advantage from the first leg Guardiola brought in Pinto, Adriano, Milito, Maxwell, Mascherano, Keita, Bojan and Afellay who made his first start for the team, with just Piqué, Xavi and Messi continuing from the eleven that had started against Malaga. Betis began at a tremendous pace, catching Barça cold with two goals from Jorge Molina in the first seven minutes. Suddenly, the miracle comeback seemed possible and Barça looked shaken. However, little by little Barça found their composure, and shortly before half time Messi showed devastating acceleration to burst away from two defenders before shooting through the goalkeeper's legs from the edge of the area. Betis grabbed a third goal just before half time but the intensity dropped in the second half which had only an awful penalty miss from Messi to note. Betis won 3-1 on the night but Barça were through to the semi-finals.

The defeat at Betis was just a glitch as Barça finished January with three big wins. First Racing were beaten 3-0 in the league, then Almeria received a 5-0 hammering in the Copa del Rey semi-final first leg after Barça had scored four in a magnificent first half hour, and then Hercules were finally beaten (0-3) as Barça clocked up the tenth away league win out of ten while equaling a 50 year-old record set by Madrid of 15 straight league victories. Things were looking very rosy for Barça with Messi and Pedro in particularly good form. In January alone Messi had scored ten with Pedro adding eight, and the month ended perfectly as Madrid lost 1-0 at Osasuna leaving Barça seven points clear at the top. The only negative point at this time was the injury that Puyol picked up against Racing in his left knee which would trouble him for the remainder of the season.

February began with Barça completing the job against Almeria to reach the Copa del Rey final. With a second-string lineup including a front three of Afellay, Bojan and Nolito Barça still managed to win 0-3 thanks to goals from Adriano, Thiago and Afellay who got his first goal for the club. The excellent mood at the club was exemplified by Guardiola agreeing to a new contract to continue the following season while Piqué confirmed the rumours of a romance with singer Shakira by posting a photo of the couple on Twitter.

The following Saturday Barça notched up a record-breaking 16th consecutive league victory, another Messi hat-trick, his fourth of the season and the tenth in his Barça career, earned a 3-0 win over Atlético. However, the run came to an end a week later in Gijon. With a first leg game at Arsenal in the Champions League last 16 just four days away Guardiola decided to rest Abidal, Busquets and Pedro for the game at Sporting, bringing in Milito, Mascherano and Afellay. David Barral fired Sporting into the lead in the 17th minute after exposing Milito's lack of match fitness and it wasn't until ten minutes from time that Villa produced a brilliant lob over keeper Pichu Cuellar for the equalizer. The 1-1 draw allowed Madrid to reduce the gap at the top to five points.

Barça travelled to London for the game at the Emirates at full strength except for the continued absence of Puyol. Guardiola showed his faith with the Piqué-Abidal centre back pairing with Maxwell at left back. Arsenal appeared to be in better shape than when the sides had met 11 months earlier at the quarter-final stage, Robin Van Persie was back, Fabregas was properly fit and he was supported in midfield by the 19-year old Jack Wilshere who was beginning to make a name for himself in the Premiership. The first half was nowhere near as one-sided as the previous encounter at the Emirates though Barça still created more chances and Villa opened the scoring after 27 minutes after being sent through by Messi. The score might have been 0-2 at half time but Messi's diving header was incorrectly ruled out for offside. In the second half Arsenal gradually forced their way back with a particularly impressive performance from Wilshire. Substitutions in the 67th minute demonstrated the intentions of the two coaches, with Guardiola bringing on a midfielder, Keita, for a forward, Villa, while Wenger introduced the attacking midfielder Andrei Arshavin in place of the more defensive Alex Song. Arsenal finally found an equalizer twelve minutes from time when Van Persie surprised Valdés at his near post with a cross-shot from a seemingly impossible angle. Then, in the 83rd minute, Arsenal produced the move of the game. Laurent Koscielny won the ball in defence and played it forward to Nicklas Bendtner, quick passes through Wilshere and Fabregas fed Nasri on the right and he cut inside before spotting a pass to the left where Arshavin was free to curl one inside Valdés far post. The 2-1 final score left Barça with a complicated task for the second leg at Camp Nou.

Two games without a win always led to more pressure at a club like Barça, and the following league game was at home to Athletic Club who Barça had failed to beat in either of the cup games in January. Before the game there was an additional problem when Valdés injured his left knee which meant Pinto would get a run of 3 games between the posts. Guardiola decided to play Busquets at centre back again with mixed results. In the first half especially there were some very interesting tactical changes with Busquets pushing into midfield at times and also switching positions with left back Abidal. The other main tactical point of note was that Pedro played wide on the left with Villa in the middle with Messi playing a deeper wandering role. This left the right wing with nobody but Alves, and the Brazilian full back attacked this space to great effect throughout the game. After just four minutes Alves made a forward run to reach Xavi's splendid pass with a volleyed square pass that found Villa steaming in to fire home with power and precision. However, Barça couldn't build on the lead and early in the second half a clumsy challenge from Busquets on Llorente gifted Athletic a penalty and Iraola blasted his shot past Pinto for the equalizer. Barça struggled in the search for a winner and it wasn't until the 78th minute that Xavi again found the pass through to Alves who was forward yet again, this time to provide a low cross to the near post where Messi flicked the ball past Iraizoz for his 25th league goal of the season.

Still with a five-point advantage over Madrid, Barça ended February with a trip to Mallorca. Alves and Xavi joined Valdés and Puyol on the injured list but Pinto, Adriano and Keita came in and all performed well. Seven minutes before half time Keita scooped a pass into Messi who flicked the ball past Mallorca keeper Aouate with one header before nodding into the empty net with another to open the scoring. Early in the second half

Messi sent a defence splitting pass through for Villa to add Barça's second, and Pedro fired in a wicked shot to make it 0-3. Martin Montoya got the chance for his league debut with five minues remaining and Barça held on for the points. Later that evening Madrid could only manage a goalless draw away at Deportivo and Barça's advantage at the top of the table was back to seven points.

Barça then faced a tricky Wednesday night league fixture at Valencia at the start of March. Guardiola was suffering a lot of back pain due to a herniated disc but he demonstrated his commitment by braving his discomfort to travel for the game. Alves and Xavi returned to the team and Guardiola surprised by bringing in a big tactical change. Adriano was brought in at left back but he was given an attacking role very similar to Alves on the right. To compensate for these advanced full backs Busquets was used as an extra defender between Pique and Abidal, while Mascherano came in to play the holding role in front of the defence. Xavi and Iniesta played their familiar playmaker roles in midfield while Messi roamed free behind Villa who continued in a more familiar centre-forward role. Pedro was sacrificed which meant there was very little width going forward except for the advances of Alves and Adriano, but both players played a role in many attacks and Adriano turned out to be decisive.

However, it was Valencia who started strongest, coming out to battle for the ball and pushing up on Barça's defence, winning four corners in the first six minutes. Barça soon began to settle and create chances, the best being in the 9th minute when Messi broke through and had three attempts to score. Valencia keeper Vicente Guaita stopped the first and third effort while Ricardo Costa somehow cleared the second.

Jordi Alba had the ball in Barça's net after 20 minutes but was correctly called offside, but it was Barça who were looking the better team with Adriano causing problems going forward though his finishing was not good. Then on 30 minutes Messi stole the ball from one defender, got past another, but with just Guaita to beat he chose his scoop option but only succeeded in scooping the ball over the keeper and over the bar onto the top of the net. The first half ended with a couple more half chances for Villa while Barça remained pretty solid at the back though Pinto produced the odd nervous moment playing with his feet under pressure.

The second half began with Valencia coach Unai Emery bringing on a centre forward, Roberto Soldado, in place of a winger, Joaquin, and soon Valencia began to create chances. In the 52nd minute Soldado got away from Busquets and Abidal before shooting wide, and a couple of minutes later Pablo Hernandez shot straight at Pinto. The biggest scare for Barça came in the 59th minute when Soldado found Pablo on the left and his shot went across the face of the goal and just wide of the far post. Messi shot just wide at the other end but Guardiola obviously saw that things weren't working as well now so he moved from the unusual 3-5-2 formation, taking off Mascherano, moving Busquets back to his normal midfield role, while bringing on Pedro to provide some width up front in a more familiar 4-3-3.

The game seemed to be moving towards a tactical stalemate but with just twelve minutes remaining Barça finally made the breakthrough. Adriano had reverted to a more traditional left back position but this didn't stop him getting forward. Xavi managed to thread a pass through to him, Adriano then jinked into the area before looking up and squaring to Messi who swept the ball gleefully home despite a touch from Guaita's fingertips. Villa had a couple of late chances but couldn't find a goal on his return to Mestalla while Valencia gave Barça's defence some nervous moments in the closing minutes. However, Barça held on for an extremely important victory. With only 12 games to go now the seven-point advantage was going to be very difficult for Madrid to overcome.

Valencia: (4-4-2) Guaita; Stankevicius, Dealbert, Ricardo Costa, Jordi Alba; Pablo Hernández, Tino Costa (Isco m85), Éver Banega, Mathieu (Jonas m82); Joaquín (Soldado m46), Mata.

Barça: (3-5-2) Pinto; Piqué, Busquets, Abidal; Alves, Xavi, Mascherano (Pedro m62), Iniesta (Keita m87), Adriano (Maxwell m82); Messi, Villa.

Goal: m78 Messi 0-1.

CHAPTER 28 – Barça 5 Shakhtar Donetsk 1

Guardiola would again brave the pain from his herniated disc for the visit of 15th-placed Zaragoza on Saturday 5 March 2011. Puyol was still out but Valdés made a rapid recovery from his knee injury to return in goal. With the vital Champions League return game with Arsenal just four days away Abidal, Busquets, Iniesta and Villa were rested with Milito, Maxwell, Mascherano, Keita and Bojan all starting. Keita would score the only goal of the game just before half time, sweeping the ball home after Messi's right-wing dribble to the by-line. The 1-0 victory was not so memorable but the occasion was historic for the decision of the board to give over the directors box exclusively for the use of women in recognition of the role of women throughout the club's history and in order to promote their participation in the everyday life of the club. It might be noted that the directors chose the Zaragoza game for the gesture and not the big Champions League return match with Arsenal the following Tuesday 8 March which was International Women's Day.

For the Arsenal game both Guardiola and Arsene Wenger had selection problems. Barça were still without Puyol while Piqué was suspended for the game so Guardiola paired Busquets and Abidal as centre backs while preferring Adriano over Maxwell at left back. Song and Walcott were both injured for Arsenal and were replaced by Diaby and Rosicky though there was good news for Wenger when Van Persie was unexpectedly passed fit to lead the Arsenal attack. Fabregas and Van Persie had both missed the previous year's 4-1 defeat at Camp Nou, and having their two biggest names both starting must have given Wenger hope that this year would see an improved Arsenal performance. Unfortunately, for the Arsenal coach both players would play a negative role in the game. With half time approaching and the score still goalless Fabregas tried to backheel the ball to Wilshere only thirty yards from his own goal, only to be robbed by Iniesta who darted forward before pushing a pass through to Messi who controlled with one touch, and as Almunia bore down on him, flicked the ball over the Arsenal keeper with the deftest of touches before volleying past Djorou on the line. Arsenal had not managed a shot on goal in the first half but early in the second half Nasri made a rare run forward and won a corner on the left. When Nasri's corner came in Busquets misjudged his jump and sent a header into his own net. Arsenal now led 3-2 on aggregate but they suffered another setback three minutes later when Van Persie got his marching orders. The Dutch striker had been booked at the end of the first half for an unnecessary swipe at Dani Alves, and he earned a second yellow card for shooting after the whistle had blown for offside. Van Persie gestured that he had not heard the whistle though his shot had been fairly wild; some might have interpreted it as frustration for the offside call but the Swiss referee Massimo Busacca saw it as time-wasting and Arsenal were down to ten men. Barça now stormed forward and two quick goals around the 70th minute from Xavi and a Messi penalty after Koscielny brought down Pedro swung the tie back in Barça's favour. There was a big scare for Barça in the 87th minute when a mistake from Adriano gave Bendtner a chance to go clean through but the Danish striker's first touch was poor which gave Mascherano to chance to get back and make a saving tackle. Barça held on for the final whistle and went through to the quarter finals 4-3 on aggregate.

Barça had another difficult away game the following Saturday in the league at Sevilla. Bojan had been left out of the initial 18-man squad but due to Jeffren injuring himself during the warm-up he was called in to start as one of the seven substitutes. Then just 14 minutes into the game Pedro strained a muscle and had to be taken off, giving Bojan the unexpected opportunity to come on. Fortune was smiling on the young striker as in the 30th minute he bundled the ball across the line, despite a poor first touch from Alves's pass, to give Barça a deserved lead. Having been outplayed in the first half, Sevilla fought back after the break and soon found an equalizer when Jesus Navas headed in from Alvaro Negredo's cross. The game was evenly balanced with opportunities at both ends. In the 83rd minute Abidal demonstrated his commitment to the cause, bravely heading the ball away at ground level to prevent Negredo a chance. Then in the final minutes Iniesta had two chances to win the game, hitting the bar from the edge of the area in the 85th minute and then right at the end seeing his shot cleared off the line by Gary Medel. The 1-1 draw reduced Barça's advantage at the top of the league to 5 points as Madrid had beaten Hercules 2-0 earlier in the evening. With nine league games remaining including a Bernabéu *Clásico*, there was still everything to play for.

Three days later the shocking news was released that Eric Abidal needed surgery to remove a tumour from his liver. The following Thursday the surgery was performed successfully though, at the player's request, information about his condition was kept at a minimum. On Friday 18 March the draw for the Champions League quarter-finals and semi-finals was made in Nyon pairing Barça with Shakhtar Donetsk in the quarters while throwing up the mouth-watering prospect of a semi-final with Madrid if Barça could get past Shakhtar and Madrid could beat Tottenham Hotspur. The teams were already set to meet in the league at the Bernabéu on April 16 and in the Copa del Rey final in Valencia on April 20, and now they faced a possible four *Clásicos* in 18 days if they could both get through in the Champions League.

On Saturday 19 March, with Camp Nou filled with messages of support for Abidal, Barça faced Getafe in a league game before a break for internationals. Pedro and Maxwell joined Abidal and Puyol on the injured list and Guardiola gave starts to Milito, Adriano, Mascherano and Bojan. In a frustrating game full of missed chances Barça managed to score twice, through an Alves first-half bullet from 30 yards and a deflected shot from Bojan shortly after half time. Manu de Moral pulled one back for

Getafe in the 88th minute, leaving Barça clinging on to three points which should have been wrapped up much earlier.

Due to an international break Barça were not back in action until the first Saturday of April. It was a day that Madrid had high hopes of reducing the five-point difference at the top of La Liga. At 6 pm Madrid played host to Sporting who were 15th in the table while two hours later Barça were to play away at third-placed Villarreal. However, a goal from Sporting's Miguel de las Cuevas in the 79th minute shocked the Bernabéu and Sporting held on to a surprise 0-1 win. Madrid's defeat brought an end to Mourinho's personal record of nine years and 150 games without losing a home league fixture. It was also a big boost to the Barça players who heard the news just before kicking off at Villarreal. With Xavi suspended and Messi starting on the bench due to his recent international duty the team did not look particularly strong on paper. Busquets was preferred over Milito to partner Piqué at the back, Thiago was given the big resposibility to fill in for the suspended Xavi, while in attack Afellay played a proper winger's role on the left, Villa stayed in the middle and Iniesta drifted in from the right to support midfield, leaving the right flank open for Alves to attack. With Adriano also encouraged to go forward from left back, Mascherano often slipped back between Busquets and Piqué to form a defence of three with Keita moving into the defensive midfield role. Valdés denied Rossi twice early on to keep Barça in the game and little by little Villarreal were forced back. Messi came on for Keita in the 53rd minute but it wasn't until the 69th minute that the deadlock was broken. Thiago sent in a corner from the right, Busquets flicked it on to Piqué who controlled with his chest, though the ball appeared to touch his arm after the chest, before hooking the ball past keeper Diego Lopez into the top of the net. Five minutes from the end Cazorla's volley looked a certain equalizer but Valdés somehow saved with his legs and Barça were 8 points clear at the top.

Another treble was now looking extremely possible. With just eight games to play the league was close to being in the bag. Madrid would be tough in the Copa del Rey final but with Guardiola's record of five wins out of five *Clásicos* Barça were favourites to win. Barça were also favourites to win the Champions League but there was plenty of work still to do with the quarter final first leg with Shakhtar Donetsk at Camp Nou as the next hurdle.

Barça knew Shakhtar pretty well from previous meetings. Unfortunately, Chygrynskiy had been out injured since November and would miss out on both quarter final games. Shakhtar's Champions League form so far in the season had been impressive. They had won their group, leaving Arsenal second, and then had beaten Roma in the last 16. Of their eight games they had won seven though the one defeat was a 5-1 reverse at Arsenal.

Guardiola warned against the possible dangers of the game and once more he seemed to find the way to get the players to go out and give everything. With Busquets partnering Piqué at the back it was clear that the defence was lacking pace but Barça went out with the intention of scoring enough goals to make it not matter if the odd goal was conceded. The positions of Alves and Adriano at times were so far forward that it hardly seemed right to call them full backs though the excellent physical condition of both players meant they were often seen doing defensive duties. In attack, Pedro wasn't considered fit enough to start which meant Iniesta started on the left, though he was allowed a lot of freedom to roam inside, Villa was at centre forward while Messi played a 'false' right attacking role and also drifted inside to allow Alves room to attack down the right wing. As early as the second minute Adriano attacked down the left and played the ball inside to Messi who was already now on the left side of the pitch, Messi tried to slip a pass through to Villa but a defender got a foot to the ball but only succeeded in sending it straight to Andres Iniesta who placed his shot inside the near post before shoving his thumb in his mouth for a not-so-original celebration of his recent fatherhood.

Shakhtar showed some early signs of getting a goal back and Valdés had to do well to parry a cross from Willian Borges da Silva that nearly sneaked inside the near post. Then in the 12th minute Luiz Adriano got between Piqué and Busquets and away on goal, Busquets avoided giving away the foul and fortunately for Barça the Brazilian's shot went wide of Valdés's right-hand post. Just a minute later Alves gave a poor back pass and Valdés had to come storming out of his goal to clear, the ball fell to Willian 45 yards out and the hosts were again fortunate that his attempt on the open goal was not accurate.

These were worrying moments for Barça but then Messi began to appear. First he won a corner after a blinding run into the area, then he curled a free kick just wide and in the 19th minute he robbed the unfortunate Ishchenko – who was in the team in place of Chygrynskiy – but his attempted chip over keeper Pyatov didn't get enough height.

In the 25th minute Barça almost scored a carbon copy of the goal at Villarreal but this time Piqué failed to control the ball after Busquets's flick on from the corner. Barça were beginning to up the tempo now, Messi put Alves into a great position but instead of shooting the Brazilian crossed and there was nobody to finish. The danger coming from Alves was constant all night and in the 34th minute he beat the offside line to get onto Iniesta's superb pass and with one touch to control the pass he took the ball past Pyatov before slotting it into the empty net.

The second goal was a blow for Shakhtar and for the rest of the first half Barça concentrated on possession and controlling the game. There was an early chance for Luiz Adriano at the start of the second half but his control let him down, and Barça responded with Messi again testing Pyatov with a powerful whipped volley. Then in the 53rd minute Barça won another corner on the right, Xavi fired the ball in low towards the edge of the area where Piqué had arrived to turn the ball in with the help of a deflection for his second goal in a week.

There seemed to be a slight drop in Barça's intensity after the third goal. In the 59th minute Iniesta got himself booked for not retreating 10 yards at a free kick. The fact that Iniesta was Barça's only player in danger of suspension and also the way he ignored the ref's whistle suggest he was looking for the card. Though with half an hour still to play it didn't seem the best moment to pick up a tactical booking. When the free kick was taken Barça's defence was caught sleeping, allowing Shakhtar's central defender Yaroslav Rakitskiy the chance to knee the ball past Valdés.

Barça woke up after this unpleasant surprise and went straight up the other end to score a cracker. Messi dribbled from right to left across the edge of the penalty area, drawing the defence towards him before setting up Keita who made it 4-1 with an absolute screamer into the top corner.

Shakhtar still had some life left and in the 82nd minute they were a hairsbreadth away from making it 4-2 but Luiz Adriano's shot came out off the far post before ending up fortunately in Valdés's arms. It was a sign that it wasn't to be Shakhtar's day and Xavi completed their misery, converting Alves's cross for Barça's fifth in the 86th minute. The final score of 5-1 left Shakhtar needing a miracle in the second leg.

Barça: (4-3-3) Valdés; Alves, Piqué, Busquets, Adriano (Maxwell m77); Xavi, Mascherano, Keita; Messi, Villa (Pedro m70), Iniesta (Afellay m91).

Shakhtar: (4-2-3-1) Pyatov; Srna, Ishchenko, Rakitskiy, Rat; Mkhitaryan, Hübschman (Eduardo m83); Douglas Costa, Jadson (Fernandinho m70), Willian (Teixiera m75); Luiz Adriano.

Goals: m2 Iniesta 1-0, m34 Alves 2-0, m53 Piqué 3-0, m59 Rakitskiy 3-1, m60 Keita 4-1, m86 Xavi 5-1.

CHAPTER 29 – Real Madrid 0 Barça 2

Despite the excitement created by the very big possibility of facing Madrid four times in 18 days, Guardiola needed to keep his players focused as bottom-of-the-table Almeria visited Camp Nou for a league match on Saturday 9 April. Busquets and Valdés were suspended, having both picked up late tactical yellow cards at Villarreal in order to guarantee availability for the first *Clásico* on April 16, so Pinto and Milito came in while Guardiola also decided to leave Villa and Pedro on the bench, giving a start to Bojan and Thiago. The performance was well below standard and the only thing of note in a goalless first half was the unfortunate injury to Bojan who was replaced by Villa after tearing a knee ligament which would see him miss the rest of the season. Almeria took the lead early in the second half after Albert Crusat started and finished a quick counter-attack. Messi equalized two minutes later from the penalty spot after Villa had been brought down by Almeria keeper Diego Alves. Then in the 53rd minute with the score at 1-1 Guardiola brought on Pedro for Milito with Mascherano switching back to central defence. The choice of Mascherano to play in defence was taken basically because there was nobody else available but it would prove key to the remainder of the season and also to Mascherano's career at Camp Nou. Thiago headed Barça in front from Messi's corner just after the hour and right at the end Messi made it 3-1, taking advantage of Marcelo Silva's mistake to run through and flick the ball past Diego Alves.

Mascherano kept his place in central defence for the Champions League return game at Shakhtar Donetsk. With Puyol and Abidal still out Guardiola opted for Mascherano over Milito, who was struggling to find his form, and Busquets who returned to the defensive midfield role where his lack of speed was not exposed so much. The game turned out to be fairly comfortable for Barça and Messi scored the only goal of the game just before half time. It was the Argentinian's 48th goal of the season, beating his previous season's tally of 47. The following day Madrid won 0-1 at Tottenham to complete a 0-5 aggregate victory and set up an immense 4-game battle between the two great rivals of Spanish football.

The first of the four *Clásicos* was the league game at the Bernabéu on Saturday 16 April. Madrid were without the suspended Arbeloa but Mourinho still could have played his usual strongest XI. However, that would have been the same eleven that lost 5-0 at Camp Nou the previous November and Mourinho, not wanting to allow Barça the same space, made the tactical switch of moving Pepe into midfield to form the so-called *trivote* with Khedira and Xabi Alonso. Albiol was brought in to partner Carvalho in central defence while the creative Ozil was relegated to the bench. Mascherano was suspended for Barça while Abidal and Bojan were both still out. However, there was a big boost for the visitors with the return of Puyol to the team after an absence of nearly three months.

After all the usual hype in the pre-match build-up, the game itself was somewhat disappointing. Barça dominated possession but failed to penetrate as Madrid sat back and concentrated on closing down space and breaking Barça's rhythm while occasionally trying to hit Barça on the counter-attack or from set pieces. Barça took the lead early in the second half after Villa was brought down by Albiol in the area. Albiol was sent off and Messi converted the penalty, leaving Madrid with an uphill struggle. However, the introduction of Ozil for Benzema in the 56th minute inspired Madrid while Barça lost Puyol to injury a minute later which meant Busquets moved back to defence with Keita coming on as the holding man in midfield. Barça found the game more difficult to control after the changes, and things did not improve with the next set of substitutions when Afellay came on for Pedro while Mourinho brought on Arbeloa and Adebayor in place of Di Maria and Alonso. In the 82nd minute the referee awarded a dubious penalty after Alves's challenge on Marcelo and Ronaldo beat Valdés from the spot to leave the final score at 1-1. Both teams would attempt to make a victory out of the draw: Barça because the point more or less made their 8-point advantage safe with just six more league games to play, while Madrid took heart from their ten-man comeback which was a great improvement having lost the previous five games between the teams. However, Madrid's performance was not to the liking of everyone at the club. Honorary president Alfredo Di Stefano called Madrid "a team without personality" while praising Barça at the same time, "seeing them in action is a pleasure for everyone".

Four days later and the sides met again in the Copa del Rey final at Valencia's Mestalla stadium. Barça were without Puyol but Mascherano returned to take his place alongside Piqué in defence, and the only other change was Pinto in goal as Guardiola continued with the policy of playing the second-choice keeper in the Copa. Madrid had Arbeloa back at right back which meant Ramos returned to central defence at the expense of Albiol, while Mourinho continued with Pepe in his destructive role in the midfield *trivote*. Ozil returned to the starting XI supporting Di Maria and Ronaldo up front while Benzema, Higuain and Adebayor all started on the bench. From the start Madrid sat back but imposed an aggressive physical game as soon as Barça got past the halfway line. The aggression at times went too far, such as when Arbeloa stamped on Villa who was then roughly pulled to his feet by Sergio Ramos, but the only first half cards from referee Alberto Undiano Mallenco were for Pepe and Pedro. Barça failed to get a shot on target in the first 45 minutes but just before the break Madrid came within a whisker of scoring when Pepe's header hit the inside of the post. The second half swung in favour of Barça, Pedro had a goal disallowed though he was half a yard offside, and in the 75th minute Casillas first denied Messi with a low save and soon after he just got to Pedro's effort to lift the ball over him. At this time Barça looked sure to go on to win but Casillas again saved Madrid, this time from Iniesta with nine minutes to go. Then in the final minute of normal time Di

Maria nearly won it for Madrid with a shot from 20 yards that Pinto did brilliantly to tip over. In extra time Barça failed to keep up the rhythm and Madrid came back into it. Xabi Alonso was lucky not to get a second yellow in the 100th minute after pulling Iniesta, but three minutes later Marcelo and Di Maria combined well on the left and Di Maria sent in a superb cross that was met by Ronaldo who headed firmly past Pinto. Madrid defended doggedly for the remainder of extra time and Barça were a bit over frenetic with the main weapon being to push Piqué forward. Just before the end Di Maria received his second yellow of the game but it was too late to make any difference as Madrid held on to win 1-0. The only consolation for Barça fans was to see Sergio Ramos drop the trophy under the bus during Madrid's celebration tour.

The following weekend it was back to La Liga, though everybody was now looking forward to the Champions League semi-final. Madrid played first in a 6 pm game on the Saturday at Valencia and with only Casillas and Carvalho from the cup-winning starting line-up, they recorded an impressive 3-6 win with Higuain (3), Kaka (2) and Benzema scoring the goals. Barça had a home game against Osasuna immediately after at 8 pm, Adriano had been injured near the end of the Copa del Rey final and would miss the next four weeks and Guardiola made six other changes to the team that lost at Mestalla. Villa ended a run of 11 games without a goal to give Barça a first half lead and Messi came on for the last half hour and secured the three points with a late goal.

In the build-up to the first Champions League semi-final tensions between Barça and Madrid increased to new heights. Guardiola had pointed out that if it hadn't been for the linesman's good eyesight in disallowing Pedro's goal in Valencia then Barça would have won the Copa del Rey. The point he was trying to make was that games can be decided by very small things. However, Mourinho, who during the season had already caused controversy by saying that Barça were favoured by referees and kick off times, pounced on the opportunity. In the pre-match press conference the day before the first semi-final at the Bernabéu, Mourinho reflected that, "Up until now there have been two types of coaches, a very small group who never talk about referees. And then, there is a bigger group, to which I belong, who criticize the referees when they make big errors." He went on to say, "With Pep's declaration the other day we are entering a new era with a third group, which for now includes only him, that criticizes referees when they make a correct decision". Mourinho went on to reflect that this new group could only be a result of Guardiola experiencing "the scandal of Stamford Bridge and since that moment he isn't happy when the referee gets it right".

Throughout the season Guardiola had refused to rise to Mourinho's provocation, but this time was different. Whether he simply snapped, or whether it was a predetermined decision, intended to inspire his team, is unclear. Either way, Guardiola's response was remarkable and the setting of the Bernabéu press room made it even more so. He began by saying that since señor Mourinho had the familiarity to call him Pep he would call him José, he then continued "Tomorrow at 8.45 we face each other on the pitch. Off the pitch he has already won, he's been winning all season and he will win in the future. I'll give him his own personal off-the-pitch Champions League that he can take home and enjoy with his other trophies". He went on to say that we could talk about Stamford Bridge or a thousand other things but he didn't have the people working for him – obviously inferring that Mourinho did. He then delivered his most memorable line: "*En esta sala, él es el puto jefe, el puto amo, el qué más sabe del mundo* – In this room he is the fucking boss, the fucking man, the world's most knowledgeable man". When Guardiola returned to the team hotel the players greeted him with a standing ovation.

The expectation for the match was now at fever pitch. Barça had problems to form a defence, especially as Maxwell had picked up a groin strain against Osasuna leaving Guardiola without his three left backs. Neither Puyol nor Milito was at 100% but in the end captain Puyol found the strength to return to fill in at left back leaving Mascherano to partner Piqué again. There was also a big blow when Iniesta failed a late fitness test on his injured right calf, so Keita started in midfield. Madrid were without the suspended Carvalho and the injured Khedira and there had been talk that Mourinho might abandon the *trivote*. However, when the teams were announced an hour before the game the *trivote* was there, just with Lass Diarra in place of Khedira, while Albiol came in for Carvalho. Up front Mourinho again left out all three of his recognized centre-forwards opting for Di Maria and Ozil supporting Ronaldo. When German referee Wolfgang Stark finally blew his whistle to start the game the atmosphere inside the Bernabéu was at its most electric. Barça, however, came out with a steely attitude, not wanting to be bullied as in the two previous meetings, and also showing a willingness to make a meal out of any Madrid challenges. It was a poor example to the watching neutrals though it demonstrated that Barça felt they needed to match some of Mourinho's win-at-all-costs attitude.

In the first 45 minutes Madrid sat even further back than in the previous games and there were moments when Barça were allowed to pass the ball in their own half with hardly any pressing from Madrid's forwards. After 15 minutes Ronaldo petulantly demonstrated his displeasure with Mourinho's tactics with a gesture of frustration at the lack of support he was getting. The tactics meant there were very few chances for either side in the first half. After early long shots from Xavi and Ronaldo, Villa had the first good effort cutting in from the right, where he was positioned in the first half, before sending a low shot inches wide of Casillas's far post. There had been plenty of talk about the referee but the first controversial decision went Madrid's way when Ramos was not carded for handball in the 4th minute, though in the second half Busquets was also let off for a similar offence. Barça were playing with extreme patience and there were few risks with Alves rarely going forward as he didn't want to leave any room for Madrid's possible counter attacks. Messi carved out a half chance for Xavi after 24 minutes which Casillas needed to dive low to save and that was about all Barça managed in the first half. Madrid fared no better with their only tactic seeming to be for Di Maria to try and win free kicks but Ronaldo was having an off day with his shooting. However, just before half time the Portuguese fired in a long shot that Valdés failed to hold, but then the second save from Ozil turned out to be unnecessary as Ozil was offside. There had been little football and as the first half progressed things became uglier. Busquets clashed with Marcelo in midfield and went down with his hands covering his face only to be caught on camera peeking out to see if his acting had earned Marcelo a booking. It hadn't, and as Busquets moved away he was caught again by the camera, seemingly calling Marcelo "mono" (monkey) though the player would later claim he was saying "morro" (what a cheek). The fact that Busquets was covering his mouth, left the question of why would he cover his mouth if he was only saying morro.

As the players left the pitch at half time an argument broke out between Keita and Arbeloa which led to a free-for-all with substitutes and team seconds getting involved. Pinto moved towards Arbeloa who pushed Barça's reserve keeper away, and then Madrid's match delegate Chendo got involved, grabbing Pinto by the neck from behind, Pinto turned and swung a punch which would earn him a red card and a three-match suspension.

Mourinho brought on Adebayor in place of Ozil at half time and Madrid changed tactics, now pressing much higher up field with Adebayor causing Piqué, Puyol and Busquets problems with his aggressive approach. In the 50th minute Busquets was caught in possession, Ronaldo advanced into the area but Puyol got back to block the shot. However, Madrid's raised aggression had its consequences, first Ramos was booked for a foul on Messi which meant he would be suspended for the return at Camp Nou, and then in the 61st minute Pepe followed through as Alves cleared and appeared to catch Alves's shin with his foot raised and studs up. Referee Stark had no hesitation in pulling out the red card and thus ending Pepe's part in the tie. Mourinho also got sent to the stands for sarcastically applauding the decision.

There was one more chance for Madrid but Ronaldo headed wide from Alonso's free kick, and from then on it was all Barça. It was a slow dismantling of Madrid, but Barça continued to stay patient and wait for the chance. Villa, now on the left, almost scored after cutting inside in the 68th minute but Casillas did well to parry and then Pedro couldn't quite head home the rebound despite twisting acrobatically in his attempt. Guardiola then brought on Afellay for Pedro and the substitution turned out to be decisive. In the 76th minute Xavi opened play to Afellay who found a good change of pace to take him past Marcelo before crossing low for Messi who turned the ball through Casillas's legs at the near post. Barça could have sat back on the victory but Messi had smelt blood. In the 87th minute he set off on a run from 45 yards out, his acceleration saw off Lass, he then skipped past Albiol and into the area, and with Ramos and Marcelo in close proximity he kept his head to squeeze the ball past Casillas and inside the far post. It was a truly momentous goal worthy of the enormous occasion. Unfortunately there had been little more to praise about the match. In the 90th minute Guardiola gave the 19-year-old Sergi Roberto his Champions League debut and Barça held on to the 0-2 scoreline.

In the post match press conference Mourinho played the victim. He began by explaining that the referee had sent him off for giving a thumbs-up gesture and went on to add "If I tell the referee and Uefa what I think of them, my career would be over, and as I cannot say what I feel about them I only have one question: *"Por qué?"*. Why? He then reeled off the names of referees who he considered were part of the great Barça/Uefa conspiracy. *"Por qué* Øvrebø? *Por qué* Bussaca? *Por qué* De Bleeckere? *Por qué* Stark? Why? I don't understand." He went on to reflect that maybe it was for Barça's association with UNICEF or perhaps it was down to the power of the Spanish Football Federation's president, Angel Maria

Villar, in UEFA, or maybe it was just because they were nice guys. He claimed the second leg was *"misión imposible* – even if we score there, they will kill us again". The rant went on with Mourinho continuing to ask: why? – he would ask *Por qué?* a total of 35 times during the 15 minute press conference - *"Por qué* Pepe sent off? *Por qué* four penalties not given against Chelsea? *Por qué* Motta sent off? *Por qué* Van Persie sent off?" He contemplated that for Barça, winning in this manner, "must taste differently". When asked about Guardiola's pre-match comments to award him the off-the-pitch Champions League, Mourinho - taking care to call Guardiola 'Josep Guardiola' "I'll call him *señor* Josep Guardiola if he wants" - responded by recalling his two on-the-pitch Champions Leagues with Porto and Inter, before going on to say: "Josep Guardiola is a fantastic coach, I repeat, a fantastic coach. But he has won one Champions League which I would have been ashamed to win. Because he won it with the *'escandalo de Stamford Bridge'*. And now if he goes on to win a second Champions League this season he will have done it with the *'escandalo del Bernabéu'*".

It was an incredible outburst from the Madrid coach, but in the morning the Catalan sports press reminded everybody whose day it had really been, running the headline: *Messi es el puto amo.*

Real Madrid: Casillas; Arbeola, Ramos, Albiol, Marcelo; Lass, Pepe, Alonso; Ozil (Adebayor h/t), Ronaldo, Di Maria.

Barça: Valdés; Alves, Mascherano, Piqué, Puyol; Xavi, Busquets, Keita; Pedro (Afellay m71), Messi, Villa (Sergi Roberto m90).

Goals: m76 Messi 0-1, m87 Messi 0-2.

CHAPTER 30 – Barça 3 Manchester United 1

The fallout from the first semi-final continued for some days. Barça complained to UEFA about Mourinho's accusations and Madrid responded with their own complaint about the anti-sporting behavior of six Barça players. Things got even dirtier when a video was shown on a Madrid-based TV show *Punto Pelota* that appeared to demonstrate that Pepe had made no contact with Alves in the sending-off incident. The Barcelona-based sports daily *El Sport* then produced a video that appeared to demonstrate that *Punto Pelota*'s video had been manipulated, with the frame where contact was made being removed.

Perhaps it was normal that with all the tension and accusations of the semi-final both Barça and Madrid failed to perform when they returned to league action the following Saturday. Madrid played a 6 pm game at home to Zaragoza and were beaten 2-3, giving Barça, playing at 8 pm, the chance to move to within a point of the title if they could beat Real Sociedad in San Sebastian. Of the first-choice players only Piqué, Xavi and Messi started with Pinto, Montoya, Milito, Fontás, Thiago, Keita, Jeffren and Afellay coming in. Despite taking a first half lead thanks to Thiago's neat chip Barça threw the game away with a sluggish performance that allowed Real to score twice in the last 20 minutes.

The tension didn't seem quite so great for the Champions League return game at Camp Nou played on Tuesday 3 May. Perhaps it was due to Barça's two-goal advantage from the first leg which gave Madrid, without the injured Khedria and the suspended Pepe and Ramos, little chance of qualifying, or perhaps it was down to Mourinho's absence as given his suspension for the game he preferred to watch the game at the team's hotel rather than from the Camp Nou directors box. Barça were without

Maxwell, Adriano, Milito, and Bojan but there was a massive boost as Abidal returned to the squad just six and a half weeks after his liver operation. However, Puyol continued at left back and Barça's only change from the first leg was the return of Iniesta in place of Keita. Madrid abandoned the *trivote*, reverting to their more typical 4-2-3-1 shape with Carvalho, Kaká and Higuain replacing Ramos, Pepe and Ozil from the first leg.

Madrid pressed further forward than in the first leg but neither side took many risks early on. After an initial period of very high pressure from Madrid the game settled down to the familiar pattern of Barça bossing the midfield and maintaining possession. Madrid created very little going forward as Piqué, Mascherano and Puyol were superb in defensive duties, then as the game entered the last 15 minutes of the first half Barça put together a string of chances, with Casillas having to make two very good saves to prevent Villa and Messi.

Madrid began the second half with their best spell and they were unfortunate when Higuain had a goal ruled out for a foul called against Ronaldo. Madrid would feel hard done by as Ronaldo had only brought down Mascherano as a result of his falling after making contact with Piqué. However, Madrid coming out to look for a goal meant they were more vulnerable at the back and Barça took advantage in the 54th minute when Iniesta threaded a pass through to Pedro who controlled before sweeping the ball left footed past Casillas.

Adebayor and Ozil replaced Higuain and Kaká but it was now an enormous task facing Madrid. Marcelo pulled one goal back in the 64th minute to make it 1-1 on the night but Barça held on reasonably comfortably to go through to the final 3-1 on aggregate. In the 90th minute Abidal was sent on to a tremendous ovation and at the final whistle he was thrown in the air by his teammates in an emotional celebration. The following day in the other semi-final Manchester United hammered Schalke 4-1 at Old

Trafford (6-1 on aggregate) to become Barça's opponents at Wembley in a repeat of the 2009 final.

On Friday 6 May UEFA gave its verdict on the goings on in the first leg at the Bernabéu. Mourinho was given a five-match suspension and €50,000 fine for his sending off and post-match comments, Pinto received a three-match ban for his sending off in the half time scuffle, while Pepe received a one-match ban for his red card which he had already served by missing the game at Camp Nou. There was no mention of the Busquets incident with Marcelo as it was not recorded in the referee's report.

Back in the league Barça still needed four more points from the remaining four games to retain the title. Puyol was rested for the next game, the local derby with Espanyol at Camp Nou, which gave Fontás a start at left back but the rest of the team was at full strength. In the 29th minute Fontás played the ball forward and Iniesta pounced on Galan's mistake before darting into the area, nipping past Amat and firing low past Kameni at his near post for his 8th league goal this season. Piqué made it 2-0 early in the second half, heading in from Xavi's corner, and Barça held on for a comfortable win. Abidal continued his comeback, coming on as a substitute for the final 20 minutes.

The following Wednesday, May 11, with one more point needed to take the title, Barça travelled down the coast to play Levante who despite being 10th in the table were only four points above the relegation zone. Guardiola made three changes from the Espanyol game with Abidal returning at left back in place of Fontás, while Keita and Afellay replaced Iniesta and Pedro. It was Keita who put Barça ahead after half an hour, chasing Xavi's long ball to head brilliantly past Levante keeper Gustavo Munúa. However, Levante equalized through Felipe Caicedo before half time. The second half provided just one moment of magic, a Messi dribble that ended with a shot against the post, but as the minutes passed it became clear that both sides were happy with a draw. The game drew to a close in an apparent non-aggression pact with neither side looking to score, and Barça were league champions for the third consecutive season.

All attention now turned to the Champions League final. There was a scare for Busquets on May 13 when UEFA announced it would be studying Madrid's accusation of racism, with a possible 5-match ban, which would of course include the final, if found guilty. However, three days later UEFA delivered its verdict that the evidence was not convincing or strong enough.

Barça's final two league games were used to give Abidal more minutes while Maxwell and Adriano also returned from injury. The games were also used to give experience to some youngsters such as Oriol Romeu who came on as a late substitute in the 0-0 draw at home to Depotivo, and Sergi Roberto who played the 90 minutes in the 1-3 win at Malaga. The points from these games left Barça on a total of 96 points at the end of the season, four points above second-placed Madrid.

Manchester United had clinched their 19th league title with a 1-1 draw at Blackburn Rovers on May 14, so, like Barça, they had plenty of time to prepare for the Wembley final. Sir Alex Ferguson's only doubt was over Darren Fletcher who had also missed the 2009 final through suspension. Fletcher had suffered a strange stomach virus in March and had been struggling to regain match fitness. Defensively United did not look as solid as in 2009, as shown by the 37 league goals conceded in the 2010/11 Premier League compared to only 24 in the 2008/09 season. They had won the title with 80 points (compared to 90 in 2008/09) and in the previous three months they had lost important league games at Chelsea, Liverpool and Arsenal while losing out to Man City in the Wembley FA Cup semi-final. This was all reflected in the fact that this time round Barça were clear favourites whereas two years before the two sides had been evenly fancied when they met in Rome. However, United had the advantage of playing this final in England.

Five days before the game United's preparation was affected when British Liberal Democrat MP John Hemming used his parliamentary privilege to name Ryan Giggs as the footballer who had brought out a super injunction to prevent his identity being revealed in an extra-marital affair with the model Imogen Thomas. As a married father of two, Giggs was obviously trying very hard to prevent the story coming out. However, after thousands had named Giggs on Twitter and other internet sites, Hemmings claimed that he decided to reveal the player's identity when he "showed that he was going to go after relatively normal people and try and prosecute them, for gossiping about him on a matter of trivia, I think he has to be held to account for that."

Barça's preparation was also affected by an unlikely source. A year after Iceland's Eyjafjalla volcano disrupted the journey to Milan for the Champions League semi-final with Inter, there was another eruption in Iceland, this time from the Grimsvötn volcano just seven days before the final, and flights in Europe were again threatened. Barça decided not to wait on unpredictable wind patterns and flew to London on the Tuesday before the game instead of on the Thursday as had been originally planned.

Guardiola's main doubts were in defence and the choice of Abidal or Adriano at left back and Puyol or Mascherano to partner Piqué at centre back. When the teams were announced an hour before kick-off there was a surprise to see that Puyol was only a substitute which meant Xavi wore the captain's armband. Barça lined up with Valdés, Alves, Piqué, Mascherano, Abidal, Xavi, Busquets, Iniesta, Villa, Messi and Pedro, while Ferguson played eight of the Rome eleven from two years earlier, starting with Van der Sar, Fabio da Silva, Ferdinand, Vidic, Evra, Luis Antonio Valencia, Carrick, Giggs, Park, Rooney and Javier 'Chicharito' Hernandez.

The game began with United applying a very high tempo pressing. Park, Giggs and Rooney won their first 50-50 balls with Alves, Xavi and

Busquets, respectively and Barça found themselves pinned back in their own half for the first few minutes. Chicharito robbed Busquets on the edge of the area, and after receiving Carrick's return, fired in the first shot of the game but Piqué managed to get in the way. United were also trying to catch Barça with the long ball from the back, the third time they tried it Van der Sar's kick gave Rooney the chance to show his speed against Mascherano, and Valdés had to run to the edge of his area to make a spectacular punched clearance. Messi had not been given a moment on the ball and after a loose pass from Busquets, Carrick robbed Messi for the second time, giving the ball to Giggs who sent a low vertical ball through the middle for Chicharito to chase, Piqué got there first but his risky touch back to Valdés, who was running out of his area, almost caused a mix-up but the keeper managed to make an awkward kicked clearance.

It wasn't until around the tenth minute that Xavi, Iniesta and Messi began to find each other. In Rome two years previously United had had the better of the first ten minutes before Eto'o's goal changed everything. Now, there wasn't the immediate goal but the game definitely started to swing in Barça's favour from this point. Villa had two shots in a couple of minutes that were both blocked, while Pedro called for a penalty for Evra's unintentional handball. Then in the 15th minute Villa found Xavi who sent in a low cross from the right and Pedro got in front of Ferdinand at the near post but sent his shot just wide.

United's attempts to play the quick ball forward were being frustrated by Piqué's dominance in the air and by Chicharito being caught offside while they couldn't maintain the high tempo pressing which meant Park, Giggs and Carrick began to look bewildered by Barça's quick pass-and-move game. As United backed off Barça began to find shooting opportunities from outside the area. Villa sent one effort just wide from 25 yards, and then from a bit closer to goal the Asturian striker fired in a low drive which forced Van der Sar to make his first diving save. Messi began to appear closer to goal but on two runs into the area he was prevented, first by Vidic's vital tackle, and a minute later by his own slip which allowed Ferdinand to clear the danger.

Then in the 27th minute Van der Sar sent another long kick forward. Piqué beat Rooney in the air, heading the ball forward to Xavi who knocked it back first time to Iniesta who exchanged quick sideways passes with Busquets. There are many critics who have questioned the necessity of so many horizontal passes from Barça but the exchange between Iniesta and Busquets allowed Xavi to move away from Giggs and into space, Iniesta played the ball forward and Xavi now had twenty yards to run into. As Fabio came out of defence to close the space Xavi spotted Pedro moving right to gain a yard on Vidic, the pass was inch perfect and Pedro took one touch to control before firing low past Van der Sar at the goalkeeper's near post.

Barça looked to be in the driving seat now, however, the lead lasted just seven minutes. Abidal sent a long throw-in up the line from near the corner flag, Villa, under pressure from Ferdinand, failed to control the ball and after quick passes between Fabio, Rooney and Carrick, Rooney was speeding towards goal. Piqué came out of defence to meet him and Rooney flicked the ball to Giggs, who looked marginally offside, and Rooney continued his run to meet Giggs's return with a sweeping drive high past Valdés.

The pattern didn't change after United's equalizer as Barça continued to dominate. Xavi fired over from 25 yards and then Iniesta had a long-range effort that flew straight into Van der Sar's hands. The first half ended with a break through the middle from Messi, but after playing the ball out to Villa he couldn't quite make enough contact on Villa's return to divert the ball in.

Barça continued to shoot from distance in the second half with Iniesta and Xavi both having efforts blocked. The combinations from Barça in midfield opened more spaces, Iniesta exchanged passes with Xavi and Messi again before sending Alves darting into the area but Van der Sar saved the Brazilian's shot with his feet and when Messi fired the rebound back towards goal Evra arrived to head the ball away.

Then in the 54th minute a United counter-attack broke down when Rooney lost the ball to Xavi ten yards inside the Barça half. Xavi touched the ball right to Alves and the ball moved quickly from Alves to Villa to Xavi again who exchanged passes with Iniesta before spreading the ball out left to Pedro. Moving inside Pedro played the ball square to Iniesta who again exchanged passes with Xavi before playing it on to Messi who was about 35 yards from goal. Perhaps Park should have got tighter on Messi or perhaps Evra or Vidic should have moved out more quickly to close the space. Either way, Messi spotted the space in front of him and moved into it before driving home a swerving low shot that Van der Sar might have done more to stop if he hadn't been unsighted by Vidic.

Barça didn't let up after the second goal. Messi might have had another after turning Ferdinand on the edge of the area but Van der Sar did well to make an unorthodox save. Alves gor forward again before squaring to Messi just six yards out but Vidic made a vital block. Van der Sar then had to dive full stretch to turn Xavi's 25-yard drive past the post, and soon after Iniesta fired in a bullet from 30 yards that went straight at the keeper. Then in the 69th minute Barça took a short corner on the right. The ball came back to Messi near the touchline. For a moment Messi had the ball stationary at his feet with Nani, who had come on as substitute for the injured Fabio moments earlier, facing him. With a sidestep to his left Messi threw Nani off balance before taking the ball right and accelerating for the area, the Argentinian skipped past Evra but then, with his path blocked by Ferdinand, could only touch the ball towards Carrick who was running towards his own goal. However, Messi's run had disrupted United's defence and Carrick could only touch the ball towards Nani who had to stretch in his attempt to control it which gave Busquets the chance to rob the ball inside the United area and send a short pass back to Villa who steadied himself before curling a beauty out of the diving Van der Sar's reach and into the top corner.

The third goal killed off United. They managed a couple of hopeful shots from Rooney and Nani but neither found the target, and Valdés's work was confined to another spectacular punch, well off his line, to deny Chicharito the chance to turn. There was a United appeal for hands from Villa inside the area, but like Evra's in the first half, it was unintentional. Barça concentrated on keeping possession and playing out time. Keita, Puyol and Afellay came on as substitutes, and near the end Iniesta tried to catch Van der Sar off his line with an audacious sidefoot volley from 35 yards and Afellay brought one final save from the United keeper.

The shots-on-target tally of 13-1 demonstrated Barça's dominance more clearly than the 3-1 final scoreline. Messi was awarded the Man-of-the-Match trophy though it could easily have gone to Xavi who gave more passes than anybody else and was also the player who covered most distance (11,950 metres). At the end, in one of the most moving moments you will ever see at a football match, captains Puyol and Xavi gave Eric Abidal the honour of receiving the trophy from UEFA president Michel Platini.

Barça: Valdés; Alves (Puyol m88), Piqué, Mascherano, Abidal; Xavi, Busquets, Iniesta; Villa (Keita m85), Messi, Pedro (Afellay m90).

Manchester United: Van der Sar; Fabio (Nani m68), Ferdinand, Vidic, Evra; Valencia, Carrick (Scholes m76), Giggs, Park; Rooney, Chicharito.

Goals: m27 Pedro 1-0, m34 Rooney 1-1, m54 Messi 2-1, m69 Villa 3-1.

CHAPTER 31 – Barça 3 Real Madrid 2

The celebrations for the Champions League had hardly died down when the press turned its attention to the possible new signings for the 2011/12 season. Cesc Fabregas was again top of the list while the search for a new forward focused on Villarreal's Giuseppe Rossi and the Chilean international Alexis Sanchez who had just been named as best player in the Italian Serie A for 2010/11 by *La Gazzetta dello Sport* after scoring 12 goals in 28 games for Udinese.

Carles Puyol underwent a knee operation at the start of June but the rest of the month passed and there were no signings. The rumours continued but when the first group of first team players returned for training on July 18 there were still no new additions to the squad. Barça had arranged six warm-up games before the first official game of the season which would be another *Clásico* in the Spanish Supercopa on August 14. Any new signing would have little time to intergrate. Finally, on July 21 Barça and Udinese reached an agreement and Alexis signed a five-year deal for a fee of €26 million + €11.5 million in variables.

The following day a loan deal was agreed for Bojan Krkic to join Roma where Luis Enrique had taken over as coach after three successful years in charge of Barça's B team. Having started so well in his first season as a 17-year-old under Frank Rijkaard Bojan's progression had been somewhat frustrating, but at the age of just 20 he could still boast 162 first team games for Barça in which he had scored 41 goals.

Barça's first preseason game was a disappointing 0-0 draw against Hajduk Split in Croatia. With the South American players away at the Copa America, Guardiola put out two completely different teams so there was a chance for some youngsters including Isaac Cuenca who made his first appearance for the first team, having returned to the club after a year's loan at Sabadell.

There were then two games in Bayern Munich's summer tournament, the Audi Cup. First a 2-2 draw with Porto Alegre's Internacional with Thiago Alcantara, who'd been promoted to the first team along with Andreu Fontás, and Johnathan dos Santos getting the goals. Then after winning the penalty shoot-out against Internacional, Barça beat Bayern 2-0 in the final with Thiago scoring twice, including a beautiful 25-yard curler. With Fabregas still not signed, the impressive form of Thiago left many culés feeling that maybe the Arsenal man wasn't necessary.

Barça then travelled to the U.S.A for a three-match tour with the first game in Washington being a repeat of the Champions League final with Manchester United. This time United got the better of things, winning 2-1, though Barça's goal again came from Thiago, smashing a spectacular long-range effort past United's new goalkeeper, David De Gea. Barça were again defeated in the second game of the tour, played in Miami against Mexican favourites Chivas de Guadalajara. Despite an early goal from David Villa, Barça more or less fell apart in the final half hour after a series of substitutions and Chivas ran out 4-1 winners. One of Barça's substitutes was the 17-year-old Gerard Deulofeu, making his first appearance for the first team. It was back to winning ways in the final tour game in Dallas with a 2-0 victory over another Mexican team, Club América, with goals from Villa and Seydou Keita. However, the balance of only two wins in six preseason games was hardly the best preparation for the new season.

Messi, Alves, and Mascherano rejoined the group back in Barcelona for the last week of training before the first leg game of the Supercopa at the Bernabéu. New signing Alexis also started training on August 8, however, there was little time for the group to work together as the Spanish internationals had a game against Italy on August 10.

On August 12, just two days before the *Clásico* it was announced that an agreement had been made for the signing of Cesc Fabregas. However, it wasn't until after the first leg that Fabregas finally passed his medical and signed for five years. It put to an end a very long transfer saga with a final price of €29 million + €10 million in variables being agreed with Arsenal.

It was commonly believed before the Supercopa games that Madrid were in better physical shape than Barça for the contest. Apart from the recent assimilation of Barça's South American players, Puyol was still out injured while Busquets and Piqué had both picked up knocks playing for Spain. José Mourinho was still in charge at Madrid and he'd also managed to oust Jorge Valdano from the club, leaving him with more power than any previous Madrid coach had known. Mourinho changed the policy of star signings, bringing in only one big name, Fábio Coentrão, from Benfica for €30 million, with none of the other four signings, Nuri Şahin, Hamit Altintop, Raphael Varane and José Callejon, costing more than €10 million. The bookmakers made Madrid 6/5 favourites to win the first leg with Barça at 2/1.

Mourinho began with his first-choice XI of Casillas, Ramos, Pepe, Carvalho, Marcelo, Khedira, Alonso, Ronaldo, Ozil, Di Maria and Benzema. Guardiola had to make do without Puyol and Busquets, while Xavi and Piqué were only fit enough to start on the bench, Adriano, Keita and Thiago were brought into the team while Alexis made his first start as Barça lined up with Valdés, Alves, Mascherano, Abidal, Adriano, Thiago, Keita, Iniesta, Alexis, Messi and Villa.

Madrid began the better team and early on Benzema almost scored after heading down Ronaldo's left-wing cross but as the ball bounced up off the ground Valdés sprang across to make an excellent save. Soon after, a long ball up Madrid's right side found Benzema who held the ball up, drawing Abidal and Mascherano toward him, before squaring for Ozil who had burst into the gap and Valdés could do nothing as Ozil struck the ball home.

Little by little Barça began to pass their way into the game. Messi had been very quiet but in the 36th minute he managed to make himself a bit of space before sending the ball out to Villa on the left. There didn't appear to be much danger as Villa cut in towards the edge of the area but then he let fly from close to the corner of the penalty area with a wicked shot that dipped over Casillas into the far corner.

Madrid came forward again and most culés would have been happy to hear the half time whistle, but there was still time for Messi to amaze with another piece of magic. Receiving the ball 25 yards out he held off a terrific challenge from the beefy Khedira before skipping past the floundering Pepe and shooting past Casillas to put Barça 1-2 up at half time.

Madrid must have felt well and truly mugged, but they were made of pretty stern stuff. When Barça failed to clear a corner in the 54th minute Pepe laid the ball back to Alonso who hit a crisp side-footer into the far corner. Valdés kept the score down to 2-2 with further saves from Ronaldo and Benzema. Then with just seven minutes remaining, the Barça keeper failed to hold a high cross and from the floor he raised an arm and tripped Ronaldo who was following up. The ref waved play on and Barça survived with a 2-2 draw to take back for the second leg at Camp Nou.

The return game was played just three days later and Guardiola was able to put out the Wembley XI with Piqué, Busquets, Xavi and Pedro returning to starting lineup which left new signings Alexis and Fabregas starting on the bench. Mourinho made just one change to Madrid's team with Coentrao replacing Marcelo at left back. Needing a victory or a high-scoring draw Madrid were compelled to come out and play, and both teams played a risky game that led to a great contest.

Ronaldo was particularly dangerous early on and nearly all the early shots on goal came from the Portuguese. However, with Madrid playing high up, Barça occasionally found big spaces to run into. In the 15th minute, Messi received the ball just inside his own half near the right touchline. He skipped past Coentrao and Khedira as he darted infield before sending a sublime defence-splitting pass for Iniesta to run clean through. Casillas came out to close the angle but Iniesta showed class and composure, lifting the ball neatly over the goalkeeper's right shoulder and Barça were in front.

However, as seen in the first game, Madrid were looking the fitter of the two teams and they hit back quickly when Ronaldo poked in after Benzema fired a corner back across goal. Almost immediately Pedro forced a save from Casillas after a good through pass from Iniesta and then Ronaldo hit the bar via Valdés raised fists. The game was really buzzing now with Madrid still looking more dangerous and Valdés again had to save to deny Ozil after Abidal had left him onside.

As at the Bernabéu, Madrid dropped a bit in the final minutes of the first half and this was when Messi began to come to life. He made a couple of dangerous runs, forcing Casillas to save one with his foot. And then again, just as at the Bernabéu, the Argentinian grabbed a goal on the stroke of half time after Piqué, with a neat back heel, set him up to score with a right foot chip over Casillas's dive. The goal would be especially sweet for culés for the image of Ronaldo sliding on his knees in a vain attempt to stop their Messi scoring.

The second half was more cagey in comparison though Barça controlled things better. Messi was in the game much more despite several heavy challenges. Now at the age of 24 he was looking more muscular and able to take the challenges of such strong players as Pepe and Khedira. There was a moment when Messi looked like he might retaliate after Marcelo took at kick at him while jumping for the ball, and later Pepe was fortunate not to get a straight red for the locked pointing-up elbow position he employed while body-checking Messi.

Valdés was troubled much less in the second half, but there was a warning for him when Benzema volleyed over after 69 minutes. Then two minutes later Sergio Ramos missed a good chance, heading wide unmarked at a corner. Most of Barça's problems at the back were caused at corners and with less than ten minutes remaining Kaká sent in another from the left which Barça failed to clear. The ball was headed from Pepe to Benzema who swiveled and fired low past Valdés, making it all square at 2-2 on the night and 4-4 on aggregate.

Madrid probably felt they had deserved the equalizer but there was one more chapter for Messi to write. Fabregas came on for his debut in place of Pedro in the 84th minute and Guardiola placed him on the right wing. Fabregas had been on the pitch for four minutes when Mascherano found him out by the touchline, he played a quick ball inside to Messi who played a first-time ball for Adriano on the right, and when Adriano crossed, Messi was storming in to meet the ball with a crashing volley past Casillas.

Madrid's frustration overflowed in injury time when Marcelo scythed down Fabregas near the touchline in front of the two benches. A massive free-for-all ensued with every outfield player, the two goalkeepers and both benches involved. In the midst of the pushing and shoving, Mourinho walked up casually behind Tito Vilanova and unashamedly stuck his right index finger in Vilanova's eye. Vilanova responded with a slap on the back of Mourinho's head but both actions were only seen by the TV camaras and not by the officials. The referee had shown Marcelo a straight red card almost immediately after the original foul, and when the fracas died down Villa and Ozil, who had both already been substituted, were also shown red cards for their parts in the melee.

After the game, Mourinho would feign ignorance about the eye-poke. Apparently, he didn't even know who Vilanova was, outrageously asking: "Pito who?", when asked by the press about the incident. It was a remarkable lack of respect towards a fellow professional – *pito* being a Spanish slang word for penis.

The Spanish Football Federation (RFEF) took more than six weeks to deliver a verdict on the incident. Quite incredibly Mourinho's punishment was only a two-match ban which would only correspond to future Supercopa games and a fine of €600. Vilanova received an identical fine and a one-match ban which would also only come into effect for the Supercopa. As fate would have it, 12 months later in August 2012, Barça and Madrid would meet again in the Supercopa with Mourinho still in the hot seat at Madrid and Vilanova newly instated as first-team coach at Barça. However, neither coach would have to serve their ban due to a general amnesty being declared by the RFEF's president Angel Maria Villar following Spain's triumph at Euro 2012.

Barça: Valdés; Alves, Mascherano, Piqué, Abidal; Xavi, Busquets (Keita m85,), Iniesta; Pedro (Fabregas m84,), Messi, Villa (Adriano m73).

Real Madrid: Casillas; Ramos, Pepe, Carvalho, Coentrao; Alonso, Khedira (Marcelo m45); Di María (Higuian m63), Ozil (Kaka m78), Ronaldo; Benzema.

Goals: m15 Iniesta 1-0, m20 Ronaldo 1-1, m45 Messi 2-1, m81 Benzema 2-2, m88 Messi 3-2.

CHAPTER 32 – Barça 8 Osasuna 0

The start of the 2011/2012 league season was delayed due to a players' strike. The players' union, *La Asociacion de Futbolistas Españoles* (AFE), originally announced a strike for the first two games of the new season due to failure to agree on certain points in a new agreement being negotiated with the Spanish League (LFP) concerning player payment. A settlement between the two sides was reached on August 25 but not before the first round of games, set for the weekend of August 20/21, had been postponed.

However, the strike did not affect the annual Joan Gamper trophy match played on Monday 22 against Napoles who had finished third in Serie A the previous season. It may have only been a friendly but Barça offered a blistering display of attacking football and the Italians were blown away by the passing skills of Iniesta, Thiago, Fabregas, Messi and Xavi. The numerous substitutions also gave a chance for non-first team players Marc Bartra, Johnathan dos Santos, Martin Montoya, Isaac Cuenca, Sergi Roberto and new B-team signing Kiko Femenia to show what they could do, and Barça ran out 5-0 winners with goals from Keita, Fabregas, Pedro and Messi(2).

Barça's first team squad had been trimmed down with the departures of Gabi Milito, who returned to Argentina to play for Independiente, and Jeffren Suárez, who joined Sporting Lisbon for around €4 million with a buy-back clause in the contract. The day after the Gamper match Gerard Pique tore a muscle in his left leg in training which would put him out of action for a month. With Carles Puyol still about three weeks away from regaining match fitness there were familiar problems for Guardiola to form a defence on the eve of the UEFA Super Cup Final against Europa League winners FC Porto.

The game against Porto would be particularly special for Guardiola. Johan Cruyff, who had given Guardiola his Barcelona debut back in 1990, had become Barça's most successful coach ever when his 'dream team' won eleven trophies in eight seasons between 1988 and 1996. The victory over Real Madrid in the Supercopa earlier in the month had brought Guardiola level on eleven trophies, and now he had the chance to win his twelfth in little more than three years in the job.

Guardiola used a defence of Alves, Mascherano, Abidal and Adriano to face Porto with the surprise inclusion of Keita in place of Busquets in midfield. Both teams struggled a bit with the poor pitch conditions at the Stade Louis II in Monaco but Barça had the better of the first half. Messi opened the scoring in the 39th minute after intercepting a horrendous back pass from Porto's Columbian defender Fredy Guarín, the Argentinian leaving goalkeeper Helton for dead with a shimmy to the right before going left and shooting into the empty net.

Barça stayed in control in the second half though Valdés had to be alert to make a superb save to deny Guarin's long range effort. With just the slim 1-0 lead a Porto equalizer was always on the cards until the 88th minute when substitute Fabregas controlled Messi's chipped pass on his chest before volleying the ball magnificently past Helton to sew things up for Barça. Winning twelve titles out of a possible fifteen was an extraordinary achievement but after the match Guardiola gave the credit to his players, claiming that the "reliability and competitive soul" of his team was the key to their success. "They never fail and they have demonstrated this again in frankly difficult conditions".

With the players' strike now over Barça began their league campaign on the last Monday in August with a home game against Villarreal. Alves was suspended for the game while Adriano had joined Puyol, Piqué, Maxwell and Afellay on the injured list which left Guardiola with an even bigger problem in defence. Before the game the press speculated on what

Guardiola would do, with most feeling he would call up Martin Montoya from the B team to replace Alves, and play him in the back four with Mascherano, Fontás and Abidal. However, there was a surprise when the teams were announced with just Mascherano, Busquets and Abidal in a defence of three.

Guardiola had used a defence of three before but usually it had been a variant on the classic 4-3-3 formation with Alves advancing his position from defence to play wide in midfield. With no Alves, Guardiola reverted to the most Cruyff-like 3-4-3 formation with the diamond midfield of Keita, Thiago, Iniesta and Fabregas and a front three of Alexis, Messi and Pedro. Xavi and Villa were among the substitutes.

The system worked to perfection and Villarreal had little answer to the quick passing and fluidity of movement from Barça. Alexis and Pedro stayed wide to stretch the defence while Messi and Fabregas floated between midfield and attack, supported by the forward dashes of Thiago and Iniesta. It was Thiago who shot Barça ahead after a skilful run to the edge of the area. Then Fabregas, Alexis and Messi twice, scored to complete another 5-0 rout.

Following an international break Barça were back in action with an away game at Real Sociedad. Guardiola saw fit to start with Messi, Iniesta, Abidal, Villa and Mascherano on the bench along with Carles Puyol who was included in the squad for the first time since his operation. Barça reverted to 4-3-3 with Fontás partnering Busquets in central defence and Fabregas playing the Messi false nine role. The game began perfectly for Barça with Xavi and Fabregas putting Barça 0-2 up after just 11 minutes. Things began to go wrong when Alexis pulled a hamstring that would put him out of action for seven weeks. Then Real pulled two goals back in the space of three minutes through Agirretxe and Griezmann. Barça couldn't recover from their lapse and despite the introduction of Messi and Iniesta the game ended in a 2-2 draw.

Guardiola's Barça were not accustomed to throwing away the lead. Three days later AC Milan visited Camp Nou in the first game in Group H of the 2011/12 Champions League. Zlatan Ibrahimovic missed the game through injury which meant Antonio Cassano partnered Alexandre Pato in Milan's attack. Busquets was again chosen to partner Mascherano in defence while Keita continued in the defensive midfield role, and this central core of Barça's defence was exposed almost immediately by Pato's pace. Keita was a yard behind Pato when he received the ball by the halfway line, Mascherano came out to challenge but with a delightful flick Pato knocked the ball into the space behind the Argentinian and sped off in pursuit, Busquets was the man covering and his lack of speed made evident by Pato's sprint and Valdés could do nothing as the Brazilian striker slid the ball under him to put Milan ahead. There were just 24 seconds on the clock.

The brilliance of Leo Messi was responsible for getting Barça back in the game. He had already hit the post with a curling free-kick, then, in the 36th minute, he burst into the penalty area, getting in behind Milan's right back Ignazio Abate before sending a tantalizing ball across the face of the open goal for Pedro to reach first and prod home. David Villa made the score 2-1 soon after half time with a 30-yard free-kick that drifted away from Christian Abbiati's dive, and Barça really should have finished the game off in the second half. However, despite dominating possession Barça lacked incisiveness in the search for a third goal which allowed Milan to grab an injury time equalizer when Thiago Silva headed in from Seedorf's corner.

There was mixed news on the injury front as Carles Puyol returned as a substitute against Milan for his first appearance since the Champions League final at Wembley, but Andrés Iniesta's bad luck with injuries continued with another muscle tear which would see him sidelined for a month. There were suggestions in the Madrid based press that Barça were coming to the end of an era after the two 2-2 draws in a week. The following home game against Osasuna would suggest otherwise.

Guardiola realized the need to keep the players on their toes and to guard against complacency and staleness, and perhaps this was the reason why the defence of three became a much-used option during the 2011/12 season. With Piqué, Alexis and Iniesta out injured, the Barça coach returned to the 3-4-3 (or 3-1-3-3) formation to start against Osasuna with Dani Alves employed in an attacking role on the right wing. All the early danger came from this right side. Alves had already played in a couple of crosses when in the 5th minute he got into the area to head a Busquets pass across the area into the path of Messi who had a simple tap in at the far post.

With Puyol back in defence, Busquets returned to his favoured position as defensive midfielder while the three creative midfielders Xavi, Thiago and Fabregas interchanging positions. It was Fabregas again who was making the best-timed runs forward and in the 13th minute this led to Barça's second goal. Fabregas received a pass from Thiago, chesting the ball down to Messi and then darting in to meet Messi's neat chip over the top with a cracking left-foot volley past Osasuna keeper Andrés Fernández.

Messi was causing havoc with his false-nine position, setting up Abidal of all people, to head against the bar but from an offside position, and then the Argentinian was at the far post again to head Alves's terrific cross against the inside of the post. David Villa was stuck out wide on the left; he had had one early effort on goal saved by the keeper but apart from that he was not seen too much. However, it was a disciplined performance from the Asturian and his patience paid off in the 34th minute when Abidal spotted a hole in the Osasuna defence and threaded a pass through for him to take the ball round Fernandez before firing into the empty net.

Barça were on fire now and there was time for two more goals before half time. Abidal sent a tremendous 60-yard pass forward from deep in Barça's half which gave Villa another chance to head straight for goal. This time, however, his shot hit the goalkeeper, but the unfortunate Roversio Rodrigues couldn't get out of the way as the ball rebounded off him and flew into the net. Then just a minute later Xavi played the ball into the area to Fabregas who turned to set up Messi for what was more like a goal you would see in a five-a-side game. The dominance at half time was not only reflected in the 5-0 scoreline but also in the remarkable 85% possession that Barça had.

Despite the comfortable margin Barça didn't let up in the second half though Guardiola allowed himself the luxury of resting Abidal and Puyol which left Barça with a back three of Adriano, Mascherano and Maxwell. The team continued to push forward and Alves again set up Messi who scooped the ball onto the bar. Then just before the hour Messi turned provider again with a sublime chipped pass over the top to Xavi who controlled well before calmly side-footing a lob over the advanced Fernandez to make it 6-0.

Fabregas had a superb game, linking between midfield and attack. In the 76th minute he got the ball in midfield and started running. He kept running forward as the defence backed off until finally, about 25 yards out, the defence decided to try and intervene. Here, Fabregas got a fortunate rebound, possible on his hand, and suddenly he was clean through on goal. When the goalkeeper came out to meet him he unselfishly touched the ball square to the waiting Villa who scored easily. Three minutes later, Messi made it 8-0 after playing a one-two with Fabregas and dribbling into the area to complete his hat-trick.

Barça: (3-1-3-3) Valdés; Mascherano, Puyol (Maxwell m55), Abidal (Adriano m45); Busquets; Thiago, Xavi (Afellay m61), Fabregas; Alves, Messi, Villa.

Osasuna: (4-4-2) Andrés Fernández; Marc Bertrán, Roversio, Rubén, Raitala (Cejudo m46); Damià, Lolo, Puñal (Timor m77), Lamah; Raúl García (Ibra m63); Nino.

Goals: m5 Messi 1-0, m13 Fabregas 2-0, m34 Villa 3-0, m40 Roversio o.g 4-0, m41 Messi 5-0, m57 Xavi 6-0, m76 Villa 7-0, m79 Messi 8-0.

CHAPTER 33 – AC Milan 2 Barça 3

The 3-4-3 formation had worked a treat in Barça's two home league games. However, for the first 25 minutes of the next game, away at early league leaders Valencia, it looked a complete mess. Jordi Alba and Jeremy Mathieu caused all sorts of problems to the right side of Barça's defence and Puyol was often pulled across to cover Mascherano, leaving Abidal alone to defend any crosses. After 12 minutes Mathieu got past Mascherano and when his cross came in Abidal, under pressure, could only divert the ball into his own goal. Despite a quick equalizer from Pedro and a very strong shout for a penalty from Messi, Valencia continued to provoke havoc down the left, and after just 22 minutes another Mathieu cross found Pablo Hernandez who put Valencia 2-1 up. Guardiola reverted to 4-3-3 with Alves moving back from the right wing and some order was restored. Barça worked their way back into the game but it wasn't until fifteen minutes from the end that Fabregas equalized to earn Barça a point from a thrilling 2-2 draw.

Having conceded six goals in the last four matches there were obviously a lot of concerns about the defence. However, despite Piqué and Puyol struggling with injuries Barça were about to embark on run of nine games without conceding a goal. Most of the credit for this can go to Mascherano and Abidal who both hit form at the same time, playing well whether in a defence of three or a back four, while Victor Valdés was also performing splendidly.

The run began with a blistering demolition of Atlético Madrid. Guardiola left both Puyol and Piqué on the bench, but still came out with the 3-4-3, playing Valdés, Alves, Mascherano, Abidal, Busquets, Xavi, Thiago, Fàbregas, Pedro, Messi and Villa. The superb Xavi led the orchestra, setting up Villa to put Barça into an early lead, and soon after Atlético defender João Miranda scored in his own goal after goalkeeper Thibaut Courtois had blocked Messi's effort. It was then time for Messi to begin another extraordinary display of his goalscoring abilities. First, in the 26th minute he took a throw-in near the right corner flag and received the return from Pedro, cutting inside he beat one defender to the ball then darted past two more with one quick change of direction into the area before fooling Courtois with a quickfire shot inside the near post. Messi continued to threaten throughout the second half. There was one electric run which began when he received the ball from Valdés's punch and ended with a yellow card for Luis Perea for a foul on the edge of Atlético's area. Then Messi grabbed his second of the game after another exhilarating run. Receiving the ball 40 yards out he went past Perea and Miranda as he surged into the area and when Diego Godin came across Messi fired through his legs and past Courtois into the far corner. The icing on the cake came in the 90th minute. Messi again started the move about 40 yards out. After playing a quick one-two with Villa he sped into the left side of the area to shoot low past Courtois from a tight angle to complete his hat-trick and a 5-0 victory.

In the press conference after the game Guardiola was asked about the *acción de resposibilidad* that had been presented by the club against ex-president Joan Laporta and the previous board of directors. The *acción* was demanding a payment of €47.6 million for alleged misappropriation of club funds, but Guardiola showed he was clearly against the move: "I feel a lot of affection for the previous board for giving me the chance. What's happening right now makes me sad. I understand the law, but that board of directors did extraordinary things, taking over the club when it was in a much more precarious situation than now, building a wonderful team. I don't know how this will end but I know they are suffering a lot and they don't deserve that...this is all doing a lot of damage to the club."

Guardiola's comment caused an uproar in the press about the possibility of a confrontation between the coach and Barça's board. Sandro Rosell travelled with the team for Barça's first ever visit to Belarus the following Wednesday for the Champions League clash with BATE Borisov. Before the match he was pictured shaking hands with Guardiola, and he would later say that "the subject is closed, it is history, I have nothing more to say". Meanwhile, Isaac Cuenca was included in the squad for the first time and the team continued in fine form. Playing with Xavi as the holding man in midfield with Thiago and Keita, Barça needed a bit of luck with an own goal from Aleksandr Volodko to get started but then Pedro, Messi twice and Villa scored to complete an easy 0-5 victory.

October began with a game at bottom-of-the-table Sporting Gijon. Fabregas was injured in training the day before the game but Pedro played his role, combining through the middle with Messi as Guardiola again went with 3-4-3. Adriano was given the right wing position and he responded with the only goal of the match in the 12th minute, latching on to the rebound after Xavi hit the post. Curiously, when Abidal had to come off with a muscle strain early in the second half, Guardiola replaced him with Maxwell but then immediately brought on Piqué in place of Pedro and reverted to a back four, suggesting the importance Guardiola gave to the speedy Abidal in the risky back three system. The win put Barça top of the league on 14 points, ahead of Levante on goal difference and one point above Real Madrid.

Comfortable home wins followed over Racing Santander (3-0) and Viktoria Plsen (2-0). Andrés Iniesta returned to the team against Racing and he was instrumental in setting up Messi for two goals. In between Messi's brace Xavi Hernandez got into the area to score an old-fashioned centre-forward's goal, heading in Pedro's cross from the by-line. Iniesta then got an early goal against Viktoria though Barça didn't secure the points until Villa made it 2-0 in the 82nd minute. Isaac Cuenca got his first team debut replacing Villa near the end.

Barça began with the 3-4-3 formation for the following game at home to Sevilla. However, after a poor first 25 minutes, Guardiola switched Adriano from right wing to left back and the team reshuffled to a 4-3-3. Barça improved but still couldn't find a way through as the game remained goalless. Then in the 92nd minute Iniesta was brought down inside the area by Federico Fazio and a penalty was awarded. Frédéric Kanouté succeeded in delaying the penalty for almost three minutes, first by kicking the ball off the spot and then by tangling with Fabregas which started a melee which ended with Kanouté's sending off. The delaying tactics paid their dividends when Messi hit his penalty hesitantly and Sevilla keeper Javi Varas ended an excellent performance by diving to his left to save. The two points dropped from the goalless draw meant Levante went top of the league after nine weeks, a point above Real Madrid and two points above third-placed Barça.

A midweek game at newly-promoted Granada followed with Guardiola giving a first start to Cuenca who played the entire game on the left side of attack. A free kick curled in by Xavi after half an hour proved to be the only goal of an uninspiring game while Pedro took a knock on the heel which would see him sidelined for a couple of weeks. Attention was drawn to the fact that Messi had now gone three games without a goal but the player responded with a first half hat-trick in the next match against Mallorca at Camp Nou. After firing home the first goal from the penalty spot Messi celebrated by giving a one-two-three gesture with his fingers while winking directly at the TV cameras in a clear reaction to the suggestion from some parts of the press that he might be in a 'crisis'. Cuenca was given another chance, this time on the right wing, and early in the second half he dribbled past Mallorca keeper Dudu Aouate before firing into the roof of the net for his first goal for the team. With half an hour remaining Guardiola decided to give the 17-year-old Gerard Deulofeu his first-team debut while Piqué and Puyol also came on, returning from their respective injuries. Dani Alves scored near the end with a splendid dipping drive that went in off the underside of the crossbar to complete Barça's favourite 5-0 scoreline.

Messi followed his three goals against Mallorca with another hat-trick at Viktoria Plsen in the Champions League. Piqué and Puyol were back in defence to help Victor Valdés go past Miguel Reina's all-time Barça record, set in the 1972/73 season, of 824 minutes without conceding a goal. Cuenca and Adriano played on the wings while false nine Messi was supported by Fabregas and Thiago from midfield, with Fabregas getting the other goal in a 0-4 win. Alexis Sanchez returned after two months out with injury to play the last twenty minutes. Before the match news had come in that Milan had only drawn 1-1 at BATE Borisov which meant Barça's victory took them two points above Milan at the top of Group H.

Valdés's unbeaten run came to an end 19 minutes into the following game at San Mames when Ander Herrera took advantage of Mascherano's slip to put Athletic Club 1-0 up in what proved to be a thrilling battle between the sides. Guardiola was a self-confessed fan of Athletic's eccentric new coach Marcelo 'El Loco' Bielsa, and both sides played a similar high pressing game. Guardiola had close to a full strength team with the exception of Pedro, so Messi began on the right with Fabregas as false nine while Adriano was preferred to Villa for the left wing. It didn't take long for Barça to equalize when Fabregas headed Abidal's cross firmly past Gorka Iraizoz. The pouring rain didn't help conditions but there were chances at both ends as the score remained 1-1. Guardiola brought on Alexis and Villa in place of Xavi and Adriano but the subsequent readjustments, with Fabregas moving back to midfield and Messi reverting to the false nine role, didn't appear to improve things. Poor concentration defending a corner ten minutes from the end led to Abidal's mishit clearance ricocheting off Fernando Llorente and then Piqué and in for an own goal. Messi made it 2-2 in the 92nd minute taking advantage of Athletic's own version of slapstick defending. A point had been saved but two had still been dropped and Madrid took advantage to go three points clear at the top of the table.

The campaign for the 2011/12 Copa del Rey began early for Barça, due to the coming participation in the FIFA Club World Cup, with a game against neighbours L'Hospitalet. Guardiola lost his South American stars plus Spanish under-21 players Cuenca and Thiago due to an international break. Johnathan Dos Santos came in at right back and the team also included Fontás and Tello. A scorching 25-yard drive from Andrés Iniesta gave Barça a 0-1 first leg lead on Hospitalet's artificial pitch and there was a first team debut for Thiago's brother Rafinha who came on for the last 15 minutes.

The international break meant Barça didn't return to action for ten days before receiving Zaragoza at Camp Nou. The game was played four days before an important Champions League match in Milan, and with that in mind Guardiola initially left Iniesta, Villa, Abidal, Mascherano, Busquets and Pedro on the bench. Alexis Sanchez made his first start for ten weeks alongside Messi and Cuenca in attack but it was a central defender, Piqué, who put Barça in front, heading home from Xavi's free kick. Messi fired in a second before half time before the other centre back, Puyol, forced in a third early in the second half. Thiago, Iniesta and Villa came on as substitutes and Villa scored the final goal in a 4-0 victory, though there was worse luck for Iniesta who finished the game with a thigh strain that would see him miss the next two games.

Barça travelled to Milan without the injured Iniesta and Adriano and the suspended Alves, but there was more worrying news when it was revealed that Tito Vilanova was also absent due to needing an operation to remove a tumour from his parotid gland. The five-hour operation took place on November 22, the day before the Milan game and Vilanova received many messages of support with perhaps the most surprising coming from José Mourinho who declared during a press conference: "I have a message for him. If last year we showed solidarity with Abidal, we do the same with Tito Vilanova. May he return quickly to his family and his team. I hope he is here full of health on the tenth (December 10 - the day of the next Madrid-Barça *Clásico*). We will be delighted to greet him." Surprisingly Vilanova would recover in time to make that trip but he would not return to training until December 7 and his reincorporation would be gradual.

Despite the undoubted quality of Milan with Zlatan Ibrahimovic leading the attack in his first game against his ex-team, Guardiola opted again for the 3-4-3, knowing that a win would confirm top spot in Champions League Group H. Milan played with a 4-4-2 system with a diamond midfield with Kevin-Prince Boateng as the attacking point of the diamond trying to surprise the Barça defence with runs towards the wings. However, Milan's system had little width going forward which gave a certain logic to Guardiola's decision. Puyol and Abidal flanked Mascherano in the defence of three with Busquets just in front of them always ready to drop back to cover. Xavi and Keita formed the next line with Thiago starting as the attacking point of the diamond, while Fabregas started as a false nine with Messi on the right and Villa on the left.

Milan started enthusiastically, pinning Barça back for the first three minutes, but then the first chance fell to the visitors after Thiago cleverly left Messi's pass for Villa who shot well over. With both teams playing the pressing game the San Siro was treated to some fantastic fast one touch passing though it looked quite risky at times as both teams played their way out from the back. Milan also posed the aerial threat and the first high ball in to Ibrahimovic ended with Thiago heading back dangerously to Valdés.

After about twelve minutes Thiago switched to the right which meant Messi came inside with Fabregas moving back to midfield. Almost immediately the move brought results as Thiago did well to maintain possession by the corner flag. The ball came back to Fabregas and then on to Messi who spotted Keita's surge forward on the left. When Keita received Messi's pass he sent a low ball across goal which Xavi would surely have converted had ex-blaugrana Marc Van Bommel not arrived first to nudge the ball over his own goal-line.

Barça might easily have made it 0-2 a couple of minutes later when Thiago went on a tricky run into the area before sending a pass through to Fabregas who volleyed goalwards only to be denied by Abbiati's legs. Milan then came back with Ibrahimovic twice causing problems with crosses from the left, the second time the ball came back across from Boateng on the right and Robinho four yards out could only turn the ball over the crossbar. Milan's effort was rewarded soon after. Seedorf received a long ball out on the left where Puyol had given him a little room, he controlled quickly and sent the ball inside to Ibrahimovic. Busquets and Mascherano couldn't react in time and the big Swede slid the ball past Valdés for the equalizer.

At this point the speed of incidence was so fast it was difficult to keep up. In the 22nd minute Xavi held on to the ball long enough to create room for Fabregas whose cross found Messi three yards out but Messi's touch hit Abate and the ball flew up and clipped the bar on the way over. The pressure again was now all coming from Barça as Villa headed wide and Abate robbed Messi in a dangerous position. Xavi made another run into the area after Fabregas flicked the ball into space, and as Xavi honed in on goal Alberto Alquilani pulled him back and a penalty was awarded. Alquilani should have been sent off for his second yellow card but Nesta fooled the ref into thinking he was the culprit and he took the yellow card instead. Messi's penalty was deemed illegal as he dummied during his run-up, earning a rather absurd yellow card. Messi was unruffled by it all and stepped up again to fire past Abbiati's dive.

Barça might have made it 1-3 soon after. Messi set off like an arrow for the area before slipping the ball left to Villa who shot but was desperately unlucky to see Abbiati's arm deflect the ball down onto the ground before bouncing up over the bar. The reply from Milan was a poor shot wide from Boateng and then Messi went on one of his impossible dribbles into the area but his shot was saved by the diving Abbiati. Milan finished the half strongly forcing cards on Mascherano and Puyol, while Keita took one between the legs in the line of duty to block a goalbound effort. The half ended with Thiago Silva heading a corner just wide in what would have been a carbon copy of his equalizer at Camp Nou.

Barça began the second half more strongly. Messi had a shot into the side-netting after a good cross from Fabregas, and Villa had another effort wide. Milan reacted with a tremendous goal out of the blue on 53 minutes. Mascherano headed the ball away and Boateng leapt acrobatically to control the ball before beating Abidal with a delightful flick and driving low past Valdés at his near post. Barça were undeterred, with no move to sit back and hold on for a valuable draw. The visitors went straight back at Milan and within ten minutes Xavi had made it 2-3 after another well timed dart into the area to get on to Messi's pass and fire low past Abbiati into the corner.

The intensity dropped in the last half an hour as Milan tired and Barça looked to control things. Alexis and Pedro came on to continue the chasing up front and Milan struggled to cause more danger. Alexis and Puyol couldn't force home Thiago's curled free kick and Xavi couldn't quite emulate Messi with a dribble through the middle. Seedorf who had a fine game for Milan caused Barça a few worries near the end with a dangerous centre but apart from that the Barça defence held out without too many problems. In the final minute Busquets did well to stretch to cut out a through ball and that was that. Barça confirmed top spot in Group H and Guardiola would now be able to rest players for the final group match against BATE Borisov which was scheduled to be played just before Barça's league visit to the Bernabéu.

AC Milan: Abbiati; Zambrotta, Nesta (Bonera m66), Thiago Silva, Abate; Van Bommel (Nocerino m72), Seedorf, Aquilani, Boateng; Ibrahimovic, Robinho (Pato m45)

Barça: Valdés; Puyol, Mascherano, Abidal; Busquets, Xavi, Keita, Fabregas (Pedro m80); Thiago (Dos Santos m91), Messi, Villa (Alexis m67).

Goals: m14 Van Bommel (o.g.) 0-1, m19 Ibrahimovic 1-1, m30 Messi (pen) 1-2, m53 Boateng 2-2, m63 Xavi 2-3.

CHAPTER 34 – Real Madrid 1 Barça 3

The victory in Milan took Barça's unbeaten run to 27 games but the sequence came to an end with a league match at lowly Getafe who only had two previous victories to their name in the season. Barça reverted to a 4-3-3 formation but showed a lack of punch up front to break through Getafe's packed defence. Getafe hardly had an attack but in the 67th minute they won their second corner of the game. When the corner came in Piqué mistimed his jump and Juan Valera got between Busquets and Keita to head past the motionless Valdés. Barça tried to react but Getafe defended solidly. In the final minute Messi looked sure to equalize but his shot came back off the far post and Getafe keeper Miguel Angel Moya saved Pedro's attempt from the rebound. The 27-game unbeaten run counted for little now as Real Madrid moved six points clear at the top of the table.

There was a chance for Barça to cut the difference with a midweek game at home to Rayo Vallecano that was brought forward due to Barça's coming participation in the FIFA Club World Cup. Early on in the game Barça struggled against Rayo's high pressing game but then Guardiola moved Dani Alves further forward while Alexis and Villa swapped wings. It was Alexis's move to the left that brought most dividends with the Chilean grabbing two quick goals before Villa added a third before half time. Messi made it 4-0 early in the second half with a magnificent goal. He received the ball on the half-way line and laid it off quickly to Alves while spinning and setting off to receive the return pass. Javi Fuego came across but Messi sped outside him and darted into the area from the right. The angle wasn't great but Messi took one touch with his right foot to line the ball up on his left with which he made no mistake squeezing the ball inside the far post. The victory reduced the gap at the top of La Liga to three points though Madrid now had a game in hand.

Guardiola kept everybody guessing about his tactics by returning to the 3-4-3 for the following home game with Levante. The system was proving to be the one that suited Fabregas best and from his attacking midfield role he opened the scoring after just three minutes with a low shot past Gustavo Munua from the edge of the area. Fabregas then headed in from Xavi's cross before Isaac Cuanca added a third before half time. The other forwards Messi and Alexis added second half goals to complete another 5-0 rout. Credit was also due to Mascherano, Puyol and Abidal who were proving to be the best defensive threesome for the 3-4-3. The team could now boast the impressive record of 39 goals scored without conceding in the nine league games played at Camp Nou since the start of the season. However, Madrid's win at Sporting maintained their three-point advantage a week before the *Clásico*.

Before meeting at the Bernabéu, Barça and Madrid both had to play the final game of their respective Champions League groups. On the Tuesday night Barça played host to BATE Borisov. Guardiola was able to reserve all eleven of the players who would start in the *Clásico*, putting out a team of youngsters that included Martin Montoya, Marc Bartra, Andreu Fontás, Sergi Roberto, Johnathan dos Santos, Isaac Cuenca and the two Alcántara brothers, Thiago and Rafinha. The youngsters put on a fine show with Sergi Roberto putting Barça in front with his first goal for the first team after half an hour. The second half belonged to Cuenca who set up Montoya and Pedro for Barça's second and third goal before being brought down for a late penalty which Pedro converted to leave the final score at 4-0. The following night Mourinho could also reserve key players for Madrid's 0-3 win at Ajax though Fabio Coentrao, Kaká, Benzema and Higuian all started the game while Xabi Alonso played the last half hour.

Barça received a massive boost for the trip to Madrid with Tito Vilanova being given medical clearance to travel to the game, though as a precaution he took the train and not the plane with the rest of Barça's expedition. Both coaches had small surprises to their team selection.

Guardiola left David Villa on the bench, Alexis started up front with Fabregas and Messi, while the in-form Mascherano was left out in favour of restoring the Piqué-Puyol partnership in a defence of four. Mourinho left out Khedira and played the more attacking Ozil in midfield in Madrid's more usual 4-2-3-1 shape.

Directly from Barça's kick off the ball came back to Valdés, and Puyol and Pique went very wide as Madrid pushed up. Valdés passed to Puyol who under pressure played the ball back to Valdés who then made a hash of his next pass sending the ball directly to Di Maria who was only 35 yards out. Puyol and Piqué were out of the game and Di Maria tried to get the ball in quickly to Benzema, Busquets managed to get in the way but the ball came back to Ozil who shot, hitting Busquets again and before anybody could react Benzema had pounced and volleyed the ball home from close range. There were only 22 seconds on the clock and it was a terrible blow for Barça to take so early.

Messi tried to get Barça straight back in the game. After robbing Sergio Ramos, he got into the area and shot under pressure from three defenders but Casillas got down low to the left to save. Madrid kept up a high pressing game but Busquets and Xavi slowly started playing Barça back into the game. Benzema had a weak header that didn't trouble Valdés too much, then in the 16th minute Cristiano Ronaldo made his first good run but Valdés kept his concentration to beat away the powerful shot. At the other end Xavi curled a free kick that Casillas punched away for a corner. Then Ronaldo had his best chance of the first half but he sent his shot well wide after Benzema had pulled Barça's defence out of position.

Soon after this, Guardiola made the tactical change that would be crucial to the win. Alves advanced his position on the right and Alexis, who had had little luck on the left, moved to the middle. On the half hour Messi collected the ball in midfield and set off on a splendid run before playing the ball into Alexis who showed strength to hold off Pepe's challenge, speed to get away from Coentrao and composure to shoot across Casillas into the far corner for the equalizer.

Madrid looked shocked, they hadn't seen this coming, and all of a sudden Barça were in control, stroking the ball around comfortably, always seeming to release the ball just before the opponent could challenge. Pepe was slightly fortunate when he swung a leg at Alexis but there was not enough contact for the referee to give a penalty. Messi, who already had a yellow card for protesting, clattered into Alonso but a second yellow would have been harsh despite the howls at the ref from the Bernabéu.

The second half began with another push from Madrid and they managed to win a couple of free kicks in dangerous positions. Ronaldo hit the first into the wall and the second was well held by Valdés after a bounce in front of him. However, it was Barça who were looking the better team, Iniesta was only prevented by a good tackle from Coentrao and a minute later Iniesta again caused problems getting into the area on the left, Madrid managed to clear the ball but only as far as Xavi who fired a vicious volley towards goal that hit Marcelo and spun out of Casillas reach bouncing in off the post. This was certainly a stroke of luck for Barça but not undeserved on the run of play.

Madrid tried to keep pressuring Barça's defence in possession and there was another kick from Valdés that might have given Benzema another chance if Alves hadn't been quick to intervene. Abidal then did well to recover after his own mistake but Madrid were struggling to get near Valdes's goal. Barça's dominance increased with time, Alexis had an angled shot stopped by Casillas's feet and Messi fired a free kick just wide. However, in the 67th minute, Madrid had the chance that could have changed everything. Xabi Alonso hadn't been seen much in forward positions but his cross found three Madrid players unmarked in front of goal, Ronaldo was about ten yards out but his header was poor and Barça breathed again. From a possible 2-2 Barça went forward with one of those long passing build-ups that are such a joy when they end in a goal. The move finished with Messi playing the ball out to Alves on the right and Alves's fine cross was met by Fabregas who had sprinted from the half way line to stay in front of Coentrao to head past Casillas at the far post from close range.

The last twenty minutes were totally controlled by Barça as Madrid were passed into submission. Iniesta was in particularly good form and in the last few minutes he made at least four charges in from the left that really should have led to another goal. However, the 1-3 final score line left no doubt about who had been the better team. Piqué and Puyol had dominated at the back, Busquets and Xavi had organised perfectly, and Messi and Iniesta had driven Madrid's defenders nuts with their mazy runs. With the Club World Cup in Japan next on the agenda Barça were looking back to their brilliant best.

Real Madrid: Casillas; Coentrao, Pepe, Sergio Ramos, Marcelo; Xabi Alonso, Lass (Khedira m64); Di Maria (Higuain m70), Ozil (Kaká m60), Ronaldo; Benzema.

Barça: Valdés; Alves, Piqué, Puyol, Abidal; Xavi, Busquets, Iniesta (Pedro m88); Messi, Fabregas (Keita m78), Alexis (Villa m83).

Goals: m1 Benzema 1-0, m30 Alexis 1-1, m53 Xavi 1-2, m68 Fabregas 1-3.

CHAPTER 35 Santos 0 Barça 4

Guardiola named 23 players for the trip to Japan for the 2011 FIFA Club World Cup. The only unavailable first team player was Ibrahim Afellay while B team players Johnathan dos Santos, Oier Olazábal and Isaac Cuenca came in to make up the numbers. Tito Vilanova remained in Barcelona to continue his recuperation process.

Barça's first test was against Qatari side Al Saad in the semi-final on Thursday 15 December. Pep Guardiola made six changes to the team that won at the Bernabéu, Valdés, Puyol, Abidal, Iniesta and Messi retained their places while Adriano, Mascherano, Keita, Thiago, Pedro and Villa came in for Alves, Piqué, Busquets, Xavi, Fabregas and Alexis.

The pattern for the semi-final was set right from the start with Al Sadd retreating into the last third of the field in a 5-4-1 shape. The problem for Barça was the lack of space around the area but the Qataris didn't look good enough to hold out for long. The Al Saad keeper Mohamed Saqr did well to save a low shot from Villa but then in the 25th minute defender Nadir Belhadj failed to clear Pedro's cross from the left, instead knocking the ball back awkwardly for his goalkeeper who hesitated for a split second as he realised he couldn't pick the ball up, allowing Adriano the chance to rush him, Saqr tried to clear but the ball hit Adriano's knee and flew into the net.

Villa was working hard in the centre forward position but he often found himself surrounded by a pack of defenders. In the 34th minute he did well to create a shooting opportunity for Iniesta and when Iniesta's shot was parried by Saqr, Villa was there to stick home the rebound only to be denied by the linesman who had correctly seen that he had drifted half a yard offside. Villa's luck got much worse a minute later. Chasing a long pass from Iniesta, he battled into the area with two defenders but he landed awkwardly on his left leg and immediately signalled to the bench. A fractured tibia would later be confirmed, bringing an end to the Asturian's season.

Alexis came on and went straight to centre forward and Barça continued to dominate totally. Just before half time Thiago stabbed a quick vertical pass for Adriano's diagonal run from the right and Adriano grabbed his second with a low shot that Saqr will feel he should have done more to stop. Keita and Maxwell added second half goals to earn a 4-0 win and put Barça into the final against the winners of the Copa Libertadores, Santos. However, Alexis had to come off with a strained thigh muscle which would leave Guardiola with selection doubts for the final. Messi's failure to get on the score sheet left him needing a goal against Santos to equal Pedro's 2009 record of scoring in six club competitions in one calendar year.

The great Pele had led Santos to two Intercontinental Cups back in 1962 and 1963 but this was their first intercontinental final since then. Now the star for Santos was undoubtedly the 19–year-old Neymar da Silva Santos Júnior who was being hailed by some as Pele's heir with even Pele saying: "Neymar has the ability to be better than me". Santos had plenty more talent with Paulo Henrique Ganso and Elano Blumer in midfield, Danilo Luiz da Silva at right back and main striker Humberlito Borges. Neymar, Danilo and Borges had scored the goals in Santos's 3-1 win over Japanese champions Kashiwa Reysol in the other semi-final.

With Alexis, Villa and Afellay all unavailable for the final, Guardiola had fewer options for who to play up front with Messi. Pedro and Cuenca were the only other true forwards though the versatility of Adriano, Iniesta, Fabregas and Thiago offered plenty of solutions. In the end Guardiola opted for his 3-4-3 formation with Thiago on the left wing and Alves on the right. Busquets, Xavi, Fabregas and Iniesta made up an imposing quartet in midfield, while Puyol, Piqué and Abidal formed the defence of three in front of Valdés.

From the kick off Santos sat back in a 4-3-1-2 formation and for the first few minutes they managed to prevent Barça's one-twos from getting into the area. Neymar got his first run in the 8th minute after Alves's poor pass but Puyol, who was excellent throughout at the back, was on top of the youngster to clear up. Then in the 13th minute Piqué gave a risky ball out of defence but the ball came through to Messi who got his first chance to run at the Santos defence, Messi's shot was parried by keeper Rafael Cabral and Thiago's rebound lacked power which allowed Cabral time to recover.

Barça had been warned of the danger of Santos's free kicks and in the 14th minute Borges won a free kick off Piqué on the edge of the area but when Neymar touched the free kick to Ganso, the midfielder fired wide. There may have been an early illusion of equality but it wasn't to last long. Alves showed one of the reasons for Barça's success by chasing back 50 yards to rob Neymar in full flight. Within a minute Barça were in front. Fabregas combined with Messi on the right and Xavi showed his immense class to control Fabregas's pass that was flying past his right side a metre off the ground by lifting his leg backwards and to the side, the control was sublime and then we had the speed of vision as Xavi found Messi in the area, and the Argentinian equalled Pedro's 6 in 6 record with a little flick over the advancing goalkeeper that also eluded the spectacular effort from Edu Dracena to clear off the line.

The goal gave Barça confidence and with the constant interchanging of positions and fast movement of the ball, gaps began to appear in the Brazilian defence. In the 24th minute Alves found Xavi on the edge of the area and after another excellent control he fired low under Cabral from 14 yards to make it 2-0, leaving Santos with an uphill struggle. Messi nearly made it three soon after but Dracena got in a last minute tackle after Messi's one-two with Fabregas. Santos had a brief reaction when Ganso found Borges who got a yard away from Iniesta to shoot but Valdés got down low to his right to save.

There wasn't much more from Santos in the first half although Piqué got a yellow card for a foul on Neymar. Fabregas might have added Barça's third after ghosting in to beat the offside trap but his shot came out off the post. But Fabregas would get his goal just before the break after Alves and Messi had caused havoc in the Santos defence. Messi's backheel found Alves running to the byline, Alves's cross was pushed out by the diving Cabral who also managed to get in the way of Thiago's header but he could do nothing as Fabregas coolly placed his shot just inside the post.

Despite being 3-0 up Barça came out for the second half showing ambition for more goals. Straight after the kick off Fabregas won the ball in the Santos half but when Messi returned the ball Fabregas's shot was well saved low by the post by Cabral. There were more chances as Alves inexplicably headed Thiago's cross back to Thiago instead of into the gaping net, and then Messi had a chance from Fabregas's cross but Cabral closed his legs in time to save. Santos showed their class with a good counter attack with Neymar and Ganso combining to set up Borges but Valdés was out quickly to close the angle and save. Then perhaps Barça got too over-confident as Xavi got caught out for once allowing Ganso to send a good ball for Neymar to chase, but Valdés did well again to save as Neymar shot under pressure from Abidal.

Barça seems to awake to the danger of the Santos counter and began restoring order to the game. Puyol was magnificent in denying Ganso but the Santos threat was fading. As the game neared the end Barça looked for a fourth, Fabregas was denied by the keeper's feet and then Alves was denied by the post after substitute Pedro had taken advantage of a moment of hesitation in the Santos defence. Then, in the 82nd minute, Alves played in Messi who skipped round Cabral to score into the empty net. Another classy finish but all in a day's work for Messi. Alves had a fine game on the right of attack but he was destined not to score himself. Right near the end he fired over from a good position after Pedro's chest down. Perhaps a *manita* would have been too much to ask for.

Santos coach Muricy Ramalho was full of praise for the victors. "I think people already knew about the quality of Barcelona. They lost Alexis and Villa and they put another player in midfield. They played a 3-7-0, a system that would be absurd in Brazil." For the second time in three years Barça were champions of the world. For Guardiola it meant an incredible thirteenth title out of sixteen played for.

Santos: (4-3-1-2) Cabral; Danilo (Elano m31), Dracena, Bruno Rodrigo, Leo; Durval, Henrique, Arouca; Ganso (Ibsen m83); Neymar, Borges (Kardec m78).

Barça: (3-4-3) Valdés; Puyol (Fontás m85), Piqué (Mascherano m56), Abidal; Busquets, Xavi, Iniesta, Fabregas; Alves, Messi, Thiago (Pedro m79).

Goals: m17 Messi 0-1, m24 Xavi 0-2, m45 Fabregas 0-3, m82 Messi 0-4.

CHAPTER 36 – Real Madrid 1 Barça 2

There was no relaxing from the new world champions. Three days before Christmas, L'Hospitalet visited Camp Nou for the 2nd leg of the Copa del Rey tie. Seydou Keita, Eric Abidal and the South American players were given early Christmas holidays which meant that apart from Pinto in goal, the ten outfield players, and subsequently the three substitutes, had all passed through the *cantera*. It was still a very strong team put out by Guardiola with seven of Spain's World Cup winning squad in the starting XI. The 56,000 fans were treated to another blistering display of attacking football as poor Hospitalet were blown away. Pedro, Iniesta, Thiago (2), Xavi, Cristian Tello (2) and Cuenca (2) scored the goals in a 9-0 victory, Barça's biggest win since 1979. The night was not perfect as Andres Iniesta picked up a hamstring injury, though the recovery time coincided with the Christmas break. Tello gave a man-of-the-match performance after coming on for Xavi with the score already at 4-0, scoring twice and setting up one of Cuenca's goals.

Two weeks later Barça began 2012 with another Copa del Rey game at Camp Nou, this time against Osasuna in the last 16. Leo Messi was declared sick on the morning of the game, but after going home to rest he recovered enough to be named as one of the substitutes. Barça played a 3-4-3 which often became a 3-3-4 with Cuenca and Fabregas combining through the middle and within 18 minutes Fabregas had scored twice, the second a sublime lob over Osasuna's keeper Asier Riesgo. Barça continued to dominate but the third goal wouldn't come so with half an hour remaining Guardiola decided to put on Messi. The move had its desired effect with the Argentinian heading home from Fabregas's cross and then completing a 4-0 victory with a clinical finish from the edge of the area in stoppage time.

Barça returned to league action with the local derby against Espanyol at Cornellà-El Prat. Iniesta had recovered from his hamstring injury, allowing Guardiola to play the same XI that had won 1-3 at the Bernabéu a month earlier with Alves, Messi and Alexis up front in a 3-4-3 formation. However, despite Fabregas heading in the opening goal from Alves's cross on 16 minutes, Barça failed to control the game in which Espanyol showed more hunger. The home side was eventually rewarded for the effort when substitute Alvaro Vazquez escaped Puyol's attention to head in the equalizer five minutes from the end. Barça might have won the game in injury time but Gerard Piqué's shot bounced out off the crossbar and then the referee failed to see that Pedro's rebound was stopped by Raul Rodriguez's raised arm. The 1-1 draw meant that Madrid moved five points clear at the top of the table.

The following day Leo Messi picked up his third Ballon d'Or as Barça dominated the 2011 FIFA Awards. Xavi and Iniesta were voted third and fourth, respectively, Piqué and Alves were included in FIFA's best XI, and Pep Guardiola was awarded his second Coach of the Year award. In his acceptance speech Guardiola spoke in English as he recognized the work of coaches around the world while saluting the work of the thousands of people who had been involved in different capacities during more than 100 years working to make Barça one of the best football clubs in the world. He reserved a special dedication at the end in Catalan for Tito Vilanova, "my friend, my companion, my assistant...this one's for you, Tito".

On the day of the return leg of the cup tie with Osasuna it was confirmed that after 89 appearances and two goals for Barça, Maxwell Andrade would be moving to the new big money club in Europe, Paris Saint Germain. With a four-goal advantage from the first leg, Guardiola rested several regular starters putting out a young team that included Montoya, Fontás, Sergi Roberto, Thiago, Cuenca and Pedro. It was to be a disastrous night for Fontás who collapsed after just ten minutes after jarring his leg badly. A cruciate ligament injury would later be confirmed, finishing the season for the young defender. Dejan Lekic gave Osasuna brief hope of a miraculous comeback when he fired low past Pinto in the 40th minute. However, Alexis made it 1-1 on the night immediately after half time and substitute Leo Messi set up Sergi Roberto for the winner with twenty minutes remaining. The 6-1 aggregate win earned Barça a place in the quarter finals where they would face another head-to-head with Real Madrid.

Before meeting Madrid there was a home league game against tenth-placed Betis to take care of, which turned out to be more difficult than expected. Guardiola again went for a 3-4-3 with Puyol, Mascherano and Abidal at the back, the ridiculously talented quartet of Busquets, Xavi, Iniesta and Fabregas in midfield with Cuenca, Messi and Alexis up front. With Pep Guardiola and Pepe Mel in charge of the teams the entertainment was assured as both sides pressed high up the pitch. There were early chances for Betis with Valdés twice needing to save from Jorge Molina. However, Barça took the lead after ten minutes when Fabregas hit the post and Xavi was on hand to score from the rebound. A couple of minutes later Messi got away from the attentions of the defence to meet Alexis's cross and stab the ball in from close range. Betis weren't deterred by this double setback. Ruben Castro pulled a goal back after half an hour, Victor Valdés conceding his first league goal of the season at Camp Nou after Barça had scored an incredible 41 at the other end. Then five minutes into the second half Roque Santa Cruz fired in from the edge of the area to make it 2-2. Alexis was on in place of Cuenca but anxiety was creeping into Barça's game. When the referee ignored a clear penalty on Iniesta with twenty minutes to go it looked like it might not be Barça's night. However, a minute later Betis were down to ten men after Mario Alvarez received a second yellow card for illegally stopping Messi's run. The numerical advantage worked in Barça's favour; in the 75th minute Xavi sent Alexis through to fire past Betis keeper Casto, and Messi made the final score 4-2 with an injury time penalty.

The Betis game brought concerns about the freshness of the team, and while the 3-4-3 system produced some thrilling football, it was looking somewhat risky at times when consistency was needed to keep the pressure on Real Madrid. There were signs that Madrid were not in their best moment either after they needed late goals from Higuain and Jose Callejon to win 1-2 in Mallorca to retain the five-point advantage at the top of the table. Now, after already facing each other seven times in the previous nine months, the two great teams would meet again in the Copa del Rey quarter finals.

Madrid were without the injured Khedira and Di Maria while Arboloa was suspended for the first leg at the Bernabéu. Mourinho surprised by opting for Hamit Altintop at right back, while at left back Coentrao was preferred over Marcelo. Carvalho was brought in to partner Sergio Ramos in defence which allowed Pepe to be used again in a destructive role in midfield alongside Xabi Alonso and Lass Diarra. Up front, Higuain and Benzema, who usually alternated as Madrid's main striker, both started along with Cristiano Ronaldo. Mourinho's intentions were clear. Madrid would work very hard to try and close down any space near their penalty area while trying to break quickly. Guardiola went for an eleven of Pinto, Alves, Puyol, Piqué, Abidal, Xavi, Busquets, Fabregas, Alexis, Messi and Iniesta.

The contrast in the style of the two teams was evident as Barça maintained possession while Madrid sat back and tried to use their physical superiority to unsettle the visitors. Little had come of the early exchanges but in the 11th minute a Barça attack broke down and Benzema brought the ball out of defence before sending a long ball forward to Ronaldo on the left. Piqué came across to cover with Alves supporting him but Ronaldo did a quick step-over and went outside Piqué. The angle wasn't great but Ronaldo's low hard shot caught Pinto cold, beating him through his legs by the post.

Were Barça ruffled by this goal? Not in the slightest. Three minutes later, Iniesta forced Casillas into his first save. Soon after, Fabregas's delightful chip forward gave Alexis, with his back to goal, the chance to flick the ball on with his head, the ball looping over Casillas but coming back into play off the top of the post. Madrid used some heavy challenges to try and slow the flow of Barça's game. Coentrao had been let off a yellow card as early as the 10th minute after a lunge at Alexis, then in the 17th minute Pepe gave his first disgraceful challenge of the night, arriving very late to stamp on Busquets's foot and he was lucky to only see yellow.

Despite their goal advantage Madrid showed very little in attack. Ronaldo did get one more run forward after Alves lost the ball, but he wasted the chance by passing the ball straight at Abidal. Meanwhile at the other end Barça started making more chances. It wasn't easy to get through the energetic back lines of Madrid, but the gaps started to appear. First Fabregas sent Messi into the area on the left and Casillas had to get down to make a good save from the Argentinian's low effort. Then Messi sent a magnificent diagonal pass to Iniesta on the left but instead of shooting Iniesta crossed and the defence intervened. Barça kept up the pressure with Alexis neatly laying off Xavi's pass but for once Iniesta's first touch wasn't great and he sent his shot wide.

Barça kept pushing for an equalizer. Casillas was forced into a spectacular run out of his area to head clear after another well-intentioned forward pass from Messi. The Madrid defence was often reduced to hoofing the ball anywhere, and one moment near the end of the first half demonstrated perfectly the difference between the teams as Sergio Ramos whacked a clearance high out of defence and when it finally came down from the clouds Iniesta controlled the ball with a touch of exquisite delicacy. There was still time for more controversial decisions before half time as Alexis was incorrectly called offside when going through one-on-one with Casillas, and Lass also escaped without a booking after an unsporting foul on Busquets.

It seemed quite an injustice that Barça could go in a goal down at half time. The lack of ideas from Madrid was remarkable and clearly demonstrated when they managed to kick the ball into touch just six seconds after kicking off the second half. Barça kept to their game and kept moving the ball at great speed. However, when the equalizer came it was not from a typically elaborate Barça passing move but from a simple corner from the left. Barça hadn't scored from the previous 196 corners but this time Xavi flighted the ball towards the far post where captain Puyol got in front of the dormant Pepe for a spectacular diving header past Casillas.

Puyol had scored with a header at the same goal in Barça's 2-6 win at the Bernabéu in May 2009 and on the merits of the teams there might have been a similar score in this game. However, the score remained at 1-1 as Fabregas chipped in another great assist for Iniesta whose shot clipped off Ramos before cannoning off the top off the post. Madrid managed one brief period of possession which led to Altintop's cross finding Benzema at the far post and he was also denied by the post, but now it was really all Barça as Busquets headed just over from Xavi's free kick.

Mourinho brought on Ozil and Callejon but one can only wonder at his instructions when Callejon managed to get booked for fouling Messi less than two minutes after coming on. However, the game's most shameful moment followed as Pepe went over to the floored Argentinian and in a disgraceful act of cowardice, deliberately trod on his hand.

It was a clear sign of Madrid's desperation. The fouls started coming more frequently as Madrid struggled to contain Barça's flow. However, it's never easy to contain Leo Messi. In the 77th minute Messi received the ball in a central position about 30 yards out, Xabi Alonso was in close attention, Ozil came across to support and behind them there was a line of five defenders across the D of the penalty area. However, none of them picked up Eric Abidal on the left and Messi chipped in a sensational pass which the French defender controlled on his chest before stabbing the ball past Casillas into the far corner.

Abidal's celebration was a joy to behold. The man who had come back from a liver operation had only scored once before for Barça. Now he was wheeling away like a big kid, using both hands as imaginary pistols. Barça had once again gone to the Bernabéu and danced their way past the physical challenges of Los Blancos. Now Alves joined Abidal in a dance routine, popularized by the Brazilian singer Michael Teló's hit single *Ai se eu te pego*.

Poor Madrid. They hadn't beaten Barça since May 2008 and the frustration showed. Granero came on as a final sub and he committed a foul within five seconds. The fouls in the last ten minutes continued to come with one from Carvalho on Messi that should really have merited a straight red. Madrid managed not to concede again, but Barça's 1-2 win would be difficult to overturn in the return leg. It was Pep Guardiola's seventh *Clásico* at the Bernabéu as Barça's coach and he had could now boast the incredible record of five wins and two draws.

Real Madrid: Casillas; Altintop, Ramos, Carvalho, Coentrao; Lass (Ozil m66), Alonso, Pepe (Granero m80); Ronaldo, Higuaín (Callejon m66), Benzemá.

Barça: Pinto; Alves, Puyol, Piqué, Abidal, Busquets, Xavi (Thiago m86), Iniesta, Fabregas (Cuenca m88), Messi, Alexis (Adriano m82).

Goals: m11 Ronaldo 1-0, m49 Puyol 1-1, m77 Abidal 1-2.

CHAPTER 37 – Barça 7 Bayer Leverkusen 1

Before the return leg of the cup *Clásico* Barça had to visit La Rosaleda for a league game with Malaga. Since Qatari Sheik Abdullah ben Nasser Al Thani became the owner of the Andalucian club in 2010 some big name players had been signed, with Ruud van Nistelrooy, Natxo Monreal, Jerémy Toulalan, Joaquín Sánchez, Isco Alarcón, and Santi Cazorla all arriving in the summer of 2011. Malaga would finish the season in a Champions League spot but they could do nothing to stop Leo Messi who was in blistering form. The Argentinian gave Barça a first half lead with a splendid header from Adriano's cross. Then after Alexis had made it 0-2 early in the second half, Messi went on the rampage. His dribble through the middle of the defence to score his second was sublime, but the hat-trick goal, running with the ball from the halfway line before clipping the ball past Willy Caballero was an absolute beauty. José Rondon grabbed a late consolation for Malaga to make the final score 1-4, but the result might have been different if Victor Valdés hadn't made three good saves early on from the impressive 19-year-old Isco.

For the return game with Real Madrid Guardiola opted for the same XI that had won the first leg at the Bernabéu though Mourinho made three changes, bringing in Arbeloa, Ozil and Kaká, while moving Pepe into defence in a more attacking 4-2-3-1. Madrid might have taken the lead after just ten seconds when Piqué was caught napping, inexplicably allowing the ball to run past him and letting Higuain in for a scoring chance. The Argentinian striker couldn't believe his luck at getting the ball and he scuffed his shot wide of Pinto's far post. Madrid came close again midway into the first half when Ozil's 35 yard effort hit both the crossbar and the post before bouncing out. Soon after, Pinto gifted Madrid another chance but Higuain shot straight back at the Barça keeper.

Messi had been relatively quiet but he came to life in the last few minutes of the first half to great effect. First, he set off on a run through the middle, drew the Madrid defence towards him before slipping an impossible pass between Pepe and Arboloa for Pedro to shoot low past Casillas. Then just before half time another run from Messi ended with a foul from Lass Diarra who was lucky not to receive his second yellow card of the night. From the free kick Xavi's shot hit Lass, the ball spinning across the edge of the area to where Alves came running in to let fly with an absolute belter of a shot that flew past Casillas into the far top corner.

Madrid didn't deserve to go in at half time 2-0 down, and Barça now led 4-1 over the two legs. However, Madrid kept battling in the second half and two quick goals from Ronaldo and Benzema left Madrid just one more goal away from going through with eighteen minutes remaining. It was a nervous time for the Camp Nou crowd but Barça managed to hold on to go through 4-3 on aggregate.

The cup victory took its toll on Barça with Iniesta picking up a hamstring injury that would leave him sidelined for two weeks. With Villa and Afellay out with long term injuries and neither Pedro nor Alexis at 100%, Guardiola had limited options in attack for the following league game at Villarreal. Guardiola's lineup at El Madrigal was still surprising: Valdés, Puyol, Piqué, Abidal, Busquets, Xavi, Mascherano, Fabregas, Alves, Messi and Adriano in a 3-4-3 formation. With Mascherano preferred over Thiago in midfield and with Alves and Adriano employed as wingers perhaps it was not surprising that Barça had few ideas going forward. Cristian Tello came on for the last fifteen minutes and Barça began to look more dangerous, the best chance fell to Fabregas but Diego Lopez made an excellent save to tip the ball against the crossbar. Two more points dropped from the 0-0 draw and Barça were now seven adrift of leaders Real Madrid.

Barça had lacked freshness at Villarreal but there was no let up with games coming thick and fast now. Next up was the Copa del Rey semi-final first leg at Valencia and Guardiola gave starts to Cuenca, who had just signed a new first team contract, and Thiago in the hope the younger players would provide some spark. In the first half Valencia gave Barça plenty of problems and deservedly took the lead after 27 minutes through Jonas Gonçalves. Then, as at the Santiago Bernabéu two weeks previously, Carlos Puyol ghosted in at the far post to head home from a corner to level the scores. Barça could easily have won the game in the second half but had to settle for a 1-1 draw after Leo Messi had a penalty saved by Diego Alves, and Dani Alves was denied a goal by the far post.

Back in the league Barça played host to Real Sociedad on a freezing night at Camp Nou. Guardiola continued to show faith in the younger players, giving a start to Thiago in midfield and both Cuenca and Tello in attack. The biggest surprise was a rare start for Johnathan dos Santos in place of Busquets who started on the bench. Tello got Barça off to a good start, showing great pace to arrive first to Messi's pass and flip the ball past Real's keeper Claudio Bravo. Barça had plenty of chances to go further in front but the finishing was lacking while at the other end Valdés had to make two important saves from Diego Ifran and Antoine Griezmann. Messi finally made it 2-0 in the 72nd minute, clipping the ball back past Bravo from Alves's cross. However, two minutes after Messi's goal Carlos Vega pulled one back for the Basque team to set up a nervous finish for Barça. Guardiola brought on Busquets to try and control things but a gash in his knee led to him being replaced by Piqué just three minutes after coming on. However, there was very little danger to Valdés goal in the final minutes though Barça ended with a couple of uncharacteristic hoofs up the field to hold on to the 2-1 victory.

The return match with Valencia in the Copa del Rey semi-final took place the following Wednesday at Camp Nou. Xavi returned to the team and combined with Thiago to play the defensive midfield role in the absence of Busquets who'd needed fifteen stitches in his gashed knee. Valencia put up a valiant fight and were in with a shout well into the second half despite going behind to an early goal from Fabregas. However, Valencia's Sofiane Feghouli got himself stupidly sent off with fifteen minutes remaining. Soon after, Xavi grabbed Barça's second to earn a place in the final with Athletic Club.

On Saturday 11 February Barça travelled to Pamplona for the league game against Osasuna. Barça had beaten José Luis Mendilibar's men 8-0 earlier in the season and then also knocked them out of the Copa del Rey. However, the Reyno de Navarra stadium is never an easy place to visit and on this occasion there was the added problem of a frozen pitch. Busquets was still out while Xavi continued to have problems with his soleus muscle and only started on the bench. It was surprising therefore that Fabregas and Iniesta were not in the initial lineup with Guardiola opting for a midfield three of Mascherano, Thiago and Sergi Roberto who had celebrated his twentieth birthday four days previously. Despite the poor condition of the pitch Barça insisted on trying to play possession football. Early on Osasuna's relentless high pressing game caused Barça defence all sorts of problems with Piqué having a particularly difficult time. In just twenty minutes Dejan Lekic had put the home side two goals in front and Barça never fully recovered. Alexis pulled a goal back early in the second half before Raul Garcia restored Osasuna's two-goal advantage soon after. Despite substitute Tello making it 3-2 with half an hour remaining Barça couldn't find an equalizer. It was only Barça's second defeat of the season but Real Madrid were now ten points clear at the top of La Liga.

Attention now turned to the Champions League with Barça paired with Bayer Leverkusen in the last 16. On the day before the first leg in Germany, Piqué, who had had a poor game at Osasuna and a generally disappointing season by his standards, lost the door of his car after leaving it open while making a quick stop in a busy street in the centre of Barcelona. The player was close to missing the flight to Leverkusen and the unimpressed Guardiola left him out of the team and he was not even included as a substitute. However, Busquets and Iniesta were back to form a stronger midfield along with Fabregas, and Barça had few problems to control the game. Leverkusen played a very defensive 4-4-1-1, allowing Barça little space until Alexis took advantage of an excellent assist from Messi to put Barça ahead just before half time. Michal Kadlec headed in an equalizer for the Germans soon after the break but just four minutes later Fabregas played in a splendid pass for Alexis who brilliantly rounded goalkeeper Bernd Leno to score his second of the night. Messi's goal near the end left Leverkusen with an almost impossible task for the return leg three weeks later.

Messi's goal was only his second in six games but he was about to go ballistic. Just eleven days after the Copa del Rey semi-final Valencia returned to Camp Nou in La Liga. Mascherano and Alves were both suspended which meant a return for Piqué and a first league start for Martin Montoya at right back. Valencia took an early lead when Piatti took advantage of a moment of hesitation between Montoya, Piqué and Valdés, but Messi responded with two goals midway through the first half, converting crosses from Pedro and Abidal. Barça were playing some scintillating football but Diego Alves kept Valencia in the game with saves from Alexis, Fabregas and Messi. Victor Valdés then had to make the best save of the game, getting down brilliantly to get a hand to Feghouli's volley. The score remained at 2-1 until fifteen minutes from the end when Messi completed his hat-trick, pouncing on the rebound after Diego Alves saved from substitute Tello. Messi put the icing on a brilliant performance with his trademark dink over the keeper for his fourth of the night before Xavi, on as a late substitute, made it 5-1 in injury time.

Having played 14 matches in the space of 47 days it was a relief after the win over Valencia to have a week without a midweek game. Besides the long term injuries to Afellay, Villa and Fontás, the squad was back to full strength with the return of Seydou Keita from the African Cup. Barça's next test was at Atlético Madrid who were already showing great improvement under new coach Diego Simeone. Atlético were unbeaten since Simeone took over from Gregorio Manzano at the end of December and with Radamel Falcao leading the attack they were a difficult opponent. Dani Alves gave Barça the lead from Fabregas's cross near the end of the first half but Falcao struck with a volleyed equalizer straight after the break. Barça simply had to win, but as the second half progressed it was Atlético who looked the more dangerous. Cuenca and Pedro replaced Alves and Fabregas as Barça switched to a defence of three. Then in the 80th minute Pedro was fouled on the left just outside the area. Xavi and Messi stood over the ball and as Thibaut Courtois moved to his near post to line up the defensive wall Messi took the opportunity to hit a beautiful left footer that swerved away from Courtois and into the far corner. There was still time for Atlético to search for another equalizer but Valdés was in excellent form, making saves from Juanfran and Gabi, to hold on to the 1-2 victory and keep Barça's slim title hopes alive.

Messi and Busquets both picked up their fifth yellow card against Atlético which meant they were suspended for the following week's game at home to Sporting. Thiago and Abidal had both returned from international duty with injuries and were also sidelined. Guardiola brought in Adriano at left back, Keita came into midfield while up front Pedro and Cuenca played the wide roles with Fabregas as false nine. Javier Clemente had recently taken over from Manuel Preciado as Sporting's coach which meant a very defensive approach from the visitors. Barça struggled to create chances but when Iniesta put Barça in front just before half time it seemed that the hard work was done. However, immediately after the break Piqué was sent off after bringing down Miguel de las Cuevas. Clemente responded by sending on striker David Barral and midfielder Carmelo Gonzalez and within a minute Barral had equalized. Barça's ten men were up against it now but with just over ten minutes to go Mascherano played a forward pass to Alexis who flicked the ball into the path of Keita who took the ball in his stride and from just outside the penalty area sent a magnificent left-foot curler into the far top corner. Xavi completed Barça's 3-1 victory with a delicate chip over the keeper Juan Pablo just before the end.

Alexis was injured in the win over Sporting while Puyol had a slight muscle strain in his left leg which meant both players missed the Champions League return match with Bayer Leverkusen. Thiago and Abidal were both still out but Messi and Busquets returned to the team as Barça lined up with Valdés, Alves, Piqué, Mascherano, Adriano, Xavi, Busquets, Fabregas, Pedro, Messi and Iniesta. Despite the two-goal advantage from the first leg Guardiola was taking no chances, sending out his strongest available XI.

Having missed the game against Sporting Messi was raring to go and about to give one of his most remarkable performances. Early on he threatened with a chest and volley after Fabregas's excellent chip but Leno made a good save and when Messi crossed the ball back in, Pedro couldn't force the ball home. Barça had other early attempts from free kicks, though Xavi was finding the German wall that little bit taller to curl the ball over. Then, from a free kick on the left, Leno needed to make a good save after Piqué ducked under Xavi's cross, but this was just a warm up to the main feature.

Messi got the first goal of the game in the 25th minute. Bayer were pushed up near the halfway line when Xavi played a perfectly weighted pass over the top, Messi was away and when Leno came out to close him down Messi scooped the ball over the keeper and the ball rolled into the empty net.

Just before half time, Messi scored a splendid second after a rapid counter attack. Piqué played a poor pass to an opponent on the halfway line, but Mascherano was brilliant in his anticipation to steal the ball back and surge into the Leverkusen half. Iniesta worked as the link, moving the ball on to Messi on the right who cut inside onto his left foot and fired a cool low shot inside the far post.

Barça nearly got another before half time but neither Fabregas nor Pedro could finish after Messi's superb turn and pass. Then straight after the break Fabregas was too generous trying to work the ball back to Messi after a rapid one-touch build-up between the two and Andres Iniesta. Barça's third didn't have to wait much longer. In the 50th minute Fabregas sent a brilliant pass through to Messi who controlled with his left before lifting the ball over the advanced Leno, this time with his right foot, to complete his hat-trick. Anybody who thinks Messi is a one-footed player should watch the subtlety of this fine finish.

Leverkusen were understandably dispirited and Guardiola chose the perfect moment to rest Xavi and Iniesta and bring on Seydou Keita and the speedy Cristian Tello. The young winger had only been on for about a minute when Fabregas lobbed another excellent pass into space for him to sprint in from the left before beating Leno with a side-foot finish inside the far post.

Barça were rampant now and there was little the Bayer defence could do. In the 58th minute Messi played a one-two with Fabregas and despite two defenders being in the way Messi showed his ability to sniff out a goal pouncing on Leno's slip to score his fourth and Barça's fifth. Four minutes later Alves led the charge using Messi as a decoy to the right before finding Tello in acres of space on the left and Tello's shot slipped under the goalkeeper and in. Ten minutes on the pitch and two goals from the youngster, Guardiola responded by throwing on 19-year-old Marc Muniesa at left back and Camp Nou responded by chanting Guardiola's name.

Keita might have scored the seventh but he couldn't quite get to Pedro's cross, and then a couple of minutes later his header went just wide. It had to be Messi who scored his fifth of an incredible evening firing in from 25 yards after Keita knocked back Fabregas's forward pass. With the clock on 89.59 Leverkusen scored a consolation with a fine curler from Karim Bellarabi. The game ended 7-1 and Barça were through to a quarter finals. The performance from Messi was just about as close to perfection as you will ever see on a football pitch.

Barça: Valdés; Alves, Piqué, Mascherano, Adriano (Muniesa m63); Xavi (Keita m53), Busquets, Fabregas; Pedro, Messi, Iniesta (Tello m53).

Bayer Leverkusen: Leno; Castro, Schwaab, Toprak, Kadlec; Renato Augusto (Oczipka m67), Rolfes, Reinartz, Bender (Schurrle m56); Kiessling, Derdiyok (Bellarabi m56).

Goals: m25 Messi 1-0, m43 Messi 2-0, m50 Messi 3-0, m55 Tello 4-0, m58 Messi 5-0, m62 Tello 6-0, m84 Messi 7-0, m90 Bellarabi 7-1.

CHAPTER 38 – Barça 5 Granada 3

Following the massive win over Leverkusen Barça travelled to Santander to take on relegation threatened Racing. Piqué was suspended while Abidal, Thiago, Alexis, Villa, Fontás and Afellay were all out injured, but there was good news for Guardiola with Puyol recovering in time to play. In the week running up to the game there had been a dressing room coup at Racing with coach Juan José Gonzalez being overthrown and replaced by Alvaro Cevera who until then had been coach at Recreativo Huelva. Cervera adopted a very defensive approach to try and stop Barça while Guardiola again opted for a 3-4-3. Messi continued in unstoppable form, scoring both goals in Barça's 0-2 win. The first goal came after half an hour when the Argentinian stabbed home from Fabregas's cross, and then early in the second half a soft penalty was awarded after Domingo Cisma's challenge on Fabregas and Messi sent the keeper the wrong way with the penalty for his 50th Barça goal of the season. It was still only March 11.

Just four days later a bombshell hit Camp Nou with the announcement that almost a year after having a tumor removed from his liver Eric Abidal would now have to undergo a transplant. A club statement said: "Given the development of his medical condition, Abidal will undergo a liver transplant in the coming weeks. The transplant is an option that has been considered since the beginning of his treatment, one year ago. At the express wish of the player, the club requested the utmost respect for the right to privacy and confidentiality."

It was an incredible blow for Barça but Abidal showed strength and courage and optimism throughout. The Frenchman spoke to his teammates in the dressing room to explain his situation after which Carles Puyol stated: "It is he who encourages us. His attitude is an example. We are confident that he will come through this. We will give him all the strength we have and we will support him and his family. I am convinced that soon he will be fine. He is very strong, he showed that last season and will prove it again. It's a major blow. We had the news last season and now we get it again. But this will make us even stronger." Messages of goodwill and support flooded in from around the world.

There is probably no doubt that the players pulled together even more with this dreadful news but they were going to miss Abidal's defensive qualities. The following Saturday the team wore T-shirts of support before the away game at Sevilla that read: *"Abi!!! Tornaràs a guanyar!!!"* (Abi, you will be back to win again!). Guardiola played Adriano at left back in a 4-3-3 and the Brazilian had the first chance when Sevilla allowed him to move forward and his deflected shot very nearly dipped in. Then in the 16th minute Adriano burst forward again and was fouled on the edge of the box. Xavi curled the free kick nicely over the Sevilla wall and keeper Palop was a bit slow to get across his goal and despite getting a hand to the ball couldn't prevent Xavi's ninth league goal of the season. Seven minutes later a moment of Messi genius put Barça further ahead. Fabregas looked close to losing the ball but he managed to knock the ball on to Messi who was about 45 yards out. Messi exchanged passes with Iniesta and on receiving the ball back played a sublime nutmeg through Spahic's legs before using his left foot like a nine-iron to beat Palop with a delicious chip. There were chances for Sevilla to get back in the game, particularly at the end of the first half, but Valdés was in good form and Barça ended the game the stronger side without adding to the 0-2 final scoreline. The following day a scorching free kick from Santi Cazorla earned Malaga a last-minute equalizer at Real Madrid, giving Barça a glimmer of hope as the gap at the top of La Liga was reduced to eight points with eleven games to play.

Messi's goal at Sevilla was his 231st for Barça and for some time now it had seemed inevitable that sooner or later he would overcome Cesar Rodriguez's record as Barça's highest ever official goalscorer. Cesar had always appeared in the record books as having scored 235 goals in the 1940s and 1950s but, with Messi closing in, a joint study by the club's Center of Documentation and local newspaper *La Vanguardia* revised Cesar's total to 232 a day before Granada visited Camp Nou for a Tuesday night league game.

Guardiola made five changes to the team that won in Seville with Puyol, Keita, Thiago, Alexis and Cuenca returning in place of Mascherano, Busquets, Fabregas, Pedro and Iniesta. Cuenca was positioned wide on the left and had an immediate impact on the game. In the fourth minute he sped outside David Cortes before crossing to the far post where Messi headed the ball back to Xavi who hooked the ball past Granada keeper Julio Cesar from 12 yards.

Messi had his first chance to score on 11 minutes but his powerful low shot, after Alexis's assist, was well covered by Julio Cesar. Granada were playing a reasonably high defence but they were very narrow which made it easier for Barça to get the ball out to Cuenca. In the 17th minute the young winger went past Cortes again and got in another cross which flicked off the top of Borja Gomez's head before falling nicely for Messi coming in from the right and the Argentinian hit his shot sweetly in off the far post to equal Cesar's record.

With the two-goal advantage Barça eased up a bit and the intensity dropped for the remainder of the first half. Cuenca continued to impress on the left, Alexis was denied a clear penalty after being hacked by Guilherme Siqueira but there were few clear chances. Granada offered little with the most danger coming from an excellent cross from Dani Benitez that Adriano cleared. At half time Adriano with a muscle strain had to be replaced by Mascherano.

The second half began with the same low intensity. Messi had a great chance to score the record-breaking goal after Cuenca's low cross but he screwed the ball wide - quite possibly he wanted to score a better goal for such an occasion! Then in the 55th minute Camp Nou was surprised by Granada scoring a goal out of the blue. They won a free kick out on the left and when the ball swung in Diego Mainz beat Piqué to flick a header past Valdés. If that was bad for Barça, things got much worse soon after when Benitez fooled the referee, José Antonio Teixeira Vitienes, into awarding a penalty after braking abruptly in front of Alves as soon as he reached the area. There was contact as Alves tried to avoid the Granada winger, followed by an exaggerated dive from Benitez, Teixeira Vitienes was about eight yards away and he blew for a penalty. Siqueira sent Valdés the wrong way to equalize and Camp Nou could hardly believe it.

There were some nervous minutes as the game became more and more open, but when things are tough there is nobody like Messi to sort things out. In the 68th minute Alves chipped a pass over the defence and Messi controlled before flicking a sublime chip over the keeper for his historic 233rd blaugrana goal. Tello and Iniesta came on in place of Thiago and Alexis and soon after Messi gave Tello a great chance with a killer through ball but Tello was forced too wide and then after dribbling back into the area he seemed to be brought down but this time Teixeira Vitienes was very poorly positioned to see it.

Alves never stopped coming forward. In the 82nd minute he combined with Iniesta who sent in a great ball for Messi whose powerful drive was beaten away by Julio Cesar only for Tello to fire the rebound neatly inside the far post. The cherry on the top came four minutes later when Alves again got forward to assist Messi who took the ball around the keeper before shooting past Mainz on the line. The game should have ended here with Messi's hat-trick but instead Granada were awarded a second penalty for a handball from Alves. Teixeira Vitienes showed Alves his second yellow – he'd got one for conceding the first penalty – and Siqueira again showed class to send Valdés the wrong way from the spot.

The 5-3 victory took Barça to 66 points from 28 games. The following night Real Madrid conceded another late free kick equalizer, this time from Villarreal's Marcus Senna at El Madrigal. Madrid's advantage had dropped from ten points down to six in less than a week. With ten games remaining including a Camp Nou *Clásico*, La Liga was very much alive.

Barça: Valdés; Alves, Puyol, Piqué, Adriano (Mascherano m45); Xavi, Keita, Thiago (Iniesta m71); Alexis (Tello m71), Messi, Cuenca.

Granada: Julio César; Cortes, Mainz, Borja, Siqueira; D.Benitez, Moisés (Abel m69), Mikel Rico, Jara (Uche m46), Martins; Ighalo (Geijo m78).

Goals: m4 Xavi 1-0, m17 Messi 2-0, m55 Mainz 2-1, m62 Siqueira (pen) 2-2, m68 Messi 3-2, m82 Tello 4-2, m86 Messi 5-2, m89 Siqueira (pen) 5-3.

CHAPTER 39 – Barça 2 Chelsea 2

Moving into the final few weeks of the 2011/12 season and Barça still had everything to play for. Real Madrid were not looking quite so solid and their draws with Mallorca and Valladolid suggested that their six-point advantage in La Liga could be overcome. Guardiola's men were already in the Copa del Rey final and in the Champions League quarter-finals where they were the bookmakers' favourite to go on and win the trophy. A grand slam six-out-of-six season was still on the cards but there was also an underlying concern at the club as Guardiola had still not renewed his contract. In previous seasons the coach, who had always preferred one-year contract extensions, had always made a decision by February and now it was nearly the end of March. Nobody, except perhaps those closest to him, knew his intentions, but the local press were generally optimistic that he would stay at the club.

On March 24 Barça visited Mallorca in the league. With Eric Abidal waiting for his liver operation, Guardiola had a lack of full backs for the game as Dani Alves was suspended and Adriano was injured. His solution was to return to the 3-4-3 formation with a back three of Piqué, Puyol and Mascherano. Leo Messi opened the scoring halfway through the first half when his inswinging free kick was missed by everybody and crept in off the far post. Alexis came close to adding a second but his shot bounced out off the underside of the crossbar and Barça's one-goal advantage looked very fragile when Thiago received a second yellow card for a debatable handball with half an hour remaining. Guardiola subbed on Martin Montoya for Fabregas and Barça reverted to a defence of four. Despite the slender lead Piqué found time to join a Barça attack and when Messi's shot hit the post Piqué was on hand to stab home the rebound to complete a 0-2 victory.

Barça had been drawn to face AC Milan again in the Champions League quarter-finals with a semi-final against Chelsea or Benfica as the reward for the winner. When the teams had met in the group stage earlier in the tournament Guardiola had employed a 3-4-3 at the San Siro as Barça won a thrilling match 2-3. The Barça coach was more cautious now and opted for a 4-3-3 with a midfield three of Busquets, Xavi and Keita for the first leg in Milan. It was pretty conservative by Barça's standards and despite early chances for Robinho and Ibrahimovic the defences came out on top in an intense 0-0 draw.

The following Saturday Barça played host to Athletic Club in the league. It was the first home game since Leo Messi had beaten Cesar's goalscoring record and Camp Nou received the Argentinian with a giant banner that read half in Catalan and half in Argentinian Spanish: *"Leo, ets únic, sos grande"* (Leo, you are unique, you are great). Athletic had the handicap of having played on the previous Thursday, a thrilling 2-4 win at Schalke 04 in the Europa League, which meant they had less than 48 hours between games. Coach Marcelo Bielsa made four changes to his side while Guardiola made three changes to the team that drew in Milan. Adriano recovered ahead of time to replace Puyol at left back, Thiago had had his second yellow card at Mallorca overturned on appeal and he returned in place of Xavi, and Cristian Tello played on the left wing with Iniesta moving back to midfield in place of Keita. With both teams playing a similar high pressing game there were one-on-one battles all over the pitch with Barça's superior talent proving too much for the Basques. Shortly before half time Alexis robbed Athletic's Ibai Gomez and then Messi found Iniesta who took the ball on and on into the area before blasting high into the net past the helpless Gorka Iraizoz from 8 yards out. Messi completed a 2-0 victory with a second half penalty after Javi Martinez was adjudged to have brought down Tello. It was Barça's eighth straight win in La Liga but Madrid's 1-5 win at Osasuna meant the gap was still at six points.

For the return leg of the Champions League quarter-final with Milan Guardiola surprised by including Isaac Cuenca in the starting XI with Alexis Sanchez on the bench. The need for width was obvious and Cuenca started wide on the left with the other surprise being Alves playing high up on the right wing with a back three of Mascherano, Piqué and Puyol. Busquets played just in front of the defence with Xavi close by. Barça then had Iniesta, Fabregas and Messi to interchange between midfield and attack doing their best to pull Milan out of position. Ten minutes into the game Messi was brought down in the penalty area and Dutch referee Bjorn Kuipers had no hesitation in pointing to the spot. Messi kept his cool and slotted the ball inside the post, Milan keeper Christian Abbiati guessed the right way and got a touch to the ball but he couldn't prevent it from going in. Barça's lead lasted until the 32nd minute when Ibrahimovic set up Antonio Nocerino to fire past Valdés. With the score at 1-1 Milan had the away goal in their favour but shortly before half time Alessandro Nesta was guilty of holding Sergio Busquets's shirt as a corner came in. Kuipers awarded Barça a second penalty and this time Messi sent Abbiati the wrong way to give the home side a 2-1 advantage at the break. Barça changed to 4-3-3 with Alves moving back to defence, Cuenca switching to the right wing and Iniesta moving forward to the left. A one-goal lead against Milan was never going to be safe and Barça got the necessary breathing space early in the second half. Again it was Messi who caused the problems for Milan with his run at the heart of the Milan defence. His final shot was blocked but the ball bounced kindly into the path of Iniesta who controlled with his left foot before sweeping right-footed into the far corner. Barça held on comfortably to the 3-1 lead though Piqué had to go off with a hamstring problem near the end and would miss the following two league games. The following night Chelsea beat Benfica at Stamford Bridge to set up another semi-final with Barça after the famous encounter in 2009. The other semi-final would be between Bayern Munich and Real Madrid and all the bookmakers made Barça and Madrid favourites to meet in the final.

Back in La Liga Barça went to Zaragoza looking for a ninth straight league win to maintain the pressure on Madrid. Guardiola played a midfield three of Thiago, Keita and Fabregas which meant a rest for the usual trio of Xavi, Busquets and Iniesta. Carlos Aranda gave La Romareda hope, putting Zaragoza in front after half an hour, and it could have been two-nil if Victor Valdés hadn't saved Aranda's earlier penalty. Barça turned things round with goals from Carles Puyol and Leo Messi before the break and the sending off of Abraham Minero left Zaragoza with only ten men for the entire second half. The task proved too tough for the Aragonese team, and Barça completed the job with a Messi penalty, which was his sixtieth goal of the season for Barça, and a much needed goal for Pedro in injury time. The following day Real Madrid could only manage a goalless draw at home to Valencia which left Barça just four points behind the leaders with seven games, including the Camp Nou *Clásico*, to be played.

The race for La Liga continued with a round of midweek matches with Barça playing host to Getafe on the Tuesday, the same day that Eric Abidal underwent his liver transplant. The Camp Nou crowd would remember the French defender by chanting his name in the 22nd minute (22 being Abidal's shirt number). Guardiola realized the need for his players to maintain a high level of intensity, saying it was "time for less laughter and more running". Alves had picked up a slight thigh strain in Zaragoza while Piqué was still out and Fabregas was suspended, so the coach again went for a 3-4-3 with Puyol, Mascherano and Adriano at the back, Messi playing the attacking point of a midfield diamond with Cuenca, Alexis and Pedro up front. Barça were really hitting form now, playing a high press with the magnificent Mascherano showing great anticipation in winning back the ball whenever Getafe tried to break. Alexis put Barça in front after 13 minutes with an unstoppable shot past Getafe keeper Miguel Ángel Moya from the edge of the area. Then just before half time Iniesta touched the ball off brilliantly to Messi who fired a cracker into the top corner. Barça completed a 4-0 victory with two second half headers. First, from Alexis with a brilliant old-fashioned centre forward header after Cuenca cut the ball back from the goal-line. Then, from Pedro who rose to flick Messi's free-kick with a header that looped over Moya. Barça moved to within a point of Real Madrid but the following night the gap returned to four points when a Cristiano Ronaldo hat-trick inspired Madrid to a 1-4 win at Atlético.

A week before the possible title-deciding *Clásico* at Camp Nou, and four days before the Champions League semi-final first leg at Chelsea, Barça visited fifth-placed Levante for another must-win game in the league. Alves and Piqué both travelled with the squad but neither were risked for the game as Puyol, Mascherano and Adriano continued as a three-man defence. Barça dominated early on but midway through the first half Levante won a penalty when Juanfran headed the ball against Busquets's raised arm. José Barkero coolly sent Valdés the wrong way from the spot to put Levante ahead. The goal took the wind out of Barça and the team struggled to break through Levante's packed defence. Guardiola brought on Cuenca for Xavi at half time to give the attack more width and ten minutes into the second half Iniesta replaced Pedro. With half an hour remaining the score was still 1-0 and Barça's title hopes seemed to be slipping away. Then Cuenca found Messi on the edge of the area and after a quick one-two with Alexis, the Argentinian smashed the ball past Levante keeper Gustavo Munua for the equalizer. Then in the 70th minute Cuenca went down in the area after a shove from Pedro Botelho and Messi sent Munua the wrong way with the resulting penalty. Barça held out for the 1-2 victory but the gap remained at four points as Madrid had won earlier against Sporting.

Barça now faced a massive week. Chelsea away on the Wednesday, followed by Madrid at Camp Nou on the Saturday and the return game at home to Chelsea the following Tuesday. Guardiola named a 22-man squad for the trip to London with Ibrahim Afellay making the list for the first time after seven months out injured. Alves returned to the starting XI in a defence of four but there was no place for Piqué as Barça lined up with

Valdés, Alves, Mascherano, Puyol, Adriano, Xavi, Busquets, Fabregas, Alexis, Messi and Iniesta. Chelsea's season was back on track since Roberto Di Matteo had taken over from Andre Villas-Boas as first team coach. The Italian had restored faith in Chelsea's older players and Chelsea started with Cech, Ivanović, Cahill, Terry, Cole, Lampard, Mikel, Ramires, Meireles, Mata and Drogba.

In the first three minutes the difference in style of the two teams was clear to see. From the kick off Barça looked to keep possession, maintaining the ball for well over a minute before Chelsea got a touch. Then in the third minute Chelsea showed the danger of route one football when Petr Cech's enormous kick sent Drogba through, but the first touch of the Chelsea forward let him down and the ball ran on to Valdés. The first real chance of the game fell to Barça in the ninth minute when Iniesta sent a splendid pass over the top to Alexis who got to the ball before Cech but his lob over the Chelsea keeper came out off the crossbar. Barça continued to dominate, working patiently to find the way through Chelsea's disciplined defence. In the 17th minute Cech could only parry Iniesta's shot straight out to Fabregas who mishit his shot with the goal gaping and Alexis couldn't react to divert the ball home.

Chelsea were showing few signs of attacking though a couple of long throws from Ivanovic caused Barça some confusion in defence and Juan Mata had one snap shot over after Busquets failed to get a better clearance. The chances were also drying up for Barça though shortly before half time Messi robbed Mikel in the centre circle and sped off towards goal. As the defence was drawn towards him Messi slipped the ball left to Fabregas, Cech came rushing out but Fabregas touched the ball past the Chelsea keeper only to see Ashley Cole scampering back to clear the ball a metre before it crossed the line. From a possible 0-1 it went to 1-0 on the stroke of half time. Messi was dispossessed by Lampard who then sent a quick crossfield ball to Ramires who took advantage of Alves being caught upfield to surge down the Chelsea left, Puyol and

Mascherano both came across leaving Drogba free in the middle, and when Ramires pulled the ball back across goal the big Ivorian striker was there to sweep the ball past Valdés.

The 1-0 scoreline suited Chelsea perfectly and in the second half they sat back even more. Barça tried to be patient but the chances were harder to find. Alexis had one good opportunity after Fabregas scooped a pass over the defence but the ball got stuck a bit too close to his feet and he pushed his shot inches wide of Cech's left post. With time running out Barça made a final push. In the 87th minute Messi's free kick was flicked on by Puyol, and Cech had to go full stretch to make a magnificent save. Then in the final minute of injury time Messi found Pedro coming in from the left. It all looked set for the equalizer. Pedro shot low and firm and with intention, the ball took the slightest deflection off Terry's heel and beat Cech before bouncing out off the far post. Busquets following up could only send the rebound flying high over the bar. Barça didn't deserve to lose but there was still a second leg at Camp Nou to put things right.

Before the return match with Chelsea there was the much-awaited league clash with Real Madrid at Camp Nou. A win for Barça would see Madrid's lead cut to one point with four matches remaining. Before the game there had been ten *Clásicos* between Guardiola's Barça and Mourinho's Madrid with the balance clearly in Guardiola's favour with five wins to Mourinho's one and four draws. Leo Messi and Cristiano Ronaldo were both on an incredible 41 league goals, their duel for the *Pichichi* added extra interest. Alexis Sanchez had been reported to be limping when he got off the plane back from London and Guardiola kept everybody guessing about who would start and in what formation. Would there be a defence of three or four? Proper wingers or not? A true central striker or not? A place for Fabregas, and if so, which role? And would Piqué return to the team? When the teams were announced before the game there were just two changes to the team that lost at Chelsea with Tello and Thiago coming in for Fabregas and Alexis. However, Alves played a more advanced role on the right side leaving a back three of Puyol, Mascherano and Adriano. Thiago played deeper than usual close to Busquets with Xavi on the right of midfield and Iniesta playing an attacking midfield role trying to support Messi, while Tello stuck to the left.

Mourinho maintained confidence in the same XI that had lost the first leg of the Champions League semi-final 2-1 at Bayern Munich. Playing in their usual 4-2-3-1 shape Madrid lined up with Casillas, Arbeloa, Pepe, Sergio Ramos, Coentrao, Xabi Alonso, Khedira, Di Maria, Ozil, Ronaldo and Benzema. From early on it seemed clear that Madrid were more tuned in for the game. Barça were caught in possession too often and Madrid's high early pressing forced Barça into some loose passing. It was not too surprising when Madrid took the lead from a corner in the 16th minute. Di Maria sent the cross to the far post, Pepe beat Adriano to the jump, Valdés made a good stop but the ball stopped dead just two yards out, Puyol tried to clear but Khedira was quicker to force the ball over the line.

With Alves and Tello playing very wide there was a lack of support for Messi as Barça struggled to find an equalizer. Madrid were working hard to close down the spaces and the few chances that Barça had were falling to Tello who was disappointing with his finishing. In the 69th minute Guardiola decided to bring on Alexis and within a minute he had put Barça level. Messi went on a run, Iniesta flicked the ball onto Tello who this time got his shot on target forcing Casillas to save, the rebound came out to Adriano, 25 yards out, and he drove the ball back in low to Alexis whose first shot was stopped by Casillas but the Chilean managed to force home the rebound.

If there was hope here that Barça could still win the league it lasted for just three minutes. Ozil was allowed too much time to pick out his pass to Ronaldo who got away from Mascherano before rounding Valdés to score. Guardiola brought on Pedro and then Fabregas but there was no coming back. In the final minutes Madrid looked closer to a third than

Barça did to an equalizer but the 1-2 final scoreline was enough to put an end to Barça's challenge for La Liga after three successive league titles.

It was a tough blow for Barça to take but the team needed to pick itself up for the return game with Chelsea three days later. Guardiola made four changes to the team that lost to Madrid, sacrificing Dani Alves to play a flat back three of Mascherano, Piqué and Puyol. Adriano, Thiago and Tello were also left out after starting against Madrid, while the big names Fabregas, Alexis and Piqué returned and Cuenca was restored to the right wing. The formation might be described as a 3-3-1-3 with Messi playing behind a front three of Cuenca, Alexis and Iniesta. Chelsea coach Roberto di Matteo played the same XI as in the first leg at Stamford Bridge.

The game began at a great pace. In the third minute, Messi and Alexis combined through the middle but Messi's shot was on his right foot and hit the side netting. With Cuenca on the right and Iniesta on the left, Fabregas was finding a lot of space supporting Messi and Alexis through the middle. In the 6th minute, Messi went past one challenge before slipping a pass to Fabregas who played Alexis into the area, Gary Cahill slipped as he covered the threat, causing himself an injury that saw him subbed off for José Bosingwa five minutes later.

The danger from Cech's long kicks up to Drogba had been seen in the first leg. In the 16th minute, the big striker chased after another huge kick from the Chelsea keeper, Piqué went with him and got the worst of things as Valdés came steaming out to clear, smashing into both players in the process. Piqué looked very groggy and had to go off for a minute. Then with Piqué back on, an electric move involving Messi and Alexis ended with Fabregas flicking the ball through his legs back to Messi but Cech saved Messi's shot well with his legs and Iniesta's rebound was cleared. Soon after, Fabregas was into the area again but his volley went into the side-netting.

A rare counter from Chelsea saw Drogba escape from Piqué before shooting wide from an angle. Guardiola took it as the sign that Piqué was not fully recovered and brought on Alves in his place. Barça were still looking very slick in their passing and the constant pressure looked sure to pay off sooner or later. The Catalans won a couple of corners on the left. Xavi and Iniesta had shots from distance that didn't trouble Cech. Terry made a good tackle on Messi on the edge of the area.

The game had been tense and thrilling for 35 minutes, then, at the end of the first half it exploded. Fabregas won a corner on the right. Xavi swung it over looking for Puyol but the defence headed it clear. The ball was recovered by Alves in a central position 35 yards out, he burst forward and as the defence came out to meet him he freed Cuenca inside the area on the left, Cech had to rush out to cover the shot but Cuenca pulled the ball across the goal and Busquets was at the far post to sweep the ball home.

Camp Nou erupted. Then just a minute later, the Chelsea captain John Terry made an absurd error that would leave his team a man down for the rest of the game. With the ball nowhere near, Terry couldn't resist giving Alexis a knee in the back of the leg. The Turkish referee, Cüneyt Çakir, didn't see it but his linesman did and called his attention. Çakir produced the red card and Terry was off.

Barça sensed blood and went for the kill. In the 44th minute, Alexis sped forward before finding Messi to his left 35 yards out. Iniesta made a run into the area and Messi timed his pass perfectly for Iniesta to stroke the ball low past Cech into the far corner. Barça were 2-0 up on the night and 2-1 up overall. With Chelsea down to ten men, there were many at this point who thought the tie was over, though the Londoners hit back immediately, and just as in the first leg they scored a crucial goal in first half injury time. Xavi and Iniesta failed to keep the ball as they looked to penetrate and Ramires broke quickly, playing the ball forward to Lampard who had moved into space between Xavi and Busquets. Mascherano rushed out of the back line to try and intercept, Lampard held off the challenge and slipped the pass into Ramires who had run into the space left by Mascherano. Neither Puyol nor Busquets could get across quickly enough and Ramires sent a cool chip over the advanced Valdés. Half time and now the tie was level at 2-2 but Chelsea had the away goal advantage which meant Barça needed to score again.

A goal just before half time is always a big blow but Barça still had everything in favour to get through. Cuenca moved to the left for the second half with Alves supplying the width on the right as Chelsea played deeper and deeper. It didn't look like Barça would have problems to create chances when Iniesta shot from inside the area in the 47th minute but his effort was deflected wide.

A minute later, Fabregas played a quick one-two with Messi on the right of the area and Drogba, who played for long periods in the left back position, brought Fabregas down. It was again the linesman who saw it and he signalled to Çakir who awarded the penalty. It was Messi's moment, his chance to put Barça back in front while taking the Champions League goalscoring record to 15 goals in a season. Perhaps it was down to Cech's intimidating size that caused Messi to shoot high. Whatever the case, Messi's shot crashed against the crossbar and something seemed to happen to Barça's belief.

Alexis headed wide at the far post from an Alves cross but the game was beginning to look complicated for Barça, and memories of ten-man Inter two years before began to creep in. Drogba then popped up at right back to rob Cuenca and after getting past Puyol almost scored an incredible goal from the half-way line as Valdés had to move quickly and dive to save.

Cuenca had a chance in the 62nd minute after good work from Messi and Iniesta opened the space, but Cech was again big in his goal and Cuenca's shot went straight at the Chelsea keeper. Guardiola brought on Tello for Cuenca and then Keita for Fabregas but the chances were drying up for Barça as Chelsea grew in confidence, encouraged by a couple of counterattacks that almost took advantage of Barça's sparse defence.

But Barça kept insisting, trying to find holes in the packed defence. In the 78th minute, Iniesta sent a deep cross towards Alves, the ball bounced down to Busquets, 15 yards out, but he was leaning back as he shot and the ball flew over. Into the last ten minutes and the tension was unbearable. Chelsea brought on Fernando Torres in place of Drogba who, despite some of his theatrics, had played a magnificent role for his team. In the 81st minute, Alexis had the ball in the net after Alves's cross, but the linesman had spotted Alves half a yard offside. Then Messi came alive to get in a shot from just outside the area but Cech managed to get a fingertip to send the ball against the base of the post. It was the fourth time over the two games that Barça had hit the Chelsea woodwork.

As time ran out Barça became more desperate. Mascherano had a long shot saved and from the resulting corner Puyol headed over. The game moved into injury time with the home team throwing men forward in search of a goal. In one final attack Barça pushed everybody so far forward that when Cole cleared from within the Chelsea area the ball came to Torres, all alone and onside as he had started his run from the Chelsea half. Torres ran through unchallenged and when Valdés came out the Chelsea substitute skipped past him to score into the empty net.

It was an incredibly tough and disappointing week for culés. However, the reaction from the Camp Nou crowd, singing support for the team after Chelsea's second goal, demonstrated the pride and belief that the public had in their team. Losing La Liga to Madrid and getting knocked out of the Champions League to three injury time goals just didn't seem right after all the tremendous work from Guardiola and the players during the season. There was still a Copa del Rey final to prepare for at the end of May but following the Champions League elimination all attention turned to Guardiola's decision. Would he stay or would he go? Following the Chelsea game the Barça coach announced that he would talk with Rosell because now it was time to take a decision.

Barça: Valdes; Mascherano, Piqué (Alves m26), Puyol; Busquets, Xavi, Fabregas (Keita m74); Messi; Cuenca (Tello m67), Alexis, Iniesta.

Chelsea: Cech; Ivanovic, Cahill (Bosingwa m12), Terry, Cole; Meireles, Mikel, Lampard, Ramires, Mata (Kalou m58); Drogba (Torres m80)

Goals: m36 Busquets 1-0, m44 Iniesta 2-0, m45+1 Ramires 2-1, m92 Torres 2-2.

CHAPTER 40 – Barça 3 Athletic Club 0

Guardiola met Rosell two days after the Champions League disappointment and a press conference was announced for the following day, Friday 27 April at 1.30 pm. On the Thursday night rumours began to spread that Guardiola would not continue though there was still a lot of optimism from fans. The eagerly-awaited press conference began with Rosell who wasted no time in confirming that Guardiola would not renew his contract.

Guardiola then declared that he had taken the decision the previous autumn and that he had told the club's directors but not the players. He confessed that his decision to renew his contract year by year may have been a mistake as it created uncertainty. He also stated that the only reason for not continuing was tiredness. He obviously did not feel capable of maintaining the high intensity needed to do the job as well as he felt was necessary. When Guardiola finished speaking, Rosell surprised everybody at the press conference by announcing that a decision on Guardiola's replacement had already been made, and that the new first team coach would be Tito Vilanova.

Guardiola's decision was another huge disappointment for the club, but the announcement that Vilanova would be taking over softened the blow considerably. The general consensus was summed up by captain Carles Puyol: "It's the best news they could give us because it means the continuation of a project. Tito knows the team better than anybody, he understands a great deal about football and he knows the philosophy perfectly. He's worked with Pep for five years. He's the ideal person to continue this project."

Barça still had four league games to play before the Copa del Rey final with Athletic Club. The first was at Rayo Vallecano on the following Sunday. When Guardiola was asked how his players had responded to his decision, he replied that they had "trained like beasts". Rayo became the victim as the Barça players also played like beasts on the Sunday. A team including youngsters Montoya and Thiago and with Pinto in goal destroyed poor Rayo with a blistering display. Two goals each from Messi and Pedro with one apiece for Keita and Thiago and an own goal from Rayo's Rober Correa completed a 0-7 demolition job. Messi's brace took his overall season total for Barça to 65 goals while he drew level again in the battle for *Pichichi* with Cristiano Ronaldo on 43 league goals.

The following Wednesday, Messi scored three more as Barça beat Malaga 4-1 at Camp Nou. Puyol opened the scoring for Barça with Malaga's José Rondon heading in an equalizer before Messi took the stage. His hat-trick, which included two penalties, took his season's total to 68 beating Gerd Müller's 39-year-old record of 67 as the most goals ever scored in a season in European football. It also took Messi's league tally to 46, the highest ever in La Liga, though Ronaldo scored one as Madrid sealed the league title with a victory over Athletic Club, to take his total to 44 which still gave him a chance of beating Messi to the top scorer's prize.

Any doubt about who would be *Pichichi* were dispelled the following Saturday when Messi knocked in four more in a 4-0 win over Espanyol in Guardiola's last game in charge at Camp Nou. Messi opened the scoring early on, curling a beautiful free kick from just outside the area, away from the reach of Espanyol keeper Alvarez and into the corner. The second came from a penalty twenty minutes into the second half. Ten minutes later, Adriano sent a fantastic crossfield ball for Messi running through the inside left position, the Argentinian entered the area and fired a low shot across Alvarez and into the far corner to complete his hat-trick. Messi's fourth came from another penalty and to celebrate his fiftieth league goal of the season he ran over to Guardiola for an embrace of mutual respect. It was an emotional goodbye for Guardiola and the Camp Nou public and after the final whistle the players threw him in the air as they had done to celebrate so many triumphs over the previous four seasons. The negative side of the Espanyol game was a knee injury to Carles Puyol that put him out for the rest of the season and also meant he would miss out on Spain's victory at Euro 2012.

Barça's final league match of the 2011/12 season was away at Betis. There was little at stake for Barça though with Pinto suffering a slight injury Valdés returned to the team, putting at risk the goalkeepers' *Zamora* trophy for the least goals conceded. If Valdés conceded three goals then Iker Casillas could sneak in and win with a clean sheet in Madrid's home game against Mallorca. At half time at the Benito Villamarin there seemed little threat to Valdés's *Zamora* as Barça led 0-1 thanks to a flicked header from Sergio Busquets. However, things became more complicated for Guardiola's men after Dani Alves was sent off early in the second half. Then, when Ruben Castro scored twice in three minutes to put Betis ahead, Valdés's fifth *Zamora* looked in serious danger. However, Betis preferred to defend their lead rather than to press for a third goal. They paid for it at the end when Keita leapt spectacularly to head home Montoya's cross to leave the final score at 2-2.

There were now just under two weeks to prepare for the Copa del Rey final. On the morning of May 16 there was a blow to Guardiola's plans when Dani Alves broke his collarbone in training. Puyol, Abidal, Fontás and Villa were already ruled out for the final and the injury to Alves left the squad looking stretched in defence. Barça B players Martin Montoya, Marc Bartra, Cristian Tello and Johnathan dos Santos all trained with the first team in the run-up to the game with Montoya in line to get the right-back spot in Alves's absence.

There was a massive boost for everybody at the club on May 21 with the news that Eric Abidal had left hospital after 40 days recovering from his liver operation. Abidal could now enjoy the Copa del Rey final four days later from the comfort of his home.

From the moment that Athletic Club and Barça won their semi-finals there had been controversy over the venue of the 2012 final. Both clubs had wanted to play at Real Madrid's Santiago Bernabéu stadium. In 2009, the same teams met in the final in Valencia and there were many thousands of fans disappointed as Mestalla only holds 55,000. However, it seemed clear from the outset that Real Madrid did not want to host the game, they claimed that the Bernabéu would be undergoing construction work at the time though it seemed to be just an excuse as they did not want to see either Barça celebrating a trophy in their stadium or the Catalan and Basque fans booing the Spanish national anthem as they had done at Mestalla three years before. Finally, Atlético Madrid's Vicente Calderón was chosen as the venue but the possible disrespectful response to the Spanish anthem continued to create controversy with the President of the Community of Madrid, Esperanza Aguirre, bizarrely calling for the game to be played behind closed doors if the Prince of Asturias or the Spanish national anthem were whistled at.

Of course in the end the game went ahead despite the fans drowning out a shortened version of the anthem. Guardiola brought Montoya in at right back and started with Pinto, Montoya, Piqué, Mascherano, Adriano, Xavi, Busquets, Iniesta, Pedro, Messi and Alexis, while Athletic's coach Marcelo Bielsa surprised by leaving both Ander Iturraspe and Ander Herrera on the bench, playing Ibai Gomez and Javi Martinez in midfield with Borja Ekiza coming into defence which meant a starting XI of Gorka Iraizoz, Andoni Iraola, Ekiza, Fernando Amorebieta, Jon Aurtentexe, Ibai, Javi Martinez, Oscar De Marcos, Markel Susaeta, Fernando Llorente and Iker Muniain.

There may have been doubts in about how Barça would respond after nearly a month since playing an important match, but in Guardiola's time as Barça's coach he had consistently demonstrated his ability to get players in the right frame of mind. Perhaps the players were sufficiently motivated by the desire to give Pep the right send-off; whatever the case Barça came out brilliantly from the start with excellent touch and movement to take immediate control.

After only 24 seconds Messi tried a curler that went just wide. Then in the second minute Alexis fed Adriano's overlap and when the cross came into the danger zone Pedro's effort was deflected wide by Ekiza. From Xavi's corner Piqué flicked the ball on, surprising Martinez who could only deflect the ball straight to Pedro who swept the ball home left-footed from twelve yards.

It was a fantastic start and Barça kept up the pressure. Bielsa's system had Athletic man marking Barça all over the pitch except for keeping one man spare at the back. This meant that Barça's spare man was usually Piqué or Mascherano, and both players were instructed to bring the ball forward quickly whenever they had the chance to try and create superiority in midfield.

Messi came close to Barça's second after 15 minutes, cutting in from the right before letting fly a terrific shot which needed an equally terrific save from Iraizoz to turn the ball round the post. On the rare occasions that Barça lost the ball the team, and especially the forwards, worked hard to harry the Athletic players and the Basques struggled to string passes together. In the 20th minute Amorebieta gave a poor ball out of defence which Busquets intercepted just inside the Athletic half. Busquets moved the ball on quickly to Messi on the right who played a first time pass infield to Iniesta. Messi continued his run, sprinting free of Aurtentexe, Iniesta spotted him and timed his pass to perfection as Amorebieta just played Messi onside. The Argentinian received the pass with his left foot before firing right foot high past Iraizoz from a tight angle. It was Messi's twelfth final under Guardiola, and he had now scored in ten of them.

Barça were now rampant and a third goal came in the 25th minute. Piqué played the ball forward to Xavi who from the edge of the area knocked it back for Pedro to curl a beauty inside the far post. Three-nil and Athletic hadn't troubled Pînto yet. This changed a minute later when Piqué's clearance went straight to Susaeta but Pinto saved his shot well. Then Messi might have made it 4-0 after Amorebieta missed a long clearance but he misjudged his lob allowing Iraizoz a simple save.

Athletic then had a reasonable shout for a penalty after it appeared that Piqué grabbed Llorente's shirt but perhaps the Athletic target man allowed himself to fall too easily. After this Barça tried to reduce the speed of the game but it was not easy given Athletic's continued high-tempo pressing game. Xavi had a volley wide and then there was an audacious attempt from Mascherano with a free kick from the halfway line but Iraizoz reacted in time. The first half ended with a poor kick from Pinto but the keeper then saved well as Muniain tried to sneak his shot inside the near post.

Athletic made a big effort early in the second half to try to grab a quick goal back, but Barça were generally very solid in defence. However, in the 52nd minute a pass inside Adriano gave Ibai Gomez a chance but his chip past Pinto went past the far post. The game began to drop in level as it became clear that for all their effort Athletic were not going to turn the game around. Consequently there were fewer chances but Messi made one remarkable run which began in the Barça half: after beating two opponents for speed in midfield, Messi beat two more as he dribbled into the area only to be denied at the end by Iraizoz's outstretched foot. Athletic had one more chance near the end when Aurtentexe got forward to head Ibai's cross just wide but it was never going to be the Basque team's day.

It was a shame for Athletic and their magnificent fans to end a fine season with two final defeats but it was a fitting finale to Guardiola's fabulous four years as Barça's first team coach. The team rose to the occasion and gave another vintage performance. Guardiola deserved it. After taking over a team that was past its best and skillfully offloading a couple of star names he had converted a group of very talented players into a team that worked brilliantly as a solid unit. His record of 3 Ligas, 2 Champions Leagues, 2 FIFA Club World Cups, 2 Copa del Reys, 2 UEFA Super Cup and 3 Spanish Supercopas all achieved in the space of four seasons was second to none.

Barça: Pinto; Montoya, Piqué, Mascherano, Adriano; Xavi (Fabregas m81), Busquets, Iniesta; Pedro (Thiago m87), Messi, Alexis (Keita m73).

Athletic: Iraizoz; Iraola, Elkiza, Amorebieta, Aurtentexe; De Marcos (Inigo Perez m46), Javi Martinez, Ibai; Susaeta (Ander Herrera m46), Llorente (Toquero m73), Muniain.

Goals: m3 Pedro 1-0, m20 Messi 2-0, m25 Pedro 3-0.

EPILOGUE

On 24 July 2013, nearly fourteen months after Pep Guardiola's last game in charge at Barça, the Catalan team travelled to Munich for their first pre-season game of the 2013/14 season against Bayern at the Allianz Arena. The German side had won the treble of Champions League, Bundesliga and German Cup in the 2012/13 season under the leadership of 68-year-old Jupp Heynckes, but now Guardiola, after a year living away from football in New York, was back in the game as Bayern's new coach.

On the way to winning the Champions League Heynckes's team had beaten Tito Vilanova's Barça 7-0 on aggregate in the semi-finals. It was a terrible blow for the Catalans but not nearly as bad as the news that Vilanova would have to stand down as Barça's coach which came just five days before starting the 2013/14 season with the friendly in Munich.

Barça's 2012/13 season had been plagued by illness. Eric Abidal spent months working tenaciously in a long slow fight to regain fitness after his liver transplant on 10 April 2012. Abidal's fortitude and bravery were finally rewarded when he was brought on as a substitute near the end of a 5-0 win over Mallorca on 6 April 2013. It was the moment of the season at Camp Nou and the 65,127 spectators rose to give him an emotional ovation. Abidal made four more appearances in La Liga but at the end of the season Barça took the unpopular decision of not renewing the Frenchman's contract, leading to him moving back to AS Monaco where he had made his professional debut in September 2000.

On 18 December 2012, the day after an impressive 4-1 win over Atlético Madrid, another small tumour was discovered in Tito Vilanova's parotid gland, 13 months on from his first surgery. Vilanova underwent another operation on 20 December but his recovery was arduous and involved spending more than two months receiving specialist treatment in New York. Although Vilanova was still officially Barça's first team coach, Jordi Roura took over his duties in running the team assisted by Aurelio Altimira. Modern technology meant that Roura and Vilanova remained in regular contact though the situation undoubtedly affected the team.

Vilanova's Barça had begun the 2012/13 season well enough. In La Liga the team set a tremendous pace, winning eighteen games and drawing one to establish a record of 55 points from the first half of the season. Left-back Jordi Alba signed from Valencia at the end of June 2012 for €14 million which, with Dani Alves on the right, gave Barça two full-backs who got forward at every opportunity. However, the team suffered in defence, partly due to the attacking-minded full backs, partly due to the diminutive size of the team which gave opposing teams too much advantage at set-pieces, and partly due to injuries and lack of adequate back-up which led to Barça conceding 40 league goals compared to 29 in the previous season.

The other summer signing of 2012 was Alex Song, bought from Arsenal for €19 million. Song was initially used as an emergency central defender after Puyol and Piqué both got injured in the autumn. The Cameroonian struggled to adapt to the position but he performed much better when filling in for Sergio Busquets in the defensive midfield role.

The record breaking start to the league season meant that by the halfway stage of the season Barça had built up an eleven-point lead over second placed Atlético Madrid while third-placed Real Madrid were eighteen points adrift, leading José Mourinho to state that it was impossible for Madrid to win the league title.

Unfortunately, the loss of Vilanova began to take its toll and the unbeaten record in La Liga went in a 3-2 defeat at Real Sociedad in January. Then when the Champions League knock-out stage began in February Barça suffered a 2-0 first leg defeat in the last 16 at AC Milan. Before the return leg with Milan Roura's Barça lost twice to Real Madrid, first in the Copa del Rey semi-finals and then in the league fixture at the Santiago Bernabéu, setting off the alarm bells in Barcelona.

The players responded by producing the performance of the season to beat Milan 4-0 in the return game at Camp Nou, while the healthy advantage at the top of La Liga was maintained, thanks in a large part to Leo Messi who was busy setting a record of scoring in 19 consecutive league games. Having scored a record-breaking total of 91 goals for club and country in 2012 Messi had picked up his fourth consecutive Ballon d'Or in January and his performances continued to astound. However, there was some concern about the Argentinian's lack of rest, and these fears were justified when he was injured during the 2-2 draw in the Champions League quarter final first leg at Paris Saint Germain shortly after Vilanova's return from New York. A half-fit Messi returned as a substitute in the second leg and he helped set up Pedro's equalizer in a 1-1 draw that was enough to see Barça through to the semi-finals on away goals. Nevertheless, Messi would continue to have problems for the remainder of the season.

The Barça squad's lack of depth was exposed by further injury problems for the Champions League semi-final with Bayern. Puyol and Mascherano missed both legs, meaning a central defensive pairing of Piqué and Bartra, while Messi and Busquets were both asked to play in the first game in Munich despite not being fully fit and Barça suffered a humiliating 4-0 defeat. Vilanova left Messi and Busquets out for the return at Camp Nou and a weakened Barça side were comfortably beaten 0-3 by the in-form Germans.

Barça's flaws had been uncovered in the season's biggest fixtures. Only one game had been won out of six against Real Madrid while the team had also only won once in six games during the knock-out stages of the

Champions League. Seydou Keita had been allowed to leave the club in the summer of 2012 to join Dalian Aerbin in the Chinese Super League. His presence was almost certainly missed in these important games.

Despite the setbacks in the big matches Barça continued to win regularly in La Liga, ending the season strongly to finish a record 15 points clear of second placed Real Madrid. In winning the title Barça also equalled the record of 100 points in 38 games set by Madrid in the previous season. Messi finished the season with 46 league goals, his injury preventing him from surpassing his record of 50 goals in La Liga 2011/12.

Shortly after the Champions League first leg defeat in Munich it had been confirmed by Barça that Vilanova would continue as first team coach for the 2013/14 season. There was plenty of excitement when it was announced that Barça would play Bayern in a preseason friendly as it would see Vilanova facing Guardiola as rival coaches for the first time. Barça fans could also get excited by the €57 million signing from Santos of 21-year-old Brazilian sensation Neymar da Silva Santos Junior who was about to star for Brazil's Confederations Cup winning team. However, Barça would make no further signings in the summer of 2013, and in the build-up towards the new season the press turned its attention to a reported spat between Vilanova and Guardiola, with Guardiola claiming the Barça board had used Vilanova's illness to attack him and Vilanova revealing that Guardiola had not visited him when he was receiving treatment in New York.

Further divisions between Barça and Guardiola were created when the German newspaper *Der Speigel* ran the story that Guardiola had made an initial unofficial approach to Bayern Munich directors Karl-Heinz Rummenigge and Uli Hoeness in July 2011, nine months before he made the official announcement that he was leaving Barça. However, just five days before the expected clash between Vilanova's Barça and Guardiola's Bayern, Sandro Rosell gave the awful news that Vilanova would be unable to continue as Barça's coach due to his need for more treatment against his illness that would make it impossible for him to do the job.

The Argentinian coach, Gerardo 'Tata' Martino, who was relatively unknown in Europe, was named as Barça's new coach four days later. Martino was unable to take charge of the team for the pre-season game with Bayern which meant a final short stint as caretaker coach for Jordi Roura. Bayern beat Barça 2-0 in the friendly and Guardiola's new team soon went on to win the UEFA Super Cup, defeating José Mourinho's Chelsea on penalties. Martino's Barça would also win a trophy in the summer of 2013, beating Atlético Madrid on away goals to lift the Spanish Supercopa. However, despite the continued triumphs of Barça and of Guardiola it seemed unlikely that they could ever repeat the incredible success achieved together between 2008 and 2012.

5775222R00152

Printed in Great Britain
by Amazon.co.uk, Ltd.,
Marston Gate.